Reading Literature

Why do we read literature? Literature enables us to develop our judgment through observation and reflection. We read literature for the many pleasures it offers. These pleasures range widely across genres, with those reading fiction and drama differing from what readers experience in their encounters with poems and essays.

Reading Literature is a practical guide ranging across the literary genres—poetry, fiction, drama, and essay. For each of these genres, Robert DiYanni outlines five "ways in" to literary works. Each section closes with the technique of "interrupted reading." *Reading Literature* helps readers experience the rich rewards literature provides; understand the complexities of human psychology; navigate the intricacies of social relationships; and take pleasure in the ways language creates alternate worlds which echo the world in which we live. It also includes sections on literary elements and the basics of literary theory. Part V uses the familiar literary elements as the basis for sample analyses of poem, story, play, essay, and epic. The final part offers an overview of a dozen critical approaches, or theoretical perspectives, on literature.

Helping readers read closely and critically, this is an essential guide to find "ways in" to reading literature to result in valuable encounters and rewarding literary experiences for general readers or those beginning literary studies courses.

Robert DiYanni is Professor of Humanities at New York University, USA, where he serves on the faculties of the School of Professional Studies and the Stern School of Business, following a decade in the College of Arts and Science. His publications include *The Pearson Guide to Critical and Creative Thinking* (2014), *Critical and Creative Thinking: A Brief Guide for Teachers* (2015), and *Critical Reading Across the Curriculum* (with Anton Borst; 2017). His *Literature: Reading Fiction, Poetry, Drama, and the Essay* went through six editions and his *Modern American Poets* (1988, 1993) was the companion text for the PBS television series *Voices and Visions* about modern American poetry. His co-authored *Scribner Handbook for Writers* went through four editions.

Reading Literature
Practical Approaches to Engaging with Literature

Robert DiYanni

LONDON AND NEW YORK

Designed cover image: Getty Images

First published 2026
by Routledge
4 Park Square, Milton Park, Abingdon, Oxon OX14 4RN

and by Routledge
605 Third Avenue, New York, NY 10158

Routledge is an imprint of the Taylor & Francis Group, an informa business

© 2026 Robert DiYanni

The right of Robert DiYanni to be identified as author of this work has been asserted in accordance with sections 77 and 78 of the Copyright, Designs and Patents Act 1988.

All rights reserved. No part of this book may be reprinted or reproduced or utilised in any form or by any electronic, mechanical, or other means, now known or hereafter invented, including photocopying and recording, or in any information storage or retrieval system, without permission in writing from the publishers.

Trademark notice: Product or corporate names may be trademarks or registered trademarks, and are used only for identification and explanation without intent to infringe.

For Product Safety Concerns and Information please contact our EU representative GPSR@taylorandfrancis.com. Taylor & Francis Verlag GmbH, Kaufingerstraße 24, 80331 München, Germany.

Every effort has been made to contact copyright-holders. Please advise the publisher of any errors or omissions, and these will be corrected in subsequent editions.

British Library Cataloguing-in-Publication Data
A catalogue record for this book is available from the British Library

ISBN: 978-1-041-02631-0 (hbk)
ISBN: 978-1-041-04334-8 (pbk)
ISBN: 978-1-003-62028-0 (ebk)

DOI: 10.4324/9781003620280

Typeset in Times New Roman
by Taylor & Francis Books

In memory of all my splendid teachers of literature, who inspired me to follow in their wake.

Contents

Preface   xi
Acknowledgments   xiv

Introduction: Print and Digital Reading   1

PART I
Reading Poetry—Five Ways In   5

    Prelude I: The Pleasures of Poetry   7

1 Speaker, Structure, Sound—William Butler Yeats: "An Irish Airman Foresees His Death"   15

2 Argument—Andrew Marvell: "To His Coy Mistress"   19

3 Tone—Stephen Crane: "War Is Kind"   22

4 Literature and the Arts—Pieter Brueghel the Elder, W. H. Auden, William Carlos Williams, and Walt Whitman   24

5 Interrupted Reading—Robert Frost: "Stopping by Woods on a Snowy Evening"   29

    Interlude I: Epic Poetry   32

PART II
Reading Fiction—Five Ways In   39

    Prelude II: The Pleasures of Fiction   41

6 Questions—Katherine Anne Porter: "Rope"   48

7 Surprises—Edgar Allan Poe: "The Cask of Amontillado"   55

8	Voices—Jane Austen: *Pride and Prejudice*	63
9	Fiction, History, Art—Ernest Hemingway: "The Revolutionist" and *A Farewell to Arms*	65
10	Interrupted Reading—Kate Chopin: "The Story of an Hour"	70
	Interlude II: The Novel and Novella	76

PART III
Reading Drama—Five Ways In   81

	Prelude III: The Pleasures of Drama	83
11	Mental Theater—August Strindberg: *The Stronger*	86
12	Subtext—Wendy Wasserstein: *Tender Offer*	92
13	Language and Style—William Shakespeare: *Othello*	94
14	Scene and Sound—William Shakespeare: *Macbeth*	97
15	Interrupted Reading—George Bernard Shaw: *Arms and the Man*	99
	Interlude III: Types of Drama	105

PART IV
Reading the Essay—Five Ways In   109

	Prelude IV: The Pleasures of the Essay	111
16	Annotation—Francis Bacon: "Of Youth and Age"	115
17	Style and Tone—Mary Wollstonecraft: *A Vindication of the Rights of Woman*	120
18	Slow Reading—Leslie Jamison: "A Street Full of Splendid Strangers"	124
19	Reading Framework—Jamaica Kincaid: "On Seeing England for the First Time"	129
20	Interrupted Reading—George Orwell: "A Hanging"	135
	Interlude IV: The Video Essay	141

PART V
Reading with Literary Elements—Five Takes 143

    Prelude V: The Value of the Literary Elements 145

21 Elements of Lyric Poetry—Gerard Manley Hopkins: "Spring and Fall: *to a young child*" 147

22 Elements of Epic Poetry—John Milton: *Paradise Lost* 152

23 Elements of Fiction—James Joyce: "Araby" 159

24 Elements of Drama—Isabella Augusta Persse, Lady Gregory: *The Rising of the Moon* 167

25 Elements of the Essay—Zora Neale Hurston: "How It Feels to Be Colored Me" 187

    Interlude V: Literary Conventions 193

PART VI
Reading Literature through Critical Lenses—Twelve Takes 195

    Prelude VI: The Value of Literary Perspectives 197

26 Formalist 200

27 Reader-Response 203

28 Biographical 205

29 Historical 207

30 Psychological 210

31 Sociological 213

32 Mythological 217

33 Structuralist 219

34 Deconstructionist 221

35 Postcolonial 224

36 Ecocritical 227

37 Influence and Values 230

Appendix: Writing about Literature 233
References 245
Index 249

Preface

I begin with a series of questions:

- Why do you read literature? What is your main purpose?
- What do you want from your experience of reading literature?
- How might you read literature more rewardingly?

Answers to these questions provide a starting point for thinking about *how* you read literature and *why* you read it the way you do. Why and how you read literary works can matter as much as which works you read.

Most of us read literature for the pleasures it brings—pleasures of story and suspense, plot and structure, conflict and resolution. Pleasures of character and conflict, voice and style, sound and sense, meaning and value. We read for the pleasures of being engaged intellectually and emotionally with a mind in the act of thinking. We read literature for how it enlarges and deepens our understanding of ourselves and the world.

Reading enlarges and deepens us in ways social media does not. Reading works our minds, provokes our thinking, stimulates the imagination. Reading literature actively engages our thinking powers.

To some extent at least, these things may well be the case for you. My goal, thus, in this book, is to help you better enjoy, appreciate, and comprehend literary works and relate them productively to your life. To that end, I offer a set of "ways in" to reading literature designed to increase your pleasure, enhance your appreciation, and deepen your understanding.

My approach is suggestive rather than prescriptive. It's less a system than a method, less a template or formula than a set of strategies for engaging with literary works pleasurably and productively.

These "ways in" are not exhaustive, of course; other approaches exist, alternative strategies to read literary works productively. But the strategies I provide have worked for me and for other readers, young and old, as well. These approaches to reading literature result, consistently for readers, in beneficial literary encounters and rewarding literary experiences.

And they can work for you.

Reading Literature ranges across poetry, fiction, drama, and essay, with each genre comprising one of the book's first four parts. For each literary genre, I identify five "ways in" to literary works. One of these, the "interrupted reading," concludes each of the genre sections. Another way in, argument, appears directly in one genre—poetry—and indirectly yet distinctly in each of the other genres as well. In Part V, I use the familiar literary elements as the basis for sample analyses of lyric poem, epic, short story, one-act play, and essay.

Part VI introduces you to a dozen critical approaches, or theoretical perspectives; each of these perspectives is a lens that highlights a different dimension of a work you are reading—psychological or sociological, historical or mythological, for example. Like the earlier parts of the book, these lenses provide other "ways in" to reading literature.

I base my approach to reading literature on the following axioms:

1. We read literary works as acts of imagination—as our imaginative (re)creations made from an author's words.
2. We read works of literature as symbolic actions, not as literal statements.
3. The characters we encounter in literary works are neither simply words on a page nor real people, but rather *potential or provisional* people, whose feelings and thoughts we can share virtually, and whose inner lives we can understand. My approach attempts to describe and illustrate ways the lives of real people are represented through the written word.
4. We read literary works as distinctive and singular, but also as part of comprehensive literary and cultural contexts. Although we experience literary works as unique creations, we read them, simultaneously, as part of an ongoing tradition.
5. Our reading of literature, although it begins in private and touches our singular intellectual and emotional being, is also social, even civic and ethical.
6. Our reading of literature is *dialogic*: we read in dialogue with authors of literary works. We also read in conversation with other readers and also with ourselves.
7. Literature enables us to develop our judgment through observation and reflection. It provides occasions for us to achieve a degree of discernment, even of wisdom.

Hermeneutics

As serious readers, we do our best to understand the literary works we read—poems plays, stories, novels, and essays, for example. We do this because words and sentences and images artfully arranged imitate and convey important aspects of the world, something outside words that we recognize as authentic and valid and real. We trust that artistic arrangements of language convey experiences beyond our own that, through reading, we absorb, and in the process come to understand and make our own.

To understand a literary work, we need to put ourselves in the circumstances—psychological, social, linguistic, and cultural—of the writer (and of a work's characters as well). This is a hermeneutical, or interpretive, responsibility, perhaps the single most important responsibility of any reader. This analytical work requires careful and sustained attention to a work's words, phrases, and sentences, to its beliefs and attitudes, and to its implied ideas and values. In the process of trying to gain access to these benefits of reading, we engage in a kind of telepathic act, as we project our minds imaginatively into the minds of others—authors and their created literary characters. We come to learn how a work of literature goes about its business—evolving into a work of literary art, while making its unique kind of sense—an art and a sense that come to matter for us and can continue to matter for us and for other readers and writers, as well. We achieve these benefits through responding to the demands literature makes upon us. In doing so productively we can widen and deepen our perceptions, having our eyes and ears and minds opened, our lives, perhaps, transformed.

To some extent, this hermeneutic effort is creative in the broad sense. It requires care in understanding what a writer has created and an appreciation of how a literary work comes to convey what it does. The art of literary interpretation requires dexterity in navigating a work's tone, temper, and texture. It requires an effort to discover how each writer creates a world by resourcefully deploying language and form, conveying meaning and feeling through images and figurative language, while both working within the constraints of genre and also on occasion breaking through them.

Hermeneutic proficiency is also based on an ability to understand another's thought and meaning, and a further ability to communicate that understanding clearly to others. Hermeneutic expertise requires readers to understand a literary work. It requires absorbing the literary work to make something new of it and then conveying it to others.

I believe that you will find my varied "ways in," or "takes," on reading literary works helpful, and the application of literary elements and theories of value. An investment in refreshing your reading practices will deepen your understanding, enhance your appreciation, and increase your enjoyment of literature. In the process, you will undergo a kind of transformation through experiencing vicariously other characters' lives in the context of writers' lives, which, through reading, commingle with our own. Why not begin experiencing these rewards and pleasures right now? Just scroll down or turn the page.

Acknowledgments

I would like to thank, first, my editor at Routledge, Karen Raith, who saw value in this book from her first encounter with it. Karen solicited a suite of helpful reviews from thoughtful readers, whose advice helped me improve it in revision.

At Routledge, my project editor, Ann-Kathrin Klein, deserves thanks for expertly shepherding the book through its various stages of production.

The book's copy editor, Neil Dowden, provided useful guidance through that important stage. His comments and questions enabled me to improve the manuscript he reviewed with his careful, critical eye.

My thanks also go to Sophie Harding, who provided expert professional assistance and proofread the manuscript scrupulously to its and my advantage.

Finally, I wish to acknowledge the many students over my half-century of teaching literature and related subjects, with whom I have experienced the pleasures of reading and teaching literature.

William Carlos Williams, "Landscape with the Fall of Icarus" from *The Collected Poems of William Carlos Williams, Volume II: 1939–1962*. Copyright © 1962 by William Carlos Williams. Reprinted with the permission of The Permissions Company, LLC on behalf of New Directions Publishing Corp, ndbooks.com.

Every effort has been made to trace copyright holders. The publishers would be pleased to hear from any copyright holders not acknowledged here so that this section may be amended at the earliest opportunity.

Introduction
Print and Digital Reading

You may be reading these words in a physical printed book you hold in your hands. Or you may be reading them on a screen as an e-book, on a computer, tablet, or phone. Or you may find yourself switching between these reading mediums.

New reading technologies coexist with older ones. Though we no longer typically read texts in the form of scrolls, their reading persists for religious purposes, The Hebrew Torah preserved on scrolls used in Jewish ritual, notably in the bar and bat mitzvah. And, of course, we regularly "scroll" through text on our smartphones, tablets, and computers.

Reading in print differs from reading online; reading books and magazines in print is not the same experience as reading them in electronically transmitted, digitized formats. What are some of these differences and their implications for different kinds of reading?

First, we tire faster from screen reading. Second, we are more easily distracted. We also tend to lose our place more readily and find it with greater difficulty.

Recent research suggests that we retain information better and comprehend texts more completely when we read them in print. Neurological studies suggest that we read print books more comprehensively, partly because of the tactile and sensuous nature of the experience, and partly because of its aesthetic quality. Digital reading can erode the kind of deep, sustained reading necessary for understanding serious books and ideas. It's more difficult to sustain our concentration when reading on screens.

And yet readers of printed books tend to have conversations about them online, the internet working synergistically with print reading to invigorate talk about reading—whether we read primarily offline or online, with print or digital texts. The internet can serve as motivation for reading; it can provide information that encourages us to read. Publisher and bookseller websites advance the cause of reading, including the reading of serious books in both print and digital form. That's one of the benefits of digital reading.

Another benefit of reading online—especially for nonfiction—is that it enables us to take advantage of hyperlinks. Reading biography this way can be especially useful, as readers can link to various forms of contextual

DOI: 10.4324/9781003620280-1

information—in particular, to historical background and to other personages with a role in the biography being read.

The two types of reading run parallel without much transfer between them. Digital reading is a kind of "hyper-reading," which includes skimming texts, scanning them, "pecking" or hyperlinking texts, as well as pulling out a few items from long texts, and "juxtaposing," or reading across texts with multiple computer windows open.

Hyper-reading behaviors can also be used when one is reading printed text in the process of doing research among books, journals, magazines, advertisements, pamphlets, brochures, broadsides, flyers, and other print media. Skimming and scanning functions of hyper-reading have been long practiced and taught in books and courses for "basic" readers. What's different about hyper-reading is that multiple texts are open simultaneously. And yet we have to recognize the seductions of distraction, not by the texts open for research, but by those available at the click of a mouse that have nothing to do with the reading project undertaken—the distractions of web browsing and internet shopping, for instance, along with the profusion of clickbait. These attractions decrease our ability to focus and concentrate for sustained periods, resulting in shallow thinking.

Think, for example, of the kinds of reading you do online as compared with the reading you do in books. Think about your own reading process in these different reading environments. Consider the extent to which there is overlap—some aspects of the process seem quite similar, while others differ dramatically, particularly a tendency, when reading online, to follow links, to break away from one page of text to visit linked sites, or to break from the electronic page to respond to email and website updates. Or consider how scrolling up and down electronic pages differs from flipping pages in a book. Many e-book readers now mimic actual book features, notably the turning of pages with a flip of the finger.

These observations about reading, however, suggest only minimally what is at stake in using the continually evolving electronic technologies for how we *think* and process information. When we turn on our computers, we are entering "an ecosystem of interruption technologies" (Carr 91), one that shortens our attention spans, limits our ability to focus and think deeply, and, over time, actually rewires the neurons in our brains to make us intellectual jugglers rather than deep thinkers. The frequent interruptions we experience while using our electronic devices—email notifications, Twitter/X and Instagram updates, ads, page crawls, and the like—scatter our thoughts, and dilute our concentration. To avoid such distracting interruptions, we can turn those features off when we read.

The two types of reading—digital and print—are necessary and valuable. Hypertextual, linked reading is useful for gaining a quick overview of material and for switching among multiple texts. Deep-attention, focused reading is necessary for understanding complex works of literature, music, math, science, and more. It's not that one kind of reading is good and the other bad, but rather that each caters to different reading and thinking purposes. For academic study and for professional work, we need skills associated with sustained reading of serious texts in print. Readers, today, need to become "bi-textual or multi-textual, able to analyze texts flexibly in different ways, with more deliberate instruction at every stage of development on the inferential, demanding aspects of any text" (Wolf 226).

We need to acknowledge the importance of detecting patterns for both kinds of reading—a valuable skill for reading across academic disciplines. And yet to detect patterns is not enough. That's a basic skill, one that follows from making observations. It's more a matter of making connections among observations, detecting relationships. Those two related reading skills are foundational, critically important for reading texts both online and in print. Readers also need to make inferences, and draw provisional conclusions that can be supported with textual evidence and logical reasoning. This more reflective kind of reading, I believe, is what all readers need to engage in.

In the following chapters, I provide guidance for how to engage productively with works of literature, whether digitized or in print. Throughout, I offer suggestions for how to deepen your understanding and enhance your pleasure in reading works of literature. Through your reading of literature, I believe you will deepen your awareness of your own life, the lives of others, and the world in which we all live.

And yet you may be wondering how literature can enrich your life, change your life, perhaps even more importantly in some way "save" your life. Let me provide one answer to that question by referring to some thoughts about poetry that can apply to other kinds of literary works, as well.

In the introduction to his recent book *Walking Each Other Home*, Michael Hogan offers two quotations that present opposite views about poetry. Hogan quotes the modern Anglo-American poet W. H. Auden, who wrote in one of his own poems: "Poetry makes nothing happen." The second quote is from the modern Welsh poet Dylan Thomas, who says something dramatically different: "The force that through the green fuse drives the flower / Drives my green age." Admittedly, the implications of Thomas's words are not as immediately apparent as Auden's. What's interesting is what we might make of Thomas's image of force and fuse and flower.

Here is what Michael Hogan writes:

> To me, that line provides the reconciliation of the two conflicting views of poetry. By itself, the poem makes nothing happen. If readers don't interact with it, their inner lives proceed as before with no change, no new awareness. But given a reader who is alert and receptive, a good poem can often awaken an inner self that was asleep and now has discovered a new way of seeing. The "force," to steal Thomas's metaphor—through the "green fuse" of poetry—changes those of us who make ourselves available to it, and we have a new way of seeing. And when we change the way we look at things, the things we look at change. (3)

I invite you to be that kind of reader of poems, and not only of lyric and epic poems—but of other kinds of literary works as well: stories and essays, novels and plays, and newly emerging genres, such as the video-essay. Michael Hogan notes further that poetry offers us "strategies to live more deeply and more meaningfully" (6). And so, I encourage you to follow Hogan's advice and allow the works of literature you read to effect a real change in you; let them become a catalyst for transformation.

Let your reading of literature truly enrich your life.

Part I
Reading Poetry—Five Ways In

Prelude I
The Pleasures of Poetry

Why read poetry? Why not restrict our reading of literature to fiction and perhaps drama? Readers, generally, enjoy stories. And they typically respond favorably to plays, with their vivid enactment of human behavior. Poetry, on the other hand, often challenges readers—occasionally creating impediments for them. Older poems bring difficulties with diction and syntax. Modern poems can impede understanding with literary, historical, and other kinds of allusions. Often, readers want to know right off what a poem means, and why the poet doesn't just come right out and say it. I exaggerate, perhaps, readers' reluctance to engage with poetry and their resistance to it. But I submit that these responses are real and may, on occasion, apply to you.

So, then, how do we meet these challenges? How might we better experience poetry's value and virtues? My goal for this section on reading poetry is to have you inhabit enough poems to experience some joy in reading them. With luck you will find some favorites. In the process, I hope you can experience some of poetry's many distinctive pleasures.

As we know from our more favorable encounters with poems, poetry offers pleasures of sound and sense, of image and symbol, of rhythm and rhyme, of feeling and thought. Some of poetry's pleasures are verbal, some intellectual, others emotional. We can respond to the words in poems, to the ideas they spark and the feelings they evoke. And we can respond to the sheer physical force of poems, which can make our skin tingle, our feet tap, and our fingers snap in time to a rhythmic beat.

Poetry sharpens our perception of the world since poems draw their energy from the fresh observation of life; poems heighten and intensify our sense of being alive. As Tony Hoagland has noted in *real sofistikashun*, poems help "bring the world into focus" (172), and perhaps help us bring ourselves into focus as well. Joel Conarroe suggests that in taking us away from our quotidian routines, poetry restores us to our truest selves (xvi). Poetry can calm us down, soothe our nerves, tamp down our anxieties. It can also bring us joy and beauty, and sometimes wisdom.

About the power of lyric poetry, modern novelist and critic Virginia Woolf had this to say: "The impact of poetry is so hard and direct that for the moment there is no other sensation except that of the poem itself. How sudden and complete is our immersion" (256). In her essay "How Should One Read a Book?" Woolf makes these observations with respect to one of the oldest poems in English, the medieval lyric "Western Wind."

Here is the poem in its brief entirety:

> Western wind, when wilt thou blow?
> The small rain down can rain.
> Christ, if my love were in my arms,
> And I in my bed again!

This miniature medieval lyric questions, declares, and exclaims; it invokes nature; it speaks of love and separation, of yearning and desire, of basic human needs. It's a mere twenty-six words spun over four short lines (each ending with a different mark of punctuation). In that brief space it concentrates misery and longing. It eschews fancy language and complex symbols, and we hear just a hint of rhyme. We share in the anonymous poet's imaginative enactment of a lover's embrace because the poet has molded language to embody and convey a universal human experience.

Poems like "Western Wind" slow us down: they compel us to read deliberately. They alter the pace at which we live and act; they demand a different kind, and a higher degree, of attention than our normal experience of life requires. They offer us surprises and revelations, moments of insight, shocks of recognition.

British Romantic poet Percy Bysshe Shelley wrote that "poets are the unacknowledged legislators of the world." In "A Defence of Poetry," Shelley suggests that through their imaginative and inspiring works, poets subtly shape and influence society in largely unrecognized ways. Shelley also wrote in that poetic manifesto that "poetry lifts the veil from the hidden beauty of the world."

Each of these statements makes a large claim for poetry's influence and value. While I believe, along with Shelley, that poetry does indeed help us see the beauty hidden in plain sight in everyday reality—over and over and over again—I find the claim of poetry's impact on society less convincing, although not completely, of course. That being said, I don't deny the power of poetry—of poets and their poems—to effect profound change. But I think this occurs for us as individuals, personally, one at a time. Poetry can have immense value for each of us. Its value resides, as Shelley suggests, in something to do with beauty—not only with the beauty it reveals to us by calling our attention to its appearance in the world, but also in its own intrinsic beauty of language and form.

What are some other values poetry holds for us? These, at least, I think.

Poems reveal to us things we didn't know we knew, and they sharpen our perception of things we knew only vaguely. A poem can change the way we see the world; it can alter how we look at life. In *Why Poetry*, Matthew Zapruder notes that a poem can bring us "closer to what is vital and elusive, what can never be fully explained" (xiii). Mark Doty echoes this idea of a poem's incompleteness, its recognition that no vision is final, no description all-encompassing, that no poem entirely conveys or captures the elusive reality it approximates (30–31).

Poems can be puzzling and, on occasion, mystifying. Who hasn't been baffled when reading a poem by John Donne, Emily Dickinson, Wallace Stevens, Paul Celan, Tomas Tranströmer, Ezra Pound, Paul Muldoon, Adrienne Rich—pick your challenging poets. Yet we can be moved and stunned by poems even when we don't fully comprehend them.

Dana Gioia suggests that the power of poetry, like that of music, derives from how it takes us out of our ordinary selves. Rather than knowledge and wisdom, suggests Gioia, poems awe us; they astonish us with their beauty. From this perspective, we experience poetry aesthetically rather than intellectually or ethically. Comprehension isn't at issue; the crux is rather poetry's "bewildering beauty."

Former U.S. Poet Laureate Billy Collins highlights how poems stimulate and provide access to our interior life. He suggests that poems enhance our ways of perceiving through memorization (102–106). Memorizing poems enables us to make them our own, to bring them into our hearts as well as our heads. We typically describe memorizing a poem as learning it "by heart." Knowing poems in this intimate way allows us to access them any time, any place, to satisfy any need. They offer us a refuge from the noise of everyday life.

When we memorize a poem, we pledge "allegiance" in "an act of loyalty and deep respect," as Tom Newkirk reminds us in *The Art of Slow Reading* (76). That respect extends to the artistry of the memorized works, an artistry reflected in their distinctive styles and voices, which benefit from being heard, and in being heard repeatedly, as they are called up in memory.

Poems possess other rewards for us, as well. We can learn from poems the virtues of clarity, economy, and linguistic precision. Ezra Pound alerts us to three broad aspects of poetry—as *music*, or sound; as *picture*, or description; and as *argument*, or rhetoric (*ABC of Reading* 6–7). As sound, poetry sings; as description, it portrays visually; as argument, it persuades. It intones and speaks through lyric, epic, and drama (61).

Pound was a strong advocate for sampling and experiencing poems across centuries and in multiple languages. A contemporary poet, another former Poet Laureate, Kay Ryan, suggests that poems inhabit "a permanent time that poetry lets us into," and that poetry has "doors in all the centuries feeding into this permanent time" (4).

In an interview for *The New York Times* with podcaster Ezra Klein, contemporary poet Jane Hirshfield describes poetry as "the attempt to understand fully what is real, what is present, what is imaginable." Poems, she suggests, "exist to answer the questions that can't be otherwise answered; these great deep questions of how to navigate a human life that are not susceptible to medicine or engineering or any of the technologies of the practical world." And further: "Poems respond to questions that have no answer that's ever going to stay fixed or set. And yet, the questions will keep returning. And you'll either go back to the same poem, or you will look for a new one, or you will write a new one."

Poetry also offers us models of exhilaration; we call upon poetry at times of celebration. Poems also offer solace; they help us grieve because they capture with precision and beauty our deepest feelings. This no more so than in the wake of the COVID-19 pandemic.

But we shouldn't forget that poems are verbal constructs. Because poems are made of words, reading poetry enhances our ability to use and understand language. Don Paterson notes that "[p]oetry reveals language's underlying metrical and intonational regularity, and its tendency to pattern its sounds" (13). Tony Hoagland has argued that when poets make "real poems," they contribute to the evolutionary heritage of poetry as a tradition through the technology of language, "whose adaptations," he suggests, "are legion" (*real sofistikashun* 67). In *The Art of Voice* Hoagland suggests that it is the "*fantasia* of a poem's *language*" (his italics) that creates its compelling world, a world inextricable from the poet's stylistic idiosyncrasy (32). Poems energize and enliven language, making it forever new in literary works that are themselves freshly vitalizing.

Poems also provide various kinds of encounters. Edward Hirsch reminds us that poems provide opportunities for encounters with other lives, minds, voices. As readers, we encounter and are encountered by poems and the poets who made them. Any poem we read offers us a challenge, a provocation we may find enticing and seductive, perhaps confusing or disturbing, even daring and dangerous. Hirsch speaks of poets and readers experiencing "the shock, the swoon, and the bliss" of reading and writing poems (*How to Read a Poem* 30). He describes a poem as an outstretched hand waiting for our rejoining grasp. That outstretched hand is an invitation to a human connection, to a form of communion, perhaps even to the experience of epiphany (56). Hirsch elaborates further that "the poem that desires to sweep the reader away, to take the reader. Of reading as a form of sensual pleasure, a mode of possession, a method of travel" (115). How can we resist such poetic invitations?

Notes on Form

Form constitutes a poem's essential element, without which it simply can not exist as a poem. In one of his letters, C. S. Lewis writes that each poem "is a little incarnation, giving body to what had been before invisible and inaudible" (160). Poems do this largely through their form, the shape they take on the page and in the mind of poet and reader. A poem's form is its distinctive, singular way of emerging syllable by syllable, sound by sound, word by word, line by line, and, perhaps, stanza by stanza. The length of a poem's lines and the shape of its stanzas, the pulse of a poem's metrical pattern and the thrum of its rhythmic beat, the pattern of its soundscape and intonational contour—these and other poetic elements constitute its form.

But it's not only a poem's sounds that engage and embrace us; its silences do so as well. Don Paterson describes the power of a poem's silences—the silences that obtain at a poem's line ends; the silences that inhabit the spaces between stanzas; the silences that mark moments of punctuation; the final silence after the poem ends (20). These silent spaces are an integral part of a poem's formal properties. And, like other poetic elements, they contribute to a poem's effects.

Matthew Zapruder suggests that a poem's form offers "a space to move through" (57). Our minds move with the mind of the poet through the form the poet has created. We move across a poem's lines and down the page in time and in tune with the mind of the poet and with the speaker whose voice we hear.

Lyn Hejinian emphasizes a poem's energies—its "velocities" (cited in Robert Hass) in what Hass defines as "the way a poem embodies the energy of the gesture of its making" (7). Forms of poetry are forces as well as shapes, velocities, and dynamic impulses. Form involves both stasis and action, movement and stillness. Poetry is language, paradoxically, both still and in motion. And more generally, according to Denise Levertov in "Some Notes on Organic Form," "there is a form in all things (and in experience) which the poet can discern and reveal." And further: "form is a revelation of content" (cited in Hirsch, *The Heart of American Poetry*, 297–298).

We can understand and appreciate poetry by acquainting ourselves with poetic form. One basic distinction about form is that between highly structured and loosely structured poetic forms—"open" or "closed" forms. Poems with open structures lack a prescribed or consistent pattern of stanza form or rhyme. They are looser, less constrained than their fixed form poetic counterparts. Consider Whitman's "One's Self I Sing":

> One's Self I sing, a simple separate person,
> Yet utter the word Democratic, the word En-Masse.
>
> Of physiology from top to toe I sing,
> Not physiognomy alone nor brain alone is worthy for the Muse,
> I say the form complete is worthier far,
> The Female equally with the Male I sing.
>
> Of Life immense in passion, pulse, and power,
> Cheerful, for freest action form'd under the laws divine,
> The Modern man I sing.

Poems in open form are not without discernible structural patterns. They are just not as visible or as insistent as those in closed forms. We might note, for example, how Whitman's poem repeats the word "sing" three times at the ends of lines. And we notice, too, how those lines vary in length, and how the only bit of rhyme in the poem turns on that single word.

Closed form poems exhibit regularity across a number of features—rhythm and meter, rhyme, line length, stanza pattern, and more. An example of a closed form is the sonnet, which typically follows one of two common structures: the

Petrarchan or Italian, and the Shakespearean or English, sonnet form. A Petrarchan sonnet consists of two sections: an eight-line "octave" and a six-line "sestet." The Petrarchan sonnet rhyme scheme is typically either *abba abba cde cde* or *abba abba cd cd cd*. John Keats's "On First Looking into Chapman's Homer" exemplifies the Petrarchan sonnet form.

> Much have I travell'd in the realms of gold,
> And many goodly states and kingdoms seen;
> Round many western islands have I been
> Which bards in fealty to Apollo hold.
> Oft of one wide expanse had I been told
> That deep-brow'd Homer ruled as his demesne;
> Yet did I never breathe its pure serene
> Till I heard Chapman speak out loud and bold:
> Then felt I like some watcher of the skies
> When a new planet swims into his ken;
> Or like stout Cortez when with eagle eyes
> He star'd at the Pacific—and all his men
> Look'd at each other with a wild surmise—
> Silent, upon a peak in Darien.

You can see and hear the coherence of octave and sestet from their rhymes, *abba abba* and *cd cd cd*, respectively. The two four-line units of Keats's poem's octave are structurally parallel, with a semicolon marking the middle of each. Each four-line units ends with a strong mark of punctuation, though Keats uses a colon after line 8, which has the effect of pushing readers through to the sestet, where the energy of the sonnet gains momentum and the excited experience of its speaker comes to the fore.

The crux of Keats's sonnet inheres in the relationship between its octave and sestet, with the sestet a solution to the problem identified in the octave. The turn, or *volta*, at line 9, which begins with "Then felt I," is anticipated with the "Yet" in line 7. Keats conveys the speaker's excitement at his discovery of Chapman's translation of Homer's epics largely through comparisons. The first is a general comparison with astronomers discovering new planets (note the lovely image of sky as sea, as the planet "swims" into the astronomer's field of vision); the second comparison involves the particular occasion of Balboa's discovery of the Pacific Ocean (though Keats attributes this discovery to Hernando Cortéz). Both similes convey the speaker's exhilaration at discovering the grandeur and majesty of Homer through reading Chapman's translation. Keats's comparisons reveal the speaker's heightened emotion—exaltation even, at the discovery of Chapman's translation.

The Shakespearean or English sonnet divides into three *quatrains*, or four-line stanzas, and a *couplet* at the end. Its rhyme pattern is typically *abab cdcd efef gg*. Both types of sonnets require fourteen lines of ten syllables each, with alternating stresses of iambic pentameter.

Here's an example of this form from Shakespeare: his sonnet, "When, in disgrace with fortune and men's eyes." I encourage you to read the first line ALOUD, accenting the even-numbered syllables. Here is what an exaggerated emphasis on those syllables gives us: "When, IN disGRACE with FORtune AND men's EYES." Of course, we wouldn't read it quite like that—in that exaggerated singsong way. But it helps to highlight those stressed syllables, the better to feel the poem's metric pulse—the beat of its lines.

> When, in disgrace with fortune and men's eyes,
> I all alone beweep my outcast state,
> And trouble deaf heaven with my bootless cries,
> And look upon myself and curse my fate,
> Wishing me like to one more rich in hope,
> Featured like him, like him with friends possessed,
> Desiring this man's art and that man's scope,
> With what I most enjoy contented least;
> Yet in these thoughts myself almost despising,
> Haply I think on thee, and then my state,
> Like to the lark at break of day arising
> From sullen earth sings hymns at heaven's gate;
> For thy sweet love remembered such wealth brings
> That then I scorn to change my state with kings.

Shakespeare spins this sonnet out as a single sentence over its fourteen lines, although he includes semicolons at two junctures—following lines 8 and 12—where the sonnet's pace slows a bit. The first semicolon signals the end of an eight-line unit, which functions much like the octave of a Petrarchan sonnet. (Note the "Yet" that opens the *volta*, or turn, at line 9.) The second semicolon functions as a strong stop before the sonnet's concluding couplet. It completes the thought of the poem's three quatrains, and it prepares the reader for the couplet's concluding explanation about the power of the speaker's love to alter the course of his emotional trajectory—from darkness to light, from despair to hope, from sadness to joy.

A key facet of a poem's structure is its sense of closure, resolution, completeness. We feel that a poem is "over" when we perceive that the tensions it has raised have been resolved. This sense of closure is, in part, formal, and in part psychological. As Barbara Herrnstein Smith notes in *Poetic Closure*, a poem achieves closure, psychologically, when it is experienced as complete, coherent, and stable (2). A poem appears complete, as well, when the sequence of events it describes has logically concluded (lovers separated, for example, are reunited). The sense of finality derives from the expectations that the poem has generated are fulfilled.

Structurally, a sonnet's closure, for example, is established at the end of fourteen lines. A sonnet also typically concludes at the end of a sentence, and, depending on its abiding by the conventions of the Petrarchan or

Shakespearean sonnet form, at the end of the sestet, or with a concluding couplet. A sonnet's concluding sentence reinforces the poem's sense of closure through the nature of its content and context—as a declaration, question, lament, argument, or other form of utterance.

Poetic closure, thus, operates thematically and emotionally as well as structurally. Our sense of a poem's closure depends on its context. The patterns of rhythm and rhyme and meter, of imagery and figurative language a poet works with set it apart from less formalized and structured ways of using language. The pattern of internal coherence a poem displays, with its parts integrally related to each other, separates a poem from what lies outside it, encloses it in its own world. Within this poetic frame, Smith suggests, a poem's sense of closure is a measure, finally, of its "expressive design" (141).

One additional aspect of form to become familiar with is the concept of stanza. Most of us early on were exposed to poems in regular stanzas. Among the things to consider are that it's a stanza's repeating elements—its metrical beat and rhyme scheme, primarily—that define a poem's unique expression. In addition to sound patterns, we should notice a poem's visual patterns, how its stanzas are set off from one another by the white space separating them. A poem's stanzas allow us to pause, absorbing aurally, visually, and syntactically, its units of meaning. We come to a sense of what a poem says and suggests through its soundscape and its visual geography. A stanza is at once both a melodic unit—a unit of sound—and a visual unit—a unit of sight. It's also a semantic and rhetorical unit—a unit of meaning, of sense.

That third stanza element—sense—constitutes part of the poem's overall pattern of meaning, each stanza a single unit in relationship to the poem's other stanzas. It's those stanzaic relationships that constitute a poem's meaning. And so, we might read through a number of short poems, asking ourselves what each stanza is doing, and how each stanza relates to the ones that come before and/or after it.

1 Speaker, Structure, Sound—William Butler Yeats

"An Irish Airman Foresees His Death"

We continue our attention to poems with a more sustained consideration of a lyric by William Butler Yeats, "An Irish Airman Foresees His Death," focusing on the poem's speaker, diction, structure, and sound effects.

> I know that I shall meet my fate
> Somewhere among the clouds above;
> Those that I fight I do not hate,
> Those that I guard I do not love;
> My country is Kiltartan Cross,
> My countrymen Kiltartan's poor,
> No likely end could bring them loss
> Or leave them happier than before.
> Nor law, nor duty bade me fight,
> Nor public men, nor cheering crowds,
> A lonely impulse of delight
> Drove to this tumult in the clouds;
> I balanced all, brought all to mind,
> The years to come seemed waste of breath,
> A waste of breath the years behind
> In balance with this life, this death.

First, a bit of context. World War I had been ravaging Europe for nearly four years, beginning in 1914. Near the end of January 1918, an Italian aviator accidently shot down a thirty-seven-year-old Irish pilot, Robert Gregory, the son of Lady Gregory, a dear friend of Ireland's leading poet, William Butler Yeats. Deeply affected by the young man's death, Yeats composed a prose elegy, along with several poems, including "In Memory of Major Robert Gregory" and "An Irish Airman Foresees His Death," in which Yeats describes Gregory's sense of life, certain death, and war from the young man's perspective. While the poem illustrates what must have been a constant preoccupation for soldiers in World War I (a fear of death), it also tries to come to grips with the decision by Gregory (and many others) to participate in an ultimately senseless conflict.

We might start with a series of related questions: What is the speaker's attitude toward flying? Why does he fly? What drives him to it? What is the experience like for him? Viewing different versions of the question allows us to turn it around in our minds, to consider its implications.

It's clear from the poem's first two lines that the speaker believes he will die in the air, "meet [his] fate ... among the clouds." It's also clear that he is not flying out of a sense of duty or responsibility; he doesn't "hate" those he fights against in the air; nor does he "love" those he protects on his missions.

As these are negative answers, we still need to determine what motivates him positively. The answer comes only later in the poem. Early on, in lines 4–8, the poem's next unit, the speaker locates himself by country and socioeconomic status; he's from Ireland, Kiltartan's poor. His flying on their behalf in the war, regardless of the outcome or "end," will not change anything for them. So, no, we don't have an answer for his motivation to serve as an Irish airman in World War I in these lines.

Perhaps it comes in the lines that follow, in lines 9 and 10? There too, however, we find more negatives. Neither law nor duty, neither public men nor cheering crowds—neither individuals of influence nor crowds of common people, and certainly not any legal or moral pressure provide the reason for his desire to fly. None of these things motivate him. Only "A lonely impulse of delight" drives him into the chaos among the clouds. But that answer prompts more questions: What kind of delight could this be? What kind of satisfaction does the pilot obtain? What type of exhilaration? Is it from flying alone, or is it more from the danger of dying while flying a fighter plane? Perhaps it is a combination of these things.

The last four lines develop the speaker's explanation further: that "The years to come seemed waste of breath"; what lies ahead seems meaningless to him. And the years already lived seem to him equally unimportant: "A waste of breath the years behind."

The speaker's attitude toward his experience as a fighter pilot is complex. On one hand, it's the "impulse of delight"—a "lonely" impulse in which he finds that delight. On the other hand, flying a fighter plane gives his life meaning and purpose. Yet he refuses to acknowledge any grand purpose or exalted meaning for it. He goes out of his way, in fact, to deny the expected laudable reasons one might volunteer for dangerous wartime flying missions.

In the process of considering the motivation of Yeats's speaker, we have noticed a number of things the poet does to convey the speaker's complex attitude. Our analysis so far has emphasized the poem's thematic center—what the poem seems to say and suggest by way of its diction, its choice of words.

Let's shift our attention now to the poet's craft, from *what* it suggests to *how* it does so by focusing first on Yeats's diction, then on syntax and structure. We have already identified some of the poem's key words: "fate," "hate," "love," "country," "law," "duty," "impulse," "delight," "waste," and "breath." We have seen how Yeats uses "no," "nor," and "not" to negate conventional reasons, explanations, and expectations. Another word to note is "Drove"; the speaker was driven, impelled by a kind of force. It's almost as if he can't resist this "impulse of delight." The word "lonely" carries a positive and negative charge; it is negative in the sense that he's a lonely man seemingly without a purpose in life; it's positive in that he finds a purpose in his solo aerial activity.

The final words to notice are "balance" and "balanced," the two forms coming at the end of the poem, where the speaker explains how he has "balanced all"—how he has thought of all the aspects and implications of what he is doing. He sees a "balance" between life and death in his choice, his decision to "meet" his "fate" to balance "this life" with "this death." That word "death" is appropriate to conclude the poem. Death has been implied from the very first line's "my fate," but which has remained unspoken until the end, where it explodes with force. The word "balance" matters, also, because the poem is structured as a series of careful balances. These balances include the overall structure of four units, each of four lines.

A balancing of alternating rhymed lines persists through the entire poem. "Fate" balances "hate," "above" balances "love," and on through the poem. The last pair captures the poem's meaning—the speaker's decision to balance "breath" with "death." Death, of course, is balanced by "life," rhyming with it not in sound but sense—an opposite sense.

The balanced phrases create balanced syntax, or sentence structure: "Those that I fight" and "Those that I guard." Also: "I do not hate" and "I do not love." The symmetry is perfect. Other less perfect but quite strong syntactic balances appear elsewhere in the poem. For example, lines 7 and 8 balance "could bring them loss" with "leave them happier." Lines 9 and 10 balance "nor law" and "nor duty," and also "nor public men" with "nor cheering crowds."

The strongest and most powerful balancing comes in the poem's final four lines, in which the phrase "I balanced all" is balanced by "brought all to mind," which explains what the speaker means by "balance all." The repetition of the phrase "waste of breath" works equally with the balance of "the years to come" and "the years behind." Lines 14 and 15 form a "chiasmus," a crisscross "X" in their phrasing. And the final line of the last four-line unit in the poem balances the first line of that unit, with the words "balanced" and "balance" appearing in the same position in each line.

The poem is poised, hovering, perfectly balanced. It's as if poem and pilot, pilot and plane, are themselves hovering somewhere between life and death, the past life that the pilot renounces and the death to come that he embraces. The balanced syntax and the parallel structure of Yeats's poem endow it with a perfect equilibrium that freezes in time the poised contrasts its speaker—and poet—so elegantly express.

As we began our consideration of Yeats's poem with questions, so we conclude it. Our questions broaden out beyond the poem's details. We might ask ourselves, for example, why Robert Gregory's decision to meet his fate the way he does matters—why it matters to him and why it might matter to others. We might explore the larger questions that Yeats's poem raises about wars and about the young men who enlist in them, or are conscripted to fight in them. And we might ask why that might matter to us, and to others, as well as to them.

2 Argument—Andrew Marvell
"To His Coy Mistress"

Let's transfer our attention, now, to another way in to a poem—to its "argument." In the following seventeenth-century poem, a male speaker attempts to persuade a young woman to have sex with him. Andrew Marvell structures "To His Coy Mistress" as a formal argument, a syllogism with two premises and a conclusion—the speaker's attempt to get her to acquiesce to his sexual suggestion.

Its three sections are set up as an argument: If we had all the time in the world....But we don't....Therefore, we need to do it now. Let's seize the moment, the speaker suggests—*carpe diem* (seize the day). The poem begins in the *subjunctive* ("Had we but world enough and time"), shifts to the *indicative* ("But at my back I always hear"), and concludes with the *imperative* camouflaged as an invitation ("Now, therefore, ... let us sport us while we may").

Here's the first section:

> Had we but world enough and time,
> This coyness, lady, were no crime.
> We would sit down, and think which way
> To walk, and pass our long love's day.
> Thou by the Indian Ganges' side
> Shouldst rubies find; I by the tide
> Of Humber would complain. I would
> Love you ten years before the flood,
> And you should, if you please, refuse
> Till the conversion of the Jews.
> My vegetable love should grow
> Vaster than empires and more slow;
> An hundred years should go to praise
> Thine eyes, and on thy forehead gaze;
> Two hundred to adore each breast,
> But thirty thousand to the rest;
> An age at least to every part,
> And the last age should show your heart.
> For, lady, you deserve this state,
> Nor would I love at lower rate.

There is much to admire about these opening lines—the controlled iambic tetrameter, or four-beat line; the strong couplet rhymes; the effective use of enjambment and caesura, with lines that run over and are end-stopped, respectively; the playful hyperbole, or exaggeration; the direct address to a "lady"; along with its wit, charm, and grace.

Here, however, or at the moment, our emphasis is on rhetoric, or persuasion, particularly how the opening lines set up the argument to come, how they elongate time, stretching it from days to years to centuries to ages, accumulating the speaker's praise for the lady. The first part of the speaker's argument is given right at the beginning—that the lady's coyness is a "crime." It only would not be a crime *if* they had all the time in the world. But, of course, they don't. The word "if" is implied. Also implied is a "therefore"; *therefore* the lady's coyness in the form of her delay, to her putting him off, is a crime against life.

The poem's second and middle section cuts to the chase; it gets down to the exigencies of reality, of real mortal time.

> But at my back I always hear
> Time's wingèd chariot hurrying near;
> And yonder all before us lie
> Deserts of vast eternity.
> Thy beauty shall no more be found;
> Nor in thy marble vault, shall sound
> My echoing song; then worms shall try
> That long-preserved virginity,
> And your quaint honour turn to dust,
> And into ashes all my lust:
> The grave's a fine and private place,
> But none, I think, do there embrace.

This middle segment of the poem introduces a sense of urgency. Its tone shifts from the courtly grace of the first section to violence and threat, with images meant to frighten. The speaker starkly describes the relentlessness of time, which will silence the poet's song, shutting up both the ears and the mouths of the speaker and his mistress. The image of worms violating the lady, the pun on quaint (a variant of "cunt"), their physical bodies turned to dust, their hot desire cooled to ashes in the cold grave—all these work together rhetorically to prod the lady into sexual submission. And yet the lines retain both the wit and humor of the opening section, though they are starker, darker. This section culminates with what is perhaps the poem's wittiest and most memorable couplet: "The grave's a fine and private place, / But none, I think, do there embrace."

It remains, now, only for the poet to have his speaker conclude with the logical follow-up to the evidence he has presented. And so we get both the logical language of "therefore," now explicitly stated, along with the emphatic urgency of the moment, with the use of "now." Marvell gives us that "now," insistently, no less than three times in this final section's first sentence.

> Now therefore, while the youthful hue
> Sits on thy skin like morning dew,
> And while thy willing soul transpires
> At every pore with instant fires,
> Now let us sport us while we may,
> And now, like amorous birds of prey,
> Rather at once our time devour
> Than languish in his slow-chapped power.
> Let us roll all our strength and all
> Our sweetness up into one ball,
> And tear our pleasures with rough strife
> Thorough the iron gates of life:
> Thus, though we cannot make our sun
> Stand still, yet we will make him run.

The power of the poem's final section comes partly from the end of its tight logical argument, partly from an emphasis on the energies of physical life, and partly from its insistence on action in the moment, in which flesh is conflated with spirit, body with soul, strength with sweetness. The speaker attempts to reverse all-devouring time by consuming it. The poem moves from an earlier emphasis on "I" and "you" to "we" and "us" and "our." In sexual union the couple, although unable to stop time's charge, instead seize their day and take their pleasure. Marvell's poem leaves us with the image of desire satisfied, the man's wish fulfilled, the lady still alluring, their love/lust amorous if rapacious. All the while, however, we cannot forget the finality of the grave and the fearful images of death conjured by the poet. "To His Coy Mistress" deserves its fame for its toughness and its lyric grace, as well as for its imagistic pyrotechnics and rhetorical power.

3 Tone—Stephen Crane
"War Is Kind"

A complex aspect of a poem's language is its tone—an author's or speaker's implied attitude toward a subject. Tone is an abstraction we make from the details of a poem's language, especially from choices of words and sentence patterns, of images and figures of speech, such as metaphor, a comparison between unlike things.

Understanding the tone of a literary work, in any genre, can be challenging. This is particularly problematic when its tone shifts, or changes. While tone is a writer's attitude toward his or her subject, it also encompasses a speaker's attitude toward an implied audience and imagined self. As Tony Hoagland points out in *real sofistikashun*, the expressive possibilities of tone are infinite. He suggests, further, that a writer's tone reveals how that writer is connected to the spoken or written words and how those words are connected to the world (84).

Let's consider the tone of the following poem, Stephen Crane's "War Is Kind":

> Do not weep, maiden, for war is kind.
> Because your lover threw wild hands toward the sky
> And the affrighted steed ran on alone,
> Do not weep.
> War is kind.
>
> > Hoarse, booming drums of the regiment,
> > Little souls who thirst for fight,
> > These men were born to drill and die.
> > The unexplained glory flies above them,
> > Great is the battle-god, great, and his kingdom—
> > A field where a thousand corpses lie.
>
> Do not weep, babe, for war is kind.
> Because your father tumbled in the yellow trenches,
> Raged at his breast, gulped and died,
> Do not weep.
> War is kind.

> Swift blazing flag of the regiment,
> Eagle with crest of red and gold,
> These men were born to drill and die.
> Point for them the virtue of slaughter,
> Make plain to them the excellence of killing
> And a field where a thousand corpses lie.
>
> Mother whose heart hung humble as a button
> On the bright splendid shroud of your son,
> Do not weep.
> War is kind.

What we notice, fairly quickly, in reading this poem, is how its title makes a strange assertion about the nature of war; it's surprising, if not shocking, to hear that war is "kind."

How can that be we might wonder. It doesn't take us long to find out from the poem's details that war is anything but "kind."

And so, we see that the poem's speaker's attitude toward war is not what his words seem to indicate. When a writer's words (in this case, the poem's speaker's words) are contradicted by other details—or when they seem to suggest the opposite of what they literally say—we have irony. The literary term "irony" refers to a discrepancy or opposition between what is said and what is meant. What is said is that "War is kind." What is meant is just the opposite. This is ironic language.

Irony also refers to situations where what is expected or predicted and what actually happens differ, which is irony of situation or circumstance, something we find in both fiction and drama, as well. We know that Crane's poem is ironic, that his speaker's tone is ironic because his attitude toward war is not what the words indicate. We know this because the details of death in battle described in stanzas 2 and 4 are antithetical to the poem's consoling refrain in stanzas 1, 3, and 5. In stanzas 2 and 4 the details of supposed military glory in the first three lines of each stanza sound hollow and false, when placed against the details of the last three lines of the stanzas.

The "booming drums" and the "blazing flag" of the regiment suggesting military valor are set against the brute fact that the men marching with the drums and behind the flag "were born to drill and die." The view that war is glorious and that death in battle honorable is countered with images of slaughter in "a field where a thousand corpses lie."

4 Literature and the Arts—Pieter Brueghel the Elder, W. H. Auden, William Carlos Williams, and Walt Whitman

Part of the pleasure we take in poems lies in watching what poets do with language and form when describing, translating, or interpreting a work of art that inspired them. One of the best-known and most interesting ties between poetry and painting is that surrounding Pieter Brueghel the Elder's painting *Landscape with the Fall of Icarus*, widely available for viewing on the internet.

Brueghel, himself, was influenced by the story of Icarus and Daedalus as told by the first-century Latin poet Ovid in his *Metamorphoses*. Here are a few lines in translation from Ovid, who specified "An angler fishing with his quivering rod, / A lonely shepherd propped upon his crook, / A plowman leaning on his plow." Of the three figures named by Ovid, only the shepherd in the painting appears to notice Icarus's fall from the sky. This singular witness in Brueghel's painting swerves from what Ovid had described: all three figures "looked up / And gazed in awe and thought they must be gods / That they could fly." Ovid, clearly, refers to both Icarus and his father, Daedalus, who made wax wings for each of them.

In effect, then, Brueghel's painting is an interpretation of and a deviation from the lines from Ovid that inspired it. Here, next, are two modern poems, one each by William Carlos Williams and W. H. Auden, who take inspiration from Brueghel's painting.

First, Williams's "Landscape with the Fall of Icarus":

> According to Brueghel
> When Icarus fell
> it was spring
>
> a farmer was ploughing
> his field
> the whole pageantry
>
> of the year was
> awake tingling
> near

the edge of the sea
concerned
with itself

sweating in the sun
that melted
the wings' wax

unsignificantly
off the coast
there was

a splash quite unnoticed
this was
Icarus drowning

And now Auden's "Musée des Beaux Arts":

About suffering they were never wrong,
The Old Masters: how well they understood
Its human position: how it takes place
While someone else is eating or opening a window or just walking dully along;
How, when the aged are reverently, passionately waiting
For the miraculous birth, there always must be
Children who did not specially want it to happen, skating
On a pond at the edge of the wood:
They never forgot
That even the dreadful martyrdom must run its course
Anyhow in a corner, some untidy spot
Where the dogs go on with their doggy life and the torturer's horse
Scratches its innocent behind on a tree.

In Brueghel's *Icarus*, for instance: how everything turns away
Quite leisurely from the disaster; the ploughman may
Have heard the splash, the forsaken cry,
But for him it was not an important failure; the sun shone
As it had to on the white legs disappearing into the green
Water; and the expensive delicate ship that must have seen
Something amazing, a boy falling out of the sky,
Had somewhere to get to and sailed calmly on.

The poets approach Brueghel's painting differently. Where Williams is descriptive and factual, Auden is meditative. Where Williams limits his poem to the painting proper, Auden uses his poem to exemplify an idea about suffering. Williams makes us look; Auden makes us think.

Williams avoids rhyme and employs irregular tercets, with most lines including two stresses, regardless of their differing numbers of syllables. He eschews punctuation. The only pauses in Williams's poem are those suggested at the line breaks. Auden, in contrast, uses many caesuras, or pauses. His lines capture the flow of speech and thought; the lines break sometimes in the beginning, sometimes midway, and sometimes at the end.

Auden's poem employs an intricate rhyme scheme. Its two stanzas function much like a sonnet, with the stanza's relative lengths (thirteen lines and eight lines) roughly observing the proportion of a sonnet's octave and sestet. Auden's rhyme pattern, however, is largely hidden; it doesn't call attention to itself. Stanza 1 rhymes *abcadedbfgfge*; stanza 2, *aabcddbc*.

We can read both poems much like we read a prose sentence—if we ignore the line breaks. Each poet, however, forces us to read his poem as a poem, with line breaks emphasizing visual details—bit by bit, in Williams's poem, through larger syntactic chunks, in Auden's. These differences matter; they create distinctly different reading (and listening) experiences, while providing different ways of viewing and considering Brueghel's painting.

Williams's poem directs our gaze to Brueghel's painting one detail at a time. Tercet by tercet, line by line, Williams leads our eye through *The Fall of Icarus*. He organizes our visual experience of Brueghel's painting. Auden, on the other hand, directs our thinking about the way old masters, like Brueghel, portrayed and understood human suffering. In provoking our thought, Auden's poem cries out for interpretation—for how we might explain the relationship between its two stanzas—the abstract generalization of the first stanza and the concrete illustration of the second, signaled by "for instance."

Williams focuses our attention on imagistic details, on specifics; Auden nudges us toward generalization. Both poems zig-zag between image and idea, though in strikingly distinctive ways.

If William Carlos Williams and W. H. Auden illustrate what might be done when poems conspire with paintings, Walt Whitman demonstrates how poetry can combine with music. Poetry, of course, is an inherently musical art, one that embodies rhythm in its very nature and adds metrical patterning and numerous sound effects to make its music. Whitman incorporates some of those features in his poems, but he also illustrates other ways that poems consort with music.

Walt Whitman's most famous poem, "Song of Myself," begins with a musical motif:

"I celebrate myself, and sing myself." This motif of the singer permeates not only this longest and most elaborate of Whitman's poems but also his entire body of work, the word "song" appearing more than 150 times throughout his body of poetry. The notion of song and singer is evident, too, in the titles of many poems from *Leaves of Grass*. To cite just a handful of examples: "For Him I Sing," "I Hear America Singing," "I Sing the Body Electric," "Song of the Open Road," "Song of the Answerer," "Song of Joys,"

"Song of the Broad-Axe," "Song of the Redwood Tree," "A Song for Occupations," "Song of India," and "Old Chants," among many others.

These and many of Whitman's poems—long and short—employ musical language and musical references. Consider these lines from section 26 of the 1892 "Death-bed" edition of "Song of Myself":

> I hear bravuras of birds, bustle of growing wheat, gossip of flames, clack of sticks cooking my meals,
> I hear the sound I love, the sound of the human voice,
> I hear all sounds running together, combined, fused or following,
> ...
> I hear the violoncello, ('tis the young man's heart's complaint,)
> I hear the key'd cornet, it glides quickly in through my ears,
> It shakes mad-sweet pangs through my belly and breast.

Beyond direct musical references, many of Whitman's poems embody musical form, with fugal textures and rondo forms animating longer poems, including "Song of Myself." Among the more brilliant of Whitman's poems that employ music as motif, and that use the language of music pervasively, is his dirge on the death of President Lincoln, "When Lilacs Last in the Dooryard Bloom'd," a heartfelt lament that throbs with personal emotion as the poet echoes the grief of a nation in mourning. Here, Whitman invokes the voice of a thrush:

> In the swamp in secluded recesses,
> A shy and hidden bird is warbling a song.
>
> Solitary the thrush,
> The hermit withdrawn to himself, avoiding the settlements,
> Sings by himself a song.
> ...
> Sing on, sing on you gray-brown bird,
> Sing from the swamps, the recesses, pour your chant from the bushes,
> Limitless out of the dusk, out of the cedars and pines.
>
> Sing on dearest brother, warble your reedy song,
> Loud human song, with voice of uttermost woe.

Of all the musical strains heard in Whitman's poetry, however, it is the music of opera that commands pride of place: "I hear the chorus, it is a grand opera, / Ah this indeed is music—this suits me." Joshua Barone has catalogued the range of reference to opera in Whitman's poetry, citing operas Whitman attended in New York in the 1850s—bel canto operas of Italian composers. In "Song of Myself" he describes a tenor, Alessandro Bettini, he heard on the stage:

> A tenor large and fresh as the creation fills me,
> The orbic flex of his mouth is pouring and filling me full.

And in "Proud Music of the Storm," Whitman mentions the contralto Marietta Alboni by name:

> The teeming lady comes,
> The lustrous orb, Venus contralto, the blooming mother,
> Sister of loftiest gods, Alboni's self I hear.

Whitman envisioned opera as a way to bring people together from different social and economic strata. Everyone, he believed, could take pleasure in the sheer beauty of a soprano's singing. Nor was anyone excluded from experiencing the power of the orchestra and the ways conductor, musicians, and singers synchronized their combined conveyance of emotion and of story. The opera, for Whitman, was a place to experience and celebrate multiple forms of beauty—of voice, of orchestral instruments, of narrative and musical form, and of social solidarity and a shared communal experience of the sublime.

5 Interrupted Reading—Robert Frost
"Stopping by Woods on a Snowy Evening"

One technique I have long used to help readers gain confidence with the experience of reading poetry is a "stop-and-go," interrupted reading. This approach involves working through a poem's lines, stanzas, and larger sections one at a time.

Let's do a careful parsing of the first stanza a bit at a time, and then consider how the second stanza relates to the first. I encourage you to see what's carried over from stanza 1 and what changes in stanza 2—what the poet/speaker focuses on and alters in each upcoming stanza.

Here is Robert Frost's "Stopping by Woods on a Snowy Evening," presented one stanza at a time, with intervening questions and comments, to illustrate this method of what we might call "interrupted reading."

> Whose woods these are I think I know.
> His house is in the village though;
> He will not see me stopping here
> To watch his woods fill up with snow.

Let's begin with some general comments and questions about the speaker and situation, about what's literally happening—what's being described. My aim is to get you settled into the poem's action and situation before considering more formal questions about its style and structure, rhythm and meter, rhyme and other sound effects and poetic elements. And so, I would suggest something like this: Frost's poem opens with a speaker who seems concerned momentarily about who owns the woods. The speaker seems reassured that the owner can't see him. We might wonder why the speaker should be concerned about this and why he bothers to mention it. Does he feel that he is doing something wrong? The poem doesn't say; instead it paints a picture of man, woods, and snow. And it raises questions: Why does the speaker stop? What attracts him? Here's the second stanza:

> My little horse must think it queer
> To stop without a farmhouse near
> Between the woods and frozen lake
> The darkest evening of the year.

DOI: 10.4324/9781003620280-8

The first stanza refers to the speaker himself; the second shifts attention to his horse. Perhaps you noticed that there's no punctuation within the second stanza—only a period at the end of its sentence. This observation prompts us to look back at the first stanza to see that it contains two sentences rather than one. Noticing the end words of those two sentences prompts us to see (and hear) the rhyme on "know" and "snow" (if we hadn't noticed it on our earlier reading of the poem aloud). We can save discussion of the rhyme pattern for a bit later, however; although you will likely begin looking at and listening to it, as Frost's use of an interlocking rhyme scheme is there for the hearing.

And so, next, we should consider just where the speaker is located at this point in the poem. You might be tempted to say that the speaker is "in" the woods, though he isn't—he's "between" the woods and a frozen lake, looking *into* the woods. In the first stanza the speaker describes the scene and his own action. In this second stanza, although he describes this scene and action further, he begins by mentioning that his horse is unaccustomed to stopping without a practical reason. Used to a pause for food and rest, the horse must wonder why his master is stopping since there is no farmhouse anywhere to be seen. The horse is said to "think," but we realize, of course, that the horse's thoughts are those of the speaker—that the speaker is projecting his thinking onto the horse, perhaps because the speaker himself sees the impracticality of stopping for anything other than food or rest. Here, next is stanza 3:

> He gives his harness bells a shake
> To ask if there is some mistake.
> The only other sound's the sweep
> Of easy wind and downy flake.

We should note the details continued from previous stanzas, and what if anything differs in this new stanza—how the poem is developing. We note that the third stanza continues the emphasis of the second on the horse, as the speaker interprets the horse's shake of harness bells as a signal to move on, as if to suggest that stopping there serves no useful purpose. What's added—what's new—is an emphasis on the stillness of the night, which highlights the privacy of the moment, its spell on the speaker, which is broken only by the sound of the horse's bells. We might consider, as well, the extent to which the speaker is feeling some unease, some tension, some doubt about what he is doing, while yet enjoying the "sweep of easy wind and downy flake."

The poem concludes in an unusual way: with a repeated line, which is impossible to miss.

> The woods are lovely, dark and deep,
> But I have promises to keep,
> And miles to go before I sleep,
> And miles to go before I sleep.

Most readers notice how the last stanza rhymes all four of its lines, effectively bringing the poem's action to a close. Let's look back, now, at the third stanza and identify the rhyme words there so we can see how the word "sweep" in line 3 carries over as the rhyming sound of the last stanza. Working backwards through the poem, you notice its interlocking rhyme pattern, with each stanza containing three rhymes in its four lines, and with the fourth unrhymed line serving as the rhyme sound for the next stanza. Although we could say more about rhyme and other poetic elements—meter and rhythm, among them—I encourage you to think a bit about the poem's possible significance, what it suggests.

Here is what Frost gets me thinking about as I read this poem.

The speaker seems to answer the question of why he stopped by the woods. He stopped because he was stirred by their dark beauty. Even so, however, he feels a need to move on, a pressure to return to his obligations and responsibilities. The final stanza is serious, even solemn. Frost slows it down by including pauses at the end of each line, something he has not done in any of the previous stanzas. And so we have to look back at the earlier stanzas to notice where the pauses occur. We discover that each stanza uses a different sequence of punctuation marks, resulting in a slightly different pace for each stanza, with slightly different emphases. Those variations keep the poem from becoming monotonous.

In repeating the final stanza's third line as the poem's concluding line, Frost invites us to consider more than its literal meaning—perhaps alluding to the final "sleep" of death. If we make this interpretive leap, then we can consider "miles to go" as the time the speaker has left to live, and "promises" as the responsibilities he wants to fulfill before he dies. His stopping to look at the falling snow can be seen as a temporary respite from those responsibilities, and perhaps even further as a desire to escape from them entirely. However far we may wish to push these (and other) interpretive possibilities, one thing seems clear: there is a tug of war going on in the speaker's mind and heart, a vacillation between two possibilities—stopping to contemplate the beauty of nature and returning to the world of human obligation and responsibility.

Now that we have done interrupted reading of the poem, I suggest that you read it again, aloud, one last time. In this interruption-free reading, you can savor the pleasures you now know the poem possesses and evokes in us readers.

Interlude I
Epic Poetry

Epics pose many challenges for readers. It's usually necessary to understand the context in which the epic exists—the culture from which it emerged. We need to know something about the civilization from which Homer's *Iliad*, for example, emanates, including its place in the history of literature. Even without this background knowledge, we can make some sense of the poem's opening lines. And so, let's dive into the poem's beginning:

> Rage—Goddess, sing the rage of Peleus' son Achilles,
> murderous, doomed, that cost the Achaeans countless losses,
> hurling down to the House of Death so many sturdy souls,
> great fighters' souls, but made their bodies carrion,
> feasts for the dogs and birds,
> and the will of Zeus was moving toward its end.
> Begin, Muse, when the two first broke and clashed,
> Agamemnon lord of men and brilliant Achilles... .

The proem, or opening lines, of the *Iliad* names its epic hero, Achilles, directly from the very first line. The *Iliad*'s opening is about war, and death, and the wrath of Achilles and his disagreement and disaffection with his king, Agamemnon. The lines also emphasize the role of the gods and their control over the fate of men.

We can parse the lines, considering the meaning of words and phrases, such as "Peleus' son," "Achaeans," the "Muse"/"Goddess" being addressed. The opening of the epic identifies central themes, employs epic conventions, such as the invocation of a muse, and introduces cultural beliefs, in this case, the "House of Death" where the souls of the dead descend.

Here are some of the things we learn, some of these at the beginning of our engagement with the *Iliad*, others along the way, and some at the end.

The *Iliad* describes a short period toward the end of the Trojan War (c. 1250 BCE), the ten-year siege that a band of ancient Greek military adventurers laid against the city of Troy. The work focuses on the anger and exploits of its hero, Achilles, renowned as the greatest of all soldiers. The *Iliad* begins with a quarrel between Achilles and the Greek king and military commander Agamemnon over the beautiful Trojan woman Briseis. Agamemnon had taken Briseis as his royal right, even though Achilles believed he had earned her as his share of the battle spoils. Achilles expresses his disgust with Agamemnon by withdrawing sulkily to his tent and refusing to do battle with the enemy. Without Achilles' help, the Greeks are repeatedly defeated by the Trojans. Achilles returns to battle only after his friend Patroclus is killed. Achilles then kills Hector, the son of the Trojan king Priam, and abuses his corpse out of frustration and guilt at having let his friend Patroclus die through his anger. The source of the quarrel, the reason for Achilles' return to battle, and the military exploits Homer describes in vivid detail all reflect the warrior world and code the *Iliad* celebrates. Though the gods are present throughout to comment on the action, at the center of Homer's world are his human actors.

Although the *Iliad* glorifies great deeds performed on the battlefield, the poem also conveys a sense of war's terrible consequences. Homer vividly describes battles, with armies arrayed against one another in deadly combat. He describes with equal drama the conflicting loyalties of heroes on both sides, as they take leave of their wives and families to kill one another in defense of honor and in pursuit of military glory. These heroic values are celebrated consistently throughout the epic, though the *Iliad*'s worldview is occasionally tempered by scenes that portray other, less military virtues. Kindheartedness and forgiveness, for example, are exemplified in the scenes between the Trojan warrior Hector and his family, and in the scene describing Achilles' meeting with the old Trojan king Priam, who comes to ask Achilles for the body of his slain son Hector.

Let's look next at the beginning of Homer's *Odyssey*:

> Sing to me of the man, Muse, the man of twists and turns
> driven time and again off course, once he had plundered
> the hallowed heights of Troy.
> Many cities of men he saw and learned their minds,
> many pains he suffered, heartsick on the open sea,
> fighting to save his life and bring his comrades home.
> But he could not save them from disaster, hard as he strove –
> the recklessness of their own ways destroyed them all,
> the blind fools, they devoured the cattle of the Sun
> and the Sungod blotted out the day of their return... .

Instead of identifying Odysseus by name, Homer calls him "the man of twists and turns," a description that reflects both Odysseus' wily nature and the convolutions of the epic's plot. Homer encapsulates key narrative elements, including Odysseus' lack of success in bringing his men back home from the Trojan War, which the author attributes to their own foolish behavior when they violate a god's prohibition.

The *Odyssey* contains a number of memorable episodes. Two of the most famous concern dangerous escapes. In one episode, Odysseus is captured by the giant one-eyed Cyclops. Odysseus gets the Cyclops drunk, blinds him with a stake, and escapes from the monster's cave by clinging to the belly of a sheep. In a second adventure, Odysseus and his men sail through the dangerous seas inhabited by the Sirens, whose enchanting singing causes sailors to crash their boats on the rocky shores of their island. To avoid this fate, Odysseus plugs his men's ears with wax and then has them tie him to the mast of their ship, his ears open to hear the Sirens' seductive singing.

These and other exotic events make the *Odyssey* different in spirit and temper from the *Iliad*. Other differences concern its hero Odysseus, who after a twenty-year absence from home returns to his wife Penelope, his son Telemachus, and his father Laertes, his mother Anticlea having died and been spirited to the underworld. Whereas Achilles' strength in the *Iliad* is purely physical, Odysseus also possesses mental fortitude. Odysseus' cunning and wit enable him to escape numerous dangerous predicaments. Odysseus seems much more modern than Achilles, and his journeys toward understanding and toward "home" and all that means take place in a world much closer to our own than does the more primitive world of the *Iliad*.

Where the *Iliad* is narrowly focused on the military world, the *Odyssey*'s values are those of home and hearth, of patience and fidelity, of filial piety, of the wisdom gained through suffering. The range and depth of its depiction of women far surpasses the *Iliad*'s image of women as the property of men. In addition to Odysseus' clever and faithful wife Penelope, the *Odyssey*'s female characters include the intelligent and beautiful princess Nausicaa; the dangerously seductive witch Circe; the goddess Calypso, who offers Odysseus immortality; Athena, who serves as Odysseus' guide and protector; and Odysseus' nurse Euryclea. Moreover, when Odysseus visits the Land of the Dead, he sees not only his mother Anticlea but other famous women of heroic times as well.

Odysseus' journey home is interrupted by his one-year stay with Circe and by the eight years he remains on Calypso's island. In total, he is absent from Penelope and home for twenty years, ten for the long siege of Troy and ten for his return voyage. This long delay is due partly to Odysseus' unalterable fate and partly to his temperament. Warring within him are two contrary impulses: a wish to return to the peaceful kingdom of Ithaca, where he reigns royally, and a desire to experience adventure and test himself against dangerous challenges. This split is echoed by the clash between Odysseus' temptation to forget his identity as husband, father, and king in his adventures, and his responsibility to resume these less exotic and more stable roles upon his return to Ithaca.

The *Odyssey* makes reference at a number of points to characters and events of the *Iliad*, most notably to the death of Achilles. In an important scene near the middle of the *Odyssey*, Homer has his hero descend to the underworld, where he meets the spirit of Achilles. Odysseus also encounters the shade of Agamemnon, whose murder by his wife Clytemnestra serves as a warning of the fate that could befall a man who has been away too long.

Homer uses the tragic story of the house of Atreus in thematic counterpoint to the duties and responsibilities of husband, wife, and son that the *Odyssey* endorses. In fact, the *Odyssey* is very much a poem about the relationships between husbands and wives, as well as those between fathers and sons. It raises important questions about what it means to be a true son, a son worthy of a great father; it raises questions about what the right relationship is between husband and wife, and what true compatibility between them might look like.

Insofar as the *Iliad* and *Odyssey* reflect an entire culture's values, the Homeric poems became the basis of Greek education. The human characters in the *Iliad* and the *Odyssey* served as models of conduct—of heroism and pride, of cunning and loyalty—for later generations. The Homeric gods, however, were less models of ideal behavior than influences on human events. Homer gives them a secondary importance, choosing instead to emphasize men and women living out mysterious destinies. Although honored and worshipped by the characters, the gods are also portrayed as worthy of blame as well as praise, of laughter as well as fear.

One additional feature of the proems to Homer's two epics and the poems themselves overall bears note—that in neither the *Iliad* nor *Odyssey* do we learn the details of the fall of Troy at the hands of the Greeks. It is not until Virgil tells that story in his Latin epic the *Aeneid* that we learn how the Greeks hid within the giant Trojan Horse, which the unsuspecting Trojans wheeled within the city walls, precipitating the ambush at night, their city set on fire, their elderly king decapitated at the altar where he prays for the safety of Troy, and the anguish and suffering of the women and children as their husbands and fathers are killed, and they taken into slavery.

Retellings of the Homeric epics have engaged novelists, including Madeline Miller's *Song of Achilles* (2011), which examines the *Iliad* from a modern, feminist standpoint, and *Circe* (2018), which tells the story of Odysseus through the eyes of the witch goddess. These latest efforts at translation and fictional reimagination of classic Western epics reflect a turn away from the deeply masculine and patriarchal values embodied in them and toward a more fully human sensibility.

Virgil's *Aeneid*

Arma virumque cano, "Arms and the man, I sing," begins Virgil's *Aeneid*, in which Virgil revisits Homer's epics but shifts the perspective from the Greek heroes to those of the Trojans, especially heroic leader, Aeneas, one of the few Trojans to survive the Greeks' annihilation of Troy. In the same way that Achilles and Odysseus are characterized throughout the *Iliad* and *Odyssey*, Aeneas is characterized, shown persisting doggedly through exile and suffering, until he fulfills his destiny to found a city that will eventually become Rome. The poem's very first lines invoke the *Iliad* and the *Odyssey* directly, "arms" referring to Achilles, and "the man" a reference to Odysseus, who

Homer first identifies as "the man of twists and turns." Virgil gracefully acknowledges these earlier epics to which his epic is indebted. Homage is an important Western epic convention.

Europe's most important written epic (the Homeric epics were originally chanted orally), the *Aeneid* chronicles the events leading to the founding of the city of Rome and the Roman Empire, especially the misfortunes and deprivations that accompany the heroic deeds it recounts. The poem concerns the Trojan prince Aeneas, who flees his home as it is being destroyed at the end of the Trojan War and sails away to found a new city in Italy—the successor to the great Trojan civilization. A story of origins and destinies, the *Aeneid* is the first nationalistic epic in Western literature, in some degree, intended to honor the first Roman Emperor, Augustus Caesar.

Here are the poem's opening lines in English translation:

> I sing of arms and the man, he who, exiled by fate,
> first came from the coast of Troy to Italy, and to
> Lavinian shores—hurled about endlessly by land and sea,
> by the will of the gods, by cruel Juno's remorseless anger,
> long suffering also in war, until he founded a city
> and brought his gods to Latium: from that the Latin people
> came, the lords of Alba Longa, the walls of noble Rome.

The first of the *Aeneid*'s twelve books begins *in medias res*, as Aeneas and his men are caught in a storm and shipwrecked at Carthage on the north African coast. Dido, the Carthaginian queen, provides food and shelter, and Aeneas describes the destruction of Troy at the hands of the Greeks (Book II) and his journey to Carthage (Book III). Smitten with Aeneas, Dido urges him to remain at her court rather than travel to Italy to establish a new home for his people. When Aeneas instead leaves her to fulfill his destiny, the queen takes her own life by throwing herself on a funeral pyre, the spiking flames of which are visible to Aeneas as he sails away (Book IV). Books V and VI describe Aeneas' arrival in Italy and his journey to the underworld—a characteristic feature of epic poems. In the second half of the poem (Books VII–XII), Virgil describes Aeneas' arrival at the Tiber River, which will be the site of the future city of Rome, and the Battle of the Trojans with the Latin people who live there, a battle ultimately won by the Trojans.

Aeneas struggles with both his conscience and his destiny. He experiences danger in battle and painful anguish; and he agonizes over his abandonment of Queen Dido. Virgil celebrates Aeneas' victory and his heroism, highlighting his courage and filial piety. Beyond his epic's hero, Virgil also expresses sympathy and compassion for all human beings, whose existence is characterized by suffering and sorrow, a form of stoic understanding captured in Virgil's words from Book II, *lacrimae rerum*, "the tears of things."

Virgil mirrors Homer in a number of ways. Aeneas' wanderings echo those of Odysseus, and Virgil's gods, like Homer's, fight amongst themselves to determine what obstacles the heroes will confront on their voyages. In having Venus serve as Aeneas' protector (she is also his mother), Virgil imitates Homer, whose Athena watches over Odysseus.

Midway through Book I of his *Aeneid*, Virgil accentuates Aeneas' destiny along with the prediction that he will found a city that will ultimately become Rome, from which the Romans will take their name. Shortly after, Aeneas lands in Carthage, which he learns is ruled by a queen, Dido, who has had built a magnificent temple, replete with depictions of historical events, including the fall of Troy. Virgil describes Aeneas as he reads and interprets the images of that war in the following lines:

> He found before his eyes the Trojan battles
> In the old war, now known throughout the world—
> The great Atridae, Priam, and Achilles,
> Fierce in his rage at both sides. Here Aeneas
> Halted, and tears came.
> "What spot on earth,"
> He said, "what region of the earth, Achates,
> Is not full of the story of our sorrow?
> Look, here is Priam. Even so far away
> Great valor has due honor; they weep here
> For how the world goes, and our life that passes
> Touches their hearts."
> (*Aeneid* I: 619–630, trans. Robert Fitzgerald)

Aeneas is stirred by stories of the war, through stories about his own exploits and those of his companions. It's not long before Dido and Aeneas meet and immediately become enchanted with one another, though Dido is described as being inflamed with passion for Aeneas through the efforts of Cupid. The soon to be lovers begin their acquaintance by filling each other in on their histories, and the first book concludes with Dido inviting Aeneas to provide a fuller rendering of his adventures during the Trojan War. But this is to come only after he is rested and feasted, according to the customs of hospitality, another echo of Homer and the many scenes of hospitality included in the *Odyssey*. Dido's invitation leads to the story Aeneas tells in Book II, which includes the famous description of the Greek ruse of the Trojan Horse, the fall of the city, Aeneas' escape with his father and son (but without his wife Creusa, who gets lost in the confusion—which sets Aeneas up nicely for his love affair with Dido).

While Book II is replete with stories of war, it also references relationships other than those between enemy warriors, and other themes than those linked with military stratagems, suffering, and glory. Virgil highlights family relationships, especially Aeneas' meeting with the ghost of his dead wife at the end of Book II. Echoing Homer once again, Aeneas tries to embrace his wife's spirit three times (as Odysseus attempted to embrace the shade of his mother in the underworld). Each time, in scenes of great poignancy, the spirit of wife and of mother escape the embrace of Aeneas and of Odysseus, respectively. Other key themes discussed are those of deceit and treachery, cunning and cleverness, courage and heroism amply evident in the epic's great second book.

Book III continues Aeneas' story, with an emphasis on his wanderings at sea. Virgil pays tribute once again in this book to Homer by having Aeneas tell about Scylla and Charybdis and the Cyclops, both of which loomed so large in the *Odyssey*. Book IV shifts our attention from war and wanderings to love in Carthage, from the Trojans defending unsuccessfully their embattled city and Aeneas encountering obstacles at sea to the passionate affair of Dido and Aeneas. Replete with speeches, some of them quite long, Virgil echoes Homer yet again, though Dido's and Aeneas' initial speeches of love and joy ultimately mutate into words of sorrow, anger, and madness. Aeneas' dialogue with Dido in Book IV is a supreme example of the complex and often sorrowful relationship of men and women, with their differing hopes and dreams of what the future can hold for each of them.

Like Homer's *Iliad*, Virgil's *Aeneid* depicts the horrors and the glories of war. Aeneas differs from Achilles in being less of a tempestuous warrior and a killing machine. And he differs from Odysseus in being less of a brilliant schemer and adventurer. Like Homer's *Odyssey*, Virgil's *Aeneid* describes its hero's adventures, both dangerous and amorous. In spite of Virgil's debt to Greek epic, however, the *Aeneid* is a thoroughly Roman poem. It is saturated in Roman traditions and marked at every turn by its respect for family and country, characterized by *pietas*, a devotion to duty, especially love and honor of one's family and country, with Aeneas referred to frequently with the epithet "*pius* Aeneas," that is, dutiful Aeneas.

Aeneas differs from Homer's epic heroes further in having a greater sense of responsibility. We see him suffer anguish over the choices he must make. And though he possesses free will, it is not without limits. He must fulfill his destiny, which is far more and far different than a sense of personal fulfillment. His destiny, rather, requires a repudiation of personal happiness in fulfillment of a larger and greater duty, a sense of national, even imperial, destiny that fate has determined for him, and which he accepts with grace and courage, though accompanied by sorrow and regret. Virgil's Aeneas displays a deeper self-consciousness than Homer's heroes, and he is a more complex psychological figure.

Part II
Reading Fiction—Five Ways In

Prelude II
The Pleasures of Fiction

Most readers respond well, often enthusiastically, to fiction. They enjoy stories; they like telling them, and they like hearing them. Readers want to know what will happen next in a story. They start to care about a story's or novel's characters from the beginning. Sometimes, readers become enamored with the voice of a story's narrator, especially if it's told in the first person, as in *Adventures of Huckleberry Finn*, *Jane Eyre*, and *The Catcher in the Rye*, to cite a few notable examples.

Just what are the pleasures of fiction? Why do stories hold such appeal for readers? What is their allure for us? We read stories largely for the emotional and intellectual pleasures they bring—the pleasure of being surprised or disturbed by an unexpected turn of events, or of being satisfied as our expectations are met, or surprised when they are not. Well-told stories involve us emotionally in the lives of their characters. Stories enthrall us; their words and images bring characters and their passions to life. Stories provide us with the pleasure of recognition and the thrill of vicarious experience. They allow us to live in the minds and worlds of others, widening our circle of sympathy and enhancing our capacity for empathy.

Fiction brings other pleasures and benefits, as well. Stories large and small serve as conversation-starters; they build bridges to fellow-readers; they create a place for exploring ideas about behavior and for thoughtful risk-taking. Reading good fiction improves our ability to focus, sustain our attention, follow a complex plot and character relationships. Fiction can contribute to deepened understanding and help provide us with confidence in our increasing accumulation of knowledge.

Stories delight with their plots, taking us on journeys of adventure and discovery. They instruct by showing us things we had not noticed or known; they help us see things in new ways, often from a different perspective or an alternate reality. "[W]hat if," asks Zadie Smith, "things were other than they are?" (*Feel Free* 337). Reading stories and novels enables us to enter many differently imagined worlds, all the while enlarging our imaginative capacities, deepening our perception of the actual world, and enriching our understanding of other people and of ourselves. Thomas Newkirk, in *Minds Made for Stories*, suggests how, through stories, we understand and explain ourselves to ourselves (22–28).

DOI: 10.4324/9781003620280-11

As Christopher Booker notes in *The Seven Basic Plots*, stories help "make us whole" (quoted in Cohen 147). Booker reminds us that we spend a large part of our speaking and listening lives with stories: we tell them, listen to them, read them (and maybe write them), as well as watch them on television and movie screens. There is no human interaction that does not involve stories—stories upon stories, their plots thickening, ramifying. We often ask people we meet, "What's your story?" by which we mean, among other things, who are you and how did you get here; where are you going and what do you want from us now and later, and from life, generally?

Stories help us understand ourselves; they help us make sense of where we come from and how we have arrived at wherever we find ourselves—and hint at where we may be going with our lives. Stories trace the trajectories of our lives.

In giving our lives form and shape, they create meaning for us. With its made-up stories and invented characters and details, fiction conveys deep truths about our human experience. Fiction, paradoxically, helps us make sense of reality.

Hernán Diaz suggests that the relationship between truth and fiction is neither rivalrous, nor mutually exclusive; instead, he claims that "truth resides, in some way, at the heart of fiction" (56). Diaz's concern is less with the way fiction mimics reality, or with the way it reveals either psychological or epistemological truths (though those are certainly of interest and value), than with how readers experience the truths that fiction captures and conveys (57). He suggests, further, that, in mediating and reflecting the ways we experience the world, fiction illustrates a "distinctive relationship to truth," one in which fiction not only imitates experience, but which is, "itself, an experience" (65).

In sync with Diaz, Kate Briggs describes how the novel creates "a time-space, a duration in and within which to ask…questions about the basic conditions of being." The novel, she suggests, prompts readers to speculate about "the states of people and things and the forces that act upon them. About which processes are habitual, which ones can be continuously and steadily, securely or oppressively reproduced, and for that reason are felt as ongoing, inescapable, permanent" (57).

And Tim Parks suggests that fiction, novels especially, in all their singular particularity, introduce us to each author's "different world of feeling, which itself is part of reality." He adds that the novels of the past enable us to experience vicariously the "ethos of the time," against which we can understand our own time better (43).

Along with Diaz, Briggs, and Parks, Steven Pinker remarks that "the cliché that life imitates art is true because the function of some kinds of art is for life to imitate it" (543). This certainly seems true for fiction.

Reading fiction gives us opportunities to experience various kinds of social interaction virtually; in the process, we learn how to negotiate social situations in our actual lives. Fiction expands our experiential range of options, especially in making decisions. We see how fictional characters act and react; we observe the choices they make, including bad choices and serious mistakes, from which we can learn what not to do. Novels, especially, present us with the opportunity to get inside the minds of characters. They give us practice in making decisions; they allow us to watch characters' choices play out in their fictive lives rather than having to make such decisions in our own actual lives.

Here is one example from many—the character of Isabel Archer, protagonist of Henry James's *The Portrait of a Lady*, makes a bad decision in choosing whom to marry. Isabel's innocence leads her to marry an egotist and imposter, Gilbert Osmond, who marries her for her money and who tyrannizes over her. The novel's heroine suffers disillusionment and disappointment, forgoing divorcing the mercenary Osmond and his scheming accomplice Madame Merle. Readers get the benefit of seeing how Isabel makes her fateful choices without having to endure the pain and loss she undergoes.

Another example includes choices made by Mark Twain's Huckleberry Finn, choices that set him against the prevailing attitudes and manners and morals of late nineteenth-century America. Twain depicts Huck's conflict, his basic decency and honesty at war with what he has been taught he should do with respect to the slave Jim, who is seeking his freedom. "All right," says Huck at one point, "I'll go to Hell," thinking that in helping Jim escape he's acting immorally, going against what he's been taught is right, and that he'll pay the price in eternal damnation. Through irony in the service of satire, Twain enforces Huck's values as the right ones, in a reversal of the then conventional wisdom and common practice regarding race and enslavement. Huck's decision exemplifies a transvaluation of societal values.

One of our finest contemporary writers of short fiction, George Saunders, suggests another benefit in reading fiction. He claims that in studying the ways we read fiction, we learn how our minds work. Saunders claims that learning to read fiction attentively, while developing a capacity for finer-grained observations and responses in that reading, can transform us into "more active, curious, alert readers of reality" (8).

That's one of fiction's benefits, and simultaneously, one of its pleasures. Saunders' comment, moreover, opens the door to considerations about the relationship of fiction to reality—of how made-up stories intersect with our everyday lives. Another contemporary writer, Italian Nobel laureate Patrick Modiano, suggests that a book that profoundly moves or thrills you can make you a more sensitive person, and therefore a better one. Modiano claims, that this is the "moral function" of literature.

Another contemporary writer, Zadie Smith, asked herself whether she could get readers to "believe in the imaginary people [she] places in...fictional situations." She decided that if that was to happen, she would have to ensure that some of the feelings of her fictional characters had to experience "some passing relation to feelings [she]...had or could imagine. That [their] griefs were not entirely unrelated." Smith's goal as a storyteller, she has noted, is to make visible the "invisible griefs we might share, over and above our many manifest and significant differences." One way Smith accomplishes this is through the dialogue she creates for her characters, through the voices she gives them to express their griefs, along with their joys (quoted in Mendelson, 24).

Dialogue

Among the pleasures of fiction is dialogue, which is crucial to both short stories and novels. Dialogue, as Richard Cohen notes, "makes a story more lifelike" (105), less something we hear about and observe. We listen to characters come to life speaking to each other and reacting to what they say to each other (as they do in plays). In fiction, dialogue overlaps with its functions in drama—setting a scene, conveying tone, establishing characterization and character relationships, requiring a reader's close attention. Consider the following passage—the opening of Ernest Hemingway's story "The Short Happy Life of Francis Macomber," which prompts the reader to make a number of inferences:

> It was now lunch time and they were all sitting under the double green fly of the dining tent pretending that nothing had happened.
> "Will you have lime juice or lemon squash?" Macomber asked.
> "I'll have a gimlet," Robert Wilson told him.
> "I'll have a gimlet, too. I need something," Macomber's wife said.
> "I suppose it's the thing to do," Macomber agreed.
> "Tell him to make three gimlets."

The story's first sentence invites us to imagine that something has happened—something significant because "they" are all *pretending* that "nothing" has occurred. We, of course, strongly suspect otherwise. And we are curious about what they were ignoring. "What happened?" we wonder.

The opening conversation reveals something about the seriousness of what has happened—the title character's wife needs a drink as a result—and that conversation also suggests a character hierarchy. Whatever has caused Mrs. Macomber's need for alcohol must be serious. But she's not the one who initiates the request for a drink; her husband does that—with a question about the drink to be made. Macomber asks this question of the hunter guide Robert Wilson, who answers directly, without hesitation. Wilson knows what he wants: "a gimlet." There's no hesitation; there's no waffling. Wilson's direct, unequivocal declaration is a sign of his authority. Macomber's question indicates his inferiority. Wilson is top dog here. Macomber's wife is the one with a "need"; she responds first, and following her statement comes Francis Macomber's response, which suggests that he is a follower—of Wilson and of his wife. He is third and last in this pecking order. We don't find out why until a bit later in the story.

What's missing, however, in these examples, is straight dialogue, stripped of description. Here's an example from Denis Johnson's story "Steady Hands at

Seattle General," in which one patient in a rehab or detox center is shaving another:

> "Someday people are going to read about you in a story or poem. Will you describe yourself for those people?"
> "Oh, I don't know. I'm a fat piece of shit, I guess."
> "No, I'm serious."
> "You're not going to write about me."
> "Hey. I'm a writer."
> "Well then, just tell them I'm overweight."
> "He's overweight."
> "I been shot twice."
> "Twice?"
> "One by each wife, for a total of three bullets, making four holes, three ins and one out."
> "And you're still alive."
> "Are you going to change any of this for your poem?"
> "No. It's going in word for word."

The story concludes a bit later, with the roommate speaking first:

> "Well, I'm older than you are. You can take a couple more rides on this wheel and still get out with all your arms and legs stuck on right. Not me."
> "Hey. You're doing fine."
> "Talk into here."
> "Talk into your bullet hole?"
> "Talk into my bullet hole. Tell me I'm fine."
>
> (Davis 260)

I'm indebted to Lydia Davis for this example and for the explanation of its effectiveness. Davis suggests that Johnson's dialogue here fulfills half a dozen functions:

> (1) it sounds natural, (2) but it is more vivid and more interesting; (3) it reveals character or is in character; (4) it reveals the relationship or is true to the relationship; (5) it reveals or enhances the characters' situation; and (6) it enhances or advances the story.
>
> (259)

Rhythm

Another element of fiction we might consider is the writer's use of rhythm. Rhythm, of course, is an aspect of style. It's a feature of a writer's stylistic repertoire of options, his or her stylistic tool kit. The word "rhythm" derives from the Greek *rhythmos*, which refers to regularly recurring stylistic elements, including patterns of stress and accent, sounds and silences. Rhythm involves regular elements of repetition—of syllable, word, phrase, and clause; and it comprises patterns of sound and structure, as well. Rhythm is embedded in the musical aspect of writing. It appeals less to the mind than to the ear, less to concepts than to the way concepts are brought to life in word and image. A writer's use of rhythm embodies his or her thought, giving it breath and life through sound, including the sound of dialogue.

Look back at the passages from Hemingway's short story, and then ahead to the opening lines of Jane Austen's *Pride and Prejudice* to see how each establishes a pattern of rhythm for the dialogue between its characters—and for the inclusion of interpolated comments by each writer's narrator.

Suspense

No story, long or short, will have readers continue reading without suspense as to what comes next. Those brief bits of dialogue from "The Short Happy Life of Francis Macomber" get us wondering about what just happened to elicit them. The longer dialogue between Mr. and Mrs. Bennet from *Pride and Prejudice*, which occurs a bit later, arouses our curiosity about whether the Bennet girls will find suitable spouses—and how that might happen.

Suspense, of course, is an element of plot, of a narrative's developing action. Suspense operates, nevertheless, in dialogue and description—at the level of the paragraph and even of the sentence. A fiction writer (indeed writers of non-fiction, too) needs to create sentences and paragraphs, pages, and chapters that carry us forward—that make us want to read on to the next sentence, paragraph, page, scene, chapter. How they do this is a matter of both craft and art, as Hemingway and Austen demonstrate in their scenes from story and novel we have considered. Whereas Hemingway begins his story in the middle of things (something has already happened that we want to know about), Austen begins her novel at the beginning—all the action is yet to come. Hemingway hooks us by intriguing us, making us wonder what has happened. Austen does it by setting the stage for what will happen, creating a prelude to the ensuing action when our curiosity will be satisfied.

As Kathryn Schulz suggests, the main question regarding life concerns plot rather than meaning; we are eager to know what comes next in our lives, and then what happens after that—and with what consequences. In literature and in life, Schulz argues, "suspense is a response to uncertainties," creating "a state of agitation produced by the desire to know what the future holds"— that is, to resolve uncertainty. "Suspense," she suggests, "is central to our emotional landscape" (23).

Successful writers know how to capitalize on this fact of human experience; the greatest of them can prolong suspense—keep us waiting, as nineteenth-century British novelist Wilkie Collins advised, and then waiting again and yet again. Some writers do it with chapters that end with the proverbial "cliffhanger," named for an end-of-chapter scene in which a Thomas Hardy character chases a wind-blown hat, and finds himself actually hanging over the edge of a precipice.

Other nineteenth-century novelists like Charles Dickens, whose novels appeared serially, in monthly or bi-monthly installments, made readers wait for the next installment, leaving them hanging for a month to find out what would happen next in the novel. To maintain a hold on their readers, those writers perfected the art of the cliffhanger.

Form

And, finally, in this brief set of introductory notes on fiction, a few words about form. Or better, a few *additional* words about form, as my previous comments in Part I, on poetry, contain a longer consideration of form. Here we are concerned with how Jane Austen and Ernest Hemingway artfully arrange their dialogue and sentences, including where to place their authorial comments.

Rather than repeat here some of my comments about form found in the chapter on poetry, I will simply note that whatever experience fiction creates for readers results from a work's form. And that form (or those forms) derive from a writer's conscious and unconscious choices, reflected in patterns and arrangements of language and incident, which create in the reader a series of emotions.

Our experience of literature, works of fiction included, involves not only cognitive perception but an experience of feeling, of emotion, as well. That's what distinguishes fiction, largely, from expository and argumentative prose. In the 1868 essay "Notes on Form," George Eliot asks, "What is fiction other than an arrangement of events or feigned correspondences according to a predominant feeling?" (quoted in Diaz 66). That arrangement is a matter of form and of feeling; feeling and form exist in a mutually supporting, reciprocal relationship.

6 Questions—Katherine Anne Porter
"Rope"

Questions constitute the first way in to fiction—questions about Katherine Anne Porter's short story "Rope." Those questions focus on details of description and dialogue; character and action; repetition and contrast; cause and effect; theme and idea. A consideration of values is central to the discussion. A brief commentary is also provided for the story.

We can anchor these considerations about fiction by reading and reflecting on "Rope" with our focus on making inferences and considering implications. As you read Porter's story be alert for details of description, dialogue, and action; make connections among them; look for patterns of repetition and contrast, of cause and effect in the story's language and incidents. Consider the relationship between the story's two characters and the values each embodies and represents.

> On the third day after they moved to the country he came walking back from the village carrying a basket of groceries and a twenty-four-yard coil of rope. She came out to meet him, wiping her hands on her green smock. Her hair was tumbled, her nose was scarlet with sunburn; he told her that already she looked like a born country woman. His gray flannel shirt stuck to him, his heavy shoes were dusty. She assured him he looked like a rural character in a play.
>
> Had he brought the coffee? She had been waiting all day long for coffee. They had forgot it when they ordered at the store the first day.
>
> Gosh, no, he hadn't. Lord, now he'd have to go back. Yes, he would if it killed him. He thought, though, he had everything else. She reminded him it was only because he didn't drink coffee himself. If he did he would remember it quick enough. Suppose they ran out of cigarettes? Then she saw the rope. What was that for? Well, he thought it might do to hang clothes on, or something. Naturally she asked him if he thought they were going to run a laundry? They already had a fifty-foot line hanging right before his eyes? Why, hadn't he noticed it, really? It was a blot on the landscape to her.
>
> He thought there were a lot of things a rope might come in handy for. She wanted to know what, for instance. He thought a few seconds, but

nothing occurred. They could wait and see, couldn't they? You need all sorts of strange odds and ends around a place in the country. She said, yes, that was so; but she thought just at that time when every penny counted, it seemed funny to buy more rope. That was all. She hadn't meant anything else. She hadn't just seen, not at first, why he felt it was necessary.

Well, thunder, he had bought it because he wanted to, and that was all there was to it. She thought that was reason enough, and couldn't understand why he hadn't said so, at first. Undoubtedly it would be useful, twenty-four yards of rope, there were hundreds of things, she couldn't think of any at the moment, but it would come in. Of course. As he had said, things always did in the country.

But she was a little disappointed about the coffee, and oh, look, look, look at the eggs! Oh, my, they're all running! What had he put on top of them? Hadn't he known eggs mustn't be squeezed? Squeezed, who had squeezed them, he wanted to know. What a silly thing to say. He had simply brought them along in the basket with the other things. If they got broke it was the grocer's fault. He should know better than to put heavy things on top of eggs.

She believed it was the rope. That was the heaviest thing in the pack, she saw him plainly when he came in from the road, the rope was a big package on top of everything. He desired the whole wide world to witness that this was not a fact. He had carried the rope in one hand and the basket in the other, and what was the use of her having eyes if that was the best they could do for her?

Well, anyhow, she could see one thing plain: no eggs for breakfast. They'd have to scramble them now, for supper. It was too damned bad. She had planned to have steak for supper. No ice, meat wouldn't keep. He wanted to know why she couldn't finish breaking the eggs in a bowl and set them in a cool place.

Cool place! If he could find one for her, she'd be glad to set them there. Well, then, it seemed to him they might very well cook the meat at the same time they cooked the eggs and then warm up the meat for tomorrow. The idea simply choked her. Warmed-over meat, when they might as well have had it fresh. Second best and scraps and makeshifts, even to the meat! He rubbed her shoulder a little. It doesn't really matter so much, does it, darling? Sometimes when they were playful, he would rub her shoulder and she would arch and purr. This time she hissed and almost clawed. He was getting ready to say that they could surely manage somehow when she turned on him and said, if he told her they could manage somehow she would certainly slap his face.

He swallowed the words red hot, his face burned. He picked up the rope and started to put it on the top shelf. She would not have it on the top shelf, the jars and tins belonged there; positively she would not have the top shelf cluttered up with a lot of rope. She had borne all the clutter she meant to bear in the flat in town, there was space here at least and she meant to keep things in order.

Well, in that case, he wanted to know what the hammer and nails were doing up there? And why had she put them there when she knew very well he needed that hammer and those nails upstairs to fix the window sashes? She simply slowed down everything and made double work on the place with her insane habit of changing things around and hiding them.

She was sure she begged his pardon, and if she had had any reason to believe he was going to fix the sashes this summer she would have left the hammer and nails right where he put them; in the middle of the bedroom floor where they could step on them in the dark. And now if he didn't clear the whole mess out of there she would throw them down the well.

Oh, all right, all right—could he put them in the closet? Naturally not, there were brooms and mops and dustpans in the closet, and why couldn't he find a place for his rope outside her kitchen? Had he stopped to consider there were seven God-forsaken rooms in the house, and only one kitchen?

He wanted to know what of it? And did she realize she was making a complete fool of herself? And what did she take him for, a three-year-old idiot? The whole trouble with her was she needed something weaker than she was to heckle and tyrannize over. He wished to God now they had a couple of children she could take it out on. Maybe he'd get some rest.

Her face changed at this, she reminded him he had forgot the coffee and had bought a worthless piece of rope. And when she thought of all the things they actually needed to make the place even decently fit to live in, well, she could cry, that was all. She looked so forlorn, so lost and despairing he couldn't believe it was only a piece of rope that was causing all the racket. What was the matter, for God's sake?

Oh, would he please hush and go away, and stay away, if he could, for five minutes? By all means, yes, he would. He'd stay away indefinitely if she wished. Lord, yes, there was nothing he'd like better than to clear out and never come back. She couldn't for the life of her see what was holding him, then. It was a swell time. Here she was, stuck, miles from a railroad, with a half-empty house on her hands, and not a penny in her pocket, and everything on earth to do; it seemed the God-sent moment for him to get out from under. She was surprised he hadn't stayed in town as it was until she had come out and done the work and got things straightened out. It was his usual trick.

It appeared to him that this was going a little far. Just a touch out of bounds, if she didn't mind his saying so. Why the hell had he stayed in town the summer before? To do a half-dozen extra jobs to get the money he had sent her. That was it. She knew perfectly well they couldn't have done it otherwise. She had agreed with him at the time. And that was the only time so help him he had ever left her to do anything by herself.

Oh, he could tell that to his great-grandmother. She had her notion of what had kept him in town. Considerably more than a notion, if he wanted to know. So, she was going to bring all that up again, was she? Well, she could just think what she pleased. He was tired of explaining. It may have looked funny but he had simply got hooked in, and what could he do? It was impossible to believe that she was going to take it seriously. Yes, yes, she knew how it was with a man: if he was left by himself a minute, some woman was certain to kidnap him. And naturally he couldn't hurt her feelings by refusing!

Well, what was she raving about? Did she forget she had told him those two weeks alone in the country were the happiest she had known for four years? And how long had they been married when she said that? All right, shut up! If she thought that hadn't stuck in his craw.

She hadn't meant she was happy because she was away from him. She meant she was happy getting the devilish house nice and ready for him. That was what she had meant, and now look! Bringing up something she had said a year ago simply to justify himself for forgetting her coffee and breaking the eggs and buying a wretched piece of rope they couldn't afford. She really thought it was time to drop the subject, and now she wanted only two things in the world. She wanted him to get that rope from underfoot, and go back to the village and get her coffee, and if he could remember it, he might bring a metal mitt for the skillets, and two more curtain rods, and if there were any rubber gloves in the village, her hands were simply raw, and a bottle of milk of magnesia from the drugstore.

He looked out at the dark blue afternoon sweltering on the slopes, and mopped his forehead and sighed heavily and said, if only she could wait a minute for anything, he was going back. He had said so, hadn't he, the very instant they found he had overlooked it?

Oh, yes, well … run along. She was going to wash windows. The country was so beautiful! She doubted they'd have a moment to enjoy it. He meant to go, but he could not until he had said that if she wasn't such a hopeless melancholiac she might see that this was only for a few days. Couldn't she remember anything pleasant about the other summers? Hadn't they ever had any fun? She hadn't time to talk about it, and now would he please not leave that rope lying around for her to trip on? He picked it up, somehow it had toppled off the table, and walked out with it under his arm.

Was he going this minute? He certainly was. She thought so. Sometimes it seemed to her he had second sight about the precisely perfect moment to leave her ditched. She had meant to put the mattresses out to sun, if they put them out this minute they would get at least three hours, he must have heard her say that morning she meant to put them out. So of course he would walk off and leave her to it. She supposed he thought the exercise would do her good.

Well, he was merely going to get her coffee. A four-mile walk for two pounds of coffee was ridiculous, but he was perfectly willing to do it. The habit was making a wreck of her, but if she wanted to wreck herself there was nothing he could do about it. If he thought it was coffee that was making a wreck of her, she congratulated him: he must have a damned easy conscience.

Conscience or no conscience, he didn't see why the mattresses couldn't very well wait until tomorrow. And anyhow, for God's sake, were they living in the house, or were they going to let the house ride them to death? She paled at this, her face grew livid about the mouth, she looked quite dangerous, and reminded him that housekeeping was no more her work than it was his: she had other work to do as well, and when did he think she was going to find time to do it at this rate?

Was she going to start on that again? She knew as well as he did that his work brought in the regular money, hers was only occasional, if they depended on what she made – and she might as well get straight on this question once for all!

That was positively not the point. The question was, when both of them were working on their own time, was there going to be a division of the housework, or wasn't there? She merely wanted to know, she had to make her plans. Why, he thought that was all arranged. It was understood that he was to help. Hadn't he always, in summers?

Hadn't he, though? Oh, just hadn't he? And when, and where, and doing what? Lord, what an uproarious joke!

It was such a very uproarious joke that her face turned slightly purple, and she screamed with laughter. She laughed so hard she had to sit down, and finally a rush of tears spurted from her eyes and poured down into the lifted corners of her mouth. He dashed towards her and dragged her up to her feet and tried to pour water on her head. The dipper hung by a string on a nail and he broke it loose. Then he tried to pump water with one hand while she struggled in the other. So he gave it up and shook her instead.

She wrenched away, crying out for him to take his rope and go to hell, she had simply given him up: and ran. He heard her high-heeled bedroom slippers clattering and stumbling on the stairs.

He went out around the house and into the lane; he suddenly realized he had a blister on his heel and his shirt felt as if it were on fire. Things broke so suddenly you didn't know where you were. She could work herself into a fury about simply nothing. She was terrible, damn it: not an ounce of reason. You might as well talk to a sieve as that woman when she got going. Damned if he'd spend his life humoring her! Well, what to do now? He would take back the rope and exchange it for something else. Things accumulated, things were mountainous, you couldn't move them or sort them out or get rid of them. They just lay and rotted around. He'd take it back. Hell, why should he? He wanted it. What was it anyhow? A piece of rope. Imagine anybody caring more about a piece of rope than about a man's feelings. What earthly right had she to say a word about it? He remembered all the useless, meaningless things she bought for herself: Why? because I wanted it, that's why! He stopped and selected a large stone by the road. He would put the rope behind it. He would put it in the tool-box when he got back. He'd heard enough about it to last him a life-time.

When he came back she was leaning against the post box beside the road waiting. It was pretty late, the smell of broiled steak floated nose high in the cooling air. Her face was young and smooth and fresh-looking. Her unmanageable funny black hair was all on end. She waved to him from a distance, and he speeded up. She called out that supper was ready and waiting, was he starved?

You bet he was starved. Here was the coffee. He waved it at her. She looked at his other hand. What was that he had there?

Well, it was the rope again. He stopped short. He had meant to exchange it but forgot. She wanted to know why he should exchange it, if it was something he really wanted. Wasn't the air sweet now, and wasn't it fine to be here?

She walked beside him with one hand hooked into his leather belt. She pulled and jostled him a little as he walked, and leaned against him. He put his arm clear around her and patted her stomach. They exchanged wary smiles. Coffee, coffee for the Ootsum-Wootsums! He felt as if he were bringing her a beautiful present.

He was a love, she firmly believed, and if she had had her coffee in the morning, she wouldn't have behaved so funny ... There was a whippoor-will still coming back, imagine, clear out of season, sitting in the crab-apple tree calling all by himself. Maybe his girl stood him up. Maybe she did. She hoped to hear him once more, she loved whippoorwills ... He knew how she was, didn't he?

Sure, he knew how she was.

After reading this story, we might well find ourselves trying to predict the couple's future relationship based on what we see and hear in the story's present action. The following comments and questions can prompt consideration of its central preoccupations.

Comments

We notice that the man and woman are unnamed, and that they talk to each other largely with questions. We notice, further, that their questions affect each other, stimulate reactions in each other. Before long, we realize they are less conversing than arguing. We might wonder what their argument is about, what initiated it. We suspect that unspoken issues lie behind their argument.

We notice, also, that the story's western setting shifts from country to town and back. We might consider what each of these places means, respectively, for the man and for the woman—how town and country help us understand the characters' habits and values, as well as their relationship.

In addition, we notice differences in the kinds of language the man and woman use in speaking to each other. Her language is more polished, educated, and refined than his. He says things like "Gosh, no" and "Well, thunder." She describes him with comparisons, including a "rural character in a play," and sees the clothesline as "a blot on the landscape." Moreover, he repeats himself bluntly and stodgily, whereas she asks sarcastic questions. Their speech leads us to make inferences about linguistic and cultural gulfs between them. And we might wonder, further, just whether they can remain a couple for long under the weight of their differences. You can use the following questions to guide your analysis and thinking about "Rope."

Questions

1. To what extent is "Rope" a story about discord and misunderstanding, perhaps about the incompatibility of how men and women think and see things? To what extent is the story about struggle, hard work, and hope?
2. Do you see "Rope" as primarily about male/female relationships? About marriage? Do you think the marriage portrayed in the story has much or little chance for survival? On what textual evidence do you base your answer?
3. Whose values do you think the story favors, if it favors either character? What values influence your own reading of the story? What values are reflected in the man's attitudes and behavior? What values seem to animate the woman's attitudes and her behavior?
4. What, for you, are two critically important moments in the story? How do these moments help to advance your thinking about it? To what extent do your selected moments deepen your feelings or extend your sympathies, and for whom? To what extent do your moments reflect particular values? Which moments and which values?
5. What do you make of the story's ending—its final details? How would you characterize its tone—angry, bitter, confident, hopeful, condescending, reassuring? Use evidence from the story to support your view.
6. What values does each character reflect and represent? To what extent do the values of the wife and husband conflict? To what extent do they harmonize and complement one another?
7. Why do you think the author entitled her story "Rope"? What might the rope represent?

7 Surprises—Edgar Allan Poe
"The Cask of Amontillado"

Another way in to fiction is through a reading of short tales with a surprising twist of an ending—"The Monkey's Paw," for example, or "The Lottery," or any number of stories that end with ironic twists by O. Henry or Guy de Maupassant. Edgar Allan Poe's "The Cask of Amontillado" is one of my favorites:

> The thousand injuries of Fortunato I had borne as I best could, but when he ventured upon insult I vowed revenge. You, who so well know the nature of my soul, will not suppose, however, that gave utterance to a threat. At length I would be avenged; this was a point definitely, settled—but the very definitiveness with which it was resolved precluded the idea of risk. I must not only punish but punish with impunity. A wrong is unredressed when retribution overtakes its redresser. It is equally unredressed when the avenger fails to make himself felt as such to him who has done the wrong.
>
> It must be understood that neither by word nor deed had I given Fortunato cause to doubt my good will. I continued, as was my wont to smile in his face, and he did not perceive that my smile now was at the thought of his immolation.
>
> He had a weak point—this Fortunato—although in other regards he was a man to be respected and even feared. He prided himself on his connoisseurship in wine. Few Italians have the true virtuoso spirit. For the most part their enthusiasm is adopted to suit the time and opportunity, to practice imposture upon the British and Austrian millionaires. In painting and gemmary, Fortunato, like his countrymen, was a quack, but in the matter of old wines he was sincere. In this respect I did not differ from him materially;—I was skillful in the Italian vintages myself, and bought largely whenever I could.
>
> It was about dusk, one evening during the supreme madness of the carnival season, that I encountered my friend. He accosted me with excessive warmth, for he had been drinking much. The man wore motley. He had on a tight-fitting parti-striped dress, and his head was surmounted by the conical cap and bells. I was so pleased to see him that I thought I should never have done wringing his hand.

I said to him—"My dear Fortunato, you are luckily met. How remarkably well you are looking to-day. But I have received a pipe of what passes for Amontillado, and I have my doubts."

"How?" said he. "Amontillado, A pipe? Impossible! And in the middle of the carnival!"

"I have my doubts," I replied; "and I was silly enough to pay the full Amontillado price without consulting you in the matter. You were not to be found, and I was fearful of losing a bargain."

"Amontillado!"

"I have my doubts."

"Amontillado!"

"And I must satisfy them."

"Amontillado!"

"As you are engaged, I am on my way to Luchresi. If anyone has a critical turn it is he. He will tell me—"

"Luchesi cannot tell Amontillado from Sherry."

"And yet some fools will have it that his taste is a match for your own."

"Come, let us go."

"Whither?"

"To your vaults."

"My friend, no; I will not impose upon your good nature. I perceive you have an engagement. Luchesi—"

"I have no engagement;—come."

"My friend, no. It is not the engagement, but the severe cold with which I perceive you are afflicted. The vaults are insufferably damp. They are encrusted with nitre."

"Let us go, nevertheless. The cold is merely nothing. Amontillado! You have been imposed upon. And as for Luchesi, he cannot distinguish Sherry from Amontillado."

Thus speaking, Fortunato possessed himself of my arm; and putting on a mask of black silk and drawing a roquelaire closely about my person, I suffered him to hurry me to my palazzo.

There were no attendants at home; they had absconded to make merry in honour of the time. I had told them that I should not return until the morning, and had given them explicit orders not to stir from the house. These orders were sufficient, I well knew, to insure their immediate disappearance, one and all, as soon as my back was turned.

I took from their sconces two flambeaux, and giving one to Fortunato, bowed him through several suites of rooms to the archway that led into the vaults. I passed down a long and winding staircase, requesting him to be cautious as he followed. We came at length to the foot of the descent, and stood together upon the damp ground of the catacombs of the Montresors.

The gait of my friend was unsteady, and the bells upon his cap jingled as he strode.

"The pipe," he said.

"It is farther on," said I; "but observe the white web-work which gleams from these cavern walls."

He turned towards me, and looked into my eyes with two filmy orbs that distilled the rheum of intoxication.

"Nitre?" he asked, at length.

"Nitre," I replied. "How long have you had that cough?"

"Ugh! ugh! ugh!—ugh! ugh! ugh!—ugh! ugh! ugh!—ugh! ugh! ugh!—ugh! ugh! ugh!"

My poor friend found it impossible to reply for many minutes.

"It is nothing," he said, at last.

"Come," I said, with decision, "we will go back; your health is precious. You are rich, respected, admired, beloved; you are happy, as once I was. You are a man to be missed. For me it is no matter. We will go back; you will be ill, and I cannot be responsible. Besides, there is Luchesi—"

"Enough," he said; "the cough's a mere nothing; it will not kill me. I shall not die of a cough."

"True—true," I replied; "and, indeed, I had no intention of alarming you unnecessarily—but you should use all proper caution. A draught of this Medoc will defend us from the damps."

Here I knocked off the neck of a bottle which I drew from a long row of its fellows that lay upon the mould.

"Drink," I said, presenting him the wine.

He raised it to his lips with a leer. He paused and nodded to me familiarly, while his bells jingled.

"I drink," he said, "to the buried that repose around us."

"And I to your long life."

He again took my arm, and we proceeded.

"These vaults," he said, "are extensive."

"The Montresors," I replied, "were a great and numerous family."

"I forget your arms."

"A huge human foot d'or, in a field azure; the foot crushes a serpent rampant whose fangs are imbedded in the heel."

"And the motto?"

"Nemo me impune lacessit."

"Good!" he said.

The wine sparkled in his eyes and the bells jingled. My own fancy grew warm with the Medoc. We had passed through long walls of piled skeletons, with casks and puncheons intermingling, into the inmost recesses of the catacombs. I paused again, and this time I made bold to seize Fortunato by an arm above the elbow.

"The nitre!" I said; "see, it increases. It hangs like moss upon the vaults. We are below the river's bed. The drops of moisture trickle among the bones. Come, we will go back ere it is too late. Your cough—"

"It is nothing," he said; "let us go on. But first, another draught of the Medoc."

I broke and reached him a flagon of De Grave. He emptied it at a breath. His eyes flashed with a fierce light. He laughed and threw the bottle upwards with a gesticulation I did not understand.

I looked at him in surprise. He repeated the movement—a grotesque one.

"You do not comprehend?" he said.

"Not I," I replied.

"Then you are not of the brotherhood."

"How?"

"You are not of the masons."

"Yes, yes," I said; "yes, yes."

"You? Impossible! A mason?"

"A mason," I replied.

"A sign," he said, "a sign."

"It is this," I answered, producing from beneath the folds of my roquelaire a trowel.

"You jest," he exclaimed, recoiling a few paces. "But let us proceed to the Amontillado."

"Be it so," I said, replacing the tool beneath the cloak and again offering him my arm. He leaned upon it heavily. We continued our route in search of the Amontillado. We passed through a range of low arches, descended, passed on, and descending again, arrived at a deep crypt, in which the foulness of the air caused our flambeaux rather to glow than flame.

At the most remote end of the crypt there appeared another less spacious. Its walls had been lined with human remains, piled to the vault overhead, in the fashion of the great catacombs of Paris. Three sides of this interior crypt were still ornamented in this manner. From the fourth side the bones had been thrown down, and lay promiscuously upon the earth, forming at one point a mound of some size. Within the wall thus exposed by the displacing of the bones, we perceived a still interior crypt or recess, in depth about four feet, in width three, in height six or seven. It seemed to have been constructed for no especial use within itself, but formed merely the interval between two of the colossal supports of the roof of the catacombs, and was backed by one of their circumscribing walls of solid granite.

It was in vain that Fortunato, uplifting his dull torch, endeavoured to pry into the depth of the recess. Its termination the feeble light did not enable us to see.

"Proceed," I said; "herein is the Amontillado. As for Luchesi—"

"He is an ignoramus," interrupted my friend, as he stepped unsteadily forward, while I followed immediately at his heels. In niche, and finding an instant he had reached the extremity of the niche, and finding his progress arrested by the rock, stood stupidly bewildered. A moment more and I had fettered him to the granite. In its surface were two iron staples, distant from each other about two feet, horizontally. From one of these depended a short chain, from the other a padlock. Throwing the links about his waist, it was but the work of a few seconds to secure it. He was too much astounded to resist. Withdrawing the key I stepped back from the recess.

"Pass your hand," I said, "over the wall; you cannot help feeling the nitre. Indeed, it is very damp. Once more let me implore you to return. No? Then I must positively leave you. But I must first render you all the little attentions in my power."

"The Amontillado!" ejaculated my friend, not yet recovered from his astonishment.

"True," I replied; "the Amontillado."

As I said these words I busied myself among the pile of bones of which I have before spoken. Throwing them aside, I soon uncovered a quantity of building stone and mortar. With these materials and with the aid of my trowel, I began vigorously to wall up the entrance of the niche.

I had scarcely laid the first tier of the masonry when I discovered that the intoxication of Fortunato had in a great measure worn off. The earliest indication I had of this was a low moaning cry from the depth of the recess. It was not the cry of a drunken man. There was then a long and obstinate silence. I laid the second tier, and the third, and the fourth; and then I heard the furious vibrations of the chain. The noise lasted for several minutes, during which, that I might hearken to it with the more satisfaction, I ceased my labours and sat down upon the bones. When at last the clanking subsided, I resumed the trowel, and finished without interruption the fifth, the sixth, and the seventh tier. The wall was now nearly upon a level with my breast. I again paused, and holding the flambeaux over the mason-work, threw a few feeble rays upon the figure within.

A succession of loud and shrill screams, bursting suddenly from the throat of the chained form, seemed to thrust me violently back. For a brief moment I hesitated, I trembled. Unsheathing my rapier, I began to grope with it about the recess; but the thought of an instant reassured me. I placed my hand upon the solid fabric of the catacombs, and felt satisfied. I reapproached the wall; I replied to the yells of him who clamoured. I re-echoed, I aided, I surpassed them in volume and in strength. I did this, and the clamourer grew still.

It was now midnight, and my task was drawing to a close. I had completed the eighth, the ninth and the tenth tier. I had finished a portion of the last and the eleventh; there remained but a single stone to be fitted and plastered in. I struggled with its weight; I placed it partially in its destined position. But now there came from out the niche a low laugh that erected the hairs upon my head. It was succeeded by a sad voice, which I had difficulty in recognizing as that of the noble Fortunato. The voice said—

"Ha! ha! ha!—he! he! he!—a very good joke, indeed—an excellent jest. We will have many a rich laugh about it at the palazzo—he! he! he!—over our wine—he! he! he!"

"The Amontillado!" I said.

"He! he! he!—he! he! he!—yes, the Amontillado. But is it not getting late? Will not they be awaiting us at the palazzo, the Lady Fortunato and the rest? Let us be gone."

"Yes," I said, "let us be gone."

"For the love of God, Montresor!"

"Yes," I said, "for the love of God!"

But to these words I hearkened in vain for a reply. I grew impatient. I called aloud—

"Fortunato!"

No answer. I called again—

"Fortunato!"

No answer still. I thrust a torch through the remaining aperture and let it fall within. There came forth in return only a jingling of the bells. My heart grew sick; it was the dampness of the catacombs that made it so. I hastened to make an end of my labour. I forced the last stone into its position; I plastered it up. Against the new masonry I re-erected the old rampart of bones. For the half of a century no mortal has disturbed them. *In pace requiescat*!

Comments

This story, quite simply, is about revenge. We are told that right away. And what a surprising kind of revenge it is that Poe provides—walling up one's enemy in a dank cellar, where no one will hear his cries for help—where the victim knows that his plight is hopeless. It adds insult to injury, we might say—key terms for Poe's story.

"The Cask of Amontillado" presents a few challenges for readers. First, you need to know that a "cask" is a large barrel, and that Amontillado is a type of fortified sherry wine of good quality. You also need to know that the Latin words that conclude the story, "*In pace requiescat*," translate as "May he rest in peace." Those Latin words, in English translation, form part of the Catholic Mass for the dead, where they are meant literally. That is, congregants pray that the person who has died will, indeed, rest in peace eternally.

However, we are meant to understand that the narrator of Poe's story uses the words of that prayer for peace ironically—meaning the opposite of what they literally suggest. This is one of many ironies in Poe's story—the culminating one, for sure, but perhaps not even the most significant of those ironic twists. Let's identify a few other examples of Poe's irony.

One of the most obvious, perhaps, is the name of the victim, "Fortunato," who, it turns out, is anything but fortunate, meeting his unexpected and unimagined fate at the hands of Poe's vengeance-prone narrator. This is an irony of language—as is the example of the Latin words that conclude the story.

A second type of irony in the story—and the most prevalent one—involves the discrepancy between what Fortunato knows and what we readers know—what the narrator is actually doing. Fortunato is oblivious to the evil machinations of his enemy, the narrator. Ironically, in fact, Fortunato believes the narrator is his friend, who is about to share with him information about and enjoyment of a precious cask of sherry wine. Fortunato expects one thing; the reality is just the opposite; hence the irony.

In addition, there is both irony and evil in the ways that the narrator lures Fortunato deeper into the catacombs, playing upon Fortunato's presumed and proudly proclaimed knowledge of wines. Fortunato considers himself a connoisseur; and so, Poe's narrator uses Fortunato's pride in his expertise to advance his designs against him. Fortunato's strength of knowledge becomes, ironically, a major weakness and a key element in his downfall. It's a powerful example of how an evil character, with acute insights into human psychology, preys upon the weaknesses of another. The classic example is Shakespeare's Iago, who plays upon the play's title character, Othello, by driving him to insane fits of jealousy, such that he suffocates his innocent, loving wife, Desdemona.

I will leave you to discover and relish other examples of ironic language and action in Poe's marvelous story. But I do need to explain a couple of things that might present a challenge, largely due to Poe's extensive vocabulary. In the story's opening paragraph Poe writes: "I must not only punish but punish with impunity." The narrator, that is, needs to get his revenge without himself incurring punishment; with "impunity." He will lead Fortunato to his death without anyone knowing—and thus escaping retribution for his crime. The narrator explains further: "A wrong is unredressed when retribution overtakes its redresser." This means, essentially, that if the person getting his revenge is found out and punished—experiencing "retribution" for his crime—then the initial wrong done to him [as he imagines it] has never been properly avenged. And a bit more from our narrator on this important idea: "It is equally unredressed when the avenger [our narrator] fails to make himself felt as such to him who has done the wrong [Fortunato]." In other words, Fortunato must fully understand that the narrator is enacting revenge against him for a wrong Fortunato did to our narrator in the past.

Poe makes it clear that his narrator is out for vengeance. And that his consuming idea is "at the thought of his [Fortunato's] immolation." There's another one of Poe's Latin-based vocabulary words—immolation referring to Fortunato's complete destruction.

I might call your attention, as well, to the story's setting during a time of carnival. Fortunato is dressed in a costume of motley—multicolored clothing, with jingling bells and a traditional fool's cap, which symbolize his foolishness in believing what the narrator tells him.

And, finally (though there is much more to admire in this tightly crafted story), we should note that the narrator has kept secret his cunningly executed murder of Fortunato for half a century. And yet, we might wonder to whom the narrator is speaking. Who is listening to his grisly tale? And why is he telling it now after all these years? Has he been longing to reveal his clever stratagem—to seek his listeners' admiration for his ingenuity? Perhaps he doesn't want to go to his own grave unacknowledged for his ingenious accomplishment in defeating his unfortunate enemy in this remarkably vindictive way.

To conclude this discussion of "The Cask of Amontillado," here are a few additional questions to consider.

1. To what extent can you sympathize with the narrator's desire for revenge? Have you ever wanted to get even with someone who insulted you?
2. To what extent were you surprised (and perhaps impressed) by the degree of preparation undertaken by the narrator in avenging himself on Fortunato? To what extent were you sympathetic to the victim?
3. Why do you think the narrator insists upon the importance of making himself known to Fortunato as his avenger?
4. Identify some specific ways that the narrator lures his victim to his death? How does he use his understanding of Fortunato and of human nature generally to enact his plan?
5. Consider what the details of the story's setting contribute to its tone and mood and effect.

8 Voices—Jane Austen
Pride and Prejudice

The first thing we hear when reading a story is a voice—often the voice of the story's narrator, sometimes, however, the voice of one or another character. Depending on the author's choice of point of view and angle of vision, that voice can be the voice of the story's central character or of a secondary character; it can be a first-person voice or a third-person voice in those cases, respectively. We hear Huckleberry Finn, David Copperfield, Jane Eyre, and Holden Caulfield, for example, in their own first-person voices. We hear each of their stories told by an "I."

On the other hand, we hear the stories of Herman Melville's Captain Ahab, of F. Scott Fitzgerald's Gatsby, of George Eliot's Dorothea Brooke, and of Henry James's Isabel Archer, but not from their own mouths. Instead of their voices, we hear the voice of another narrator. In the case of Ahab and Gatsby, another character in the book tells their stories, Ishmael and Nick Carraway, respectively for *Moby-Dick* and *The Great Gatsby*. In the case of George Eliot's and Henry James's novels, their central characters' stories are told through a third-person narrator, omniscient in *Middlemarch* and with partial knowledge of characters' thoughts and feelings in *The Portrait of a Lady*.

Dialogue in fiction operates magically at the hands of the most accomplished writers—Jane Austen, of course, among them. The best loved, perhaps, of her novels, *Pride and Prejudice* contains one of her most brilliant openings. Let's listen to some of the dialogue near the beginning of her novel.

> "My dear Mr. Bennet," said his lady to him one day, "have you heard that Netherfield Park is let at last?"
> Mr. Bennet replied that he had not.
> "But it is," returned she; "for Mrs. Long has just been here, and she told me all about it."
> Mr. Bennet made no answer.
> "Do not you want to know who has taken it?" cried his wife impatiently.
> "You want to tell me, and I have no objection to hearing it."
> This was invitation enough.
> "Why, my dear, you must know, Mrs. Long says that Netherfield is taken by a young man of large fortune from the north of England; that

he came down on Monday in a chaise and four to see the place, and was so much delighted with it that he agreed with Mr. Morris immediately; that he is to take possession before Michaelmas, and some of his servants are to be in the house by the end of next week."

"What is his name?"

"Bingley."

"Is he married or single?"

"Oh! Single, my dear, to be sure! A single man of large fortune; four or five thousand a year. What a fine thing for our girls!"

"How so? How can it affect them?"

"My dear Mr. Bennet," replied his wife, "how can you be so tiresome! You must know that I am thinking of his marrying one of them."

...

Mr. Bennet was so odd a mixture of quick parts, sarcastic humour, reserve, and caprice, that the experience of three-and-twenty years had been insufficient to make his wife understand his character. *Her* mind was less difficult to develop. She was a woman of mean understanding, little information, and uncertain temper. When she was discontented, she fancied herself nervous. The business of her life was to get her daughters married; its solace was visiting and news.

In listening carefully to this dialogue, you hear three voices—the voice of the narrator in three brief comments interpolated between the voices of two characters, Mr. Bennet and Mrs. Bennet. What do you hear in each of these voices? What impression do you get in listening to the conversation between Mr. and Mrs. Bennet through what they say and how they say it?

Consider, also, the impression we gain of the narrator through the novel's three interpolated comments during the married couple's conversation. What impression do we gain of Austen's narrator? What does this narrative voice convey about Mr. and Mrs. Bennet?

Austen's opening dialogue introduces us to two things: to her novel's primary subject—marriage and its connection with money and status—and to a pair of important characters, who, we soon learn, have five daughters in need of marital partners. And so, we might say that this opening dialogue shows us what's important in the world of *Pride and Prejudice* while introducing us to its characters' values. The brief dialogue provides a quick look, too, at the novel's setting—rural England in the late 1790s, when Austen wrote the novel—though it wasn't published until 1813. Country estates, briefly mentioned here, become a major concern of the Bennet family as the novel progresses.

Here, at the beginning of *Pride and Prejudice*, we need to be especially alert to Jane Austen's tone—to the attitude she takes to Mr. and Mrs. Bennet, which is considered a bit later in Interlude II: The Novel and Novella.

9 Fiction, History, Art—Ernest Hemingway

"The Revolutionist" and *A Farewell to Arms*

Our next way in to reading fiction is to consider it in relationship to a discipline outside of literature proper, as we did in our discussion of poems by W.H. Auden and William Carlos Williams in Part I. The following discussion can be used as a way to consider this extended aspect of literary engagement.

Just as the study of history can shed light on literature, so can the study of literature illuminate history. We might consider, for instance, how F. Scott Fitzgerald's novel *The Great Gatsby* illuminates the roaring twenties, how Mark Twain's *Adventures of Huckleberry Finn* illustrates aspects of mid-nineteenth-century southwestern America, or how Gustave Flaubert's *Madame Bovary* helps us understand provincial life in early nineteenth-century France.

In studying literature, we would situate each of these novels in history to better understand their historical contexts. In studying history, we would seek to understand how the novels enrich and clarify our understanding of the times in which they were written.

Let's consider an example: Ernest Hemingway's sketch "The Revolutionist" from his first book, *In Our Time*. The opening paragraph requires historical contextualization.

> In 1919 he was traveling on the railroads in Italy, carrying a square of oilcloth from the headquarters of the party written in indelible pencil and saying here was a comrade who had suffered very much under the Whites in Budapest and requesting comrades to aid him in any way….He was a Magyar, a very nice boy and very shy. Horthy's men had done some bad things to him. He talked about it a little. In spite of Hungary, he believed altogether in the world revolution.
>
> (157)

We can't make sense of these details without understanding the text's historical references. We need to answer the following questions about historical context. What was happening in 1919 in Italy (and Europe generally)? Who were the "Whites" in Budapest? Who was Horthy, what is a Magyar, and why does the narrator say "In spite of Hungary"?

DOI: 10.4324/9781003620280-15

We also need to consider other words in the paragraph, such as "comrades," "party," and "revolution," which, in conjunction with the year 1919 indicate the Russian Revolution, which began in 1917, and, more specifically, with the events in Hungary and in Italy two years later. Even if our historical knowledge of the time is shaky, we can begin to see that, given even this briefest of explanations, the "bad things" Horthy's men did to the narrator involved torture; that "he," the narrator, was being aided by Communist comrades; and that Horthy and his men were enemies of the revolution. These details require additional clarification.

Our young narrator was imprisoned for his politics and tortured by Horthy and the "Whites" in Hungary. The young man has come to Italy, his faith in the revolution uncompromised by his former sufferings. And even though the counter-revolution of the Whites against the Reds has set back their revolutionary agenda, the young revolutionist narrator believes things will go better—in Italy especially.

The historical record of course ironically indicates the opposite, as Mussolini and the fascist right seized power against the leftist socialist revolutionaries. Hemingway's little character sketch was written after those events had taken place. There is, thus, considerable irony in his depiction of the young man's idealism foundering on the jagged rocks of history. Youthful idealism is here skewered on those sharp edges; the narrator, however, remains blithely oblivious to that cruel reality.

Once those facts are identified, we can consider Hemingway's artistry. An interdisciplinary perspective that includes both literature and history enhances our understanding and appreciation of this brief sketch. It also enlarges our understanding of the book as a whole, whose title, *In Our Time*, reflects the period of World War I and just after.

For a fuller understanding and appreciation of "The Revolutionist," moreover, a reader needs to bring an additional perspective to bear—that of art history. Consider this excerpt from a bit later in the sketch:

> He had been in many towns, walked much, and seen many pictures. Giotto, Masaccio, and Piero della Francesca he bought reproductions of and carried them wrapped in a copy of *Avanti*. Mantegna he did not like....I spoke to him about the Mantegnas in Milano. "No," he said, very shyly, he did not like Mantegna.
>
> (158)

Besides knowing that the Italian word "*avanti*" means to advance or go forward, and that *Avanti* was a Communist newspaper (linguistic and historical facts), a reader needs to know something about Renaissance art, especially the paintings of Giotto, Masaccio, Piero della Francesca, and Mantegna (art history). Only then does the young revolutionist's repugnance for the paintings of Mantegna make sense—especially if we understand who Horthy was and what he and his men did to political opponents like our idealistic revolutionist.

Here, we will note only that the works of the first three painters are typically pleasing in color and in composition. They are easy to enjoy. They are, for the most part, beautiful to behold.

Not so with the paintings of Andrea Mantegna. A look at two of Mantegna's paintings *The Dead Christ* and *The Martyrdom of St. Sebastian* will enable you to see why Hemingway's young revolutionary, having been tortured by Horthy's men, would not find those paintings to his liking. You can find them easily on the internet.

As a character in Hemingway's novel *A Farewell to Arms* puts it referring to the first painting: "lots of nail holes"—the last thing the revolutionist could stand to look at. Mantegna portrays the dead Christ with sallow complexion, sagging body protruding penis, and a drawn countenance; the painting is completely unidealized.

Mantegna depicts St. Sebastian with numerous arrows protruding from his bound body, along with bloody wounds. For a realistic writer like Hemingway, however, the unflinching and unsentimental art of Mantegna held an appeal that correlates directly with his own stark realism as a writer.

Other painters whose works influenced Hemingway's fiction and whose art requires consideration are Francisco de Goya and Paul Cézanne. Hemingway was familiar with Goya's bullfight etchings; from those he derived an appreciation not only of Goya's art but of the art of bullfighting as well, something that figures prominently in both *In Our Time* and in *The Sun Also Rises*. Hemingway also references Goya's etching from *The Disasters of War*, in which a corpse holds a stone with the word "nada" (nothing) incised. Hemingway provides a verbal counterpart to Goya's "nada" in "A Clean, Well-Lighted Place," in which the narrator travesties the Lord's prayer, negating its message of hope by casting it in a tone of despair: "our nada who art in nada, nada be thy name thy Kingdom nada thy will be nada in nada as it is in nada" (383).

The relationship between Cézanne's painting and Hemingway's writing is different. Hemingway did not reference any particular painting of Cézanne in his fiction. Instead, he attempted to do with words what Cézanne had done with paint. Hemingway once said, "I learned how to make a landscape from Mr. Paul Cézanne by walking through the Luxembourg Museum a thousand times" (60). One thing he learned was that landscapes in Cezanne's work are composed of geometric forms in a series of interlocking planes. Another was the way a landscape's colors modulate from one to another, enhancing and emphasizing those geometric shapes, as exemplified in the series of paintings Cézanne made of Mont Sainte-Victoire.

Hemingway strove to convey what he saw, heard, and felt, as immediately and directly as possible. One way he did so was by contrasting the stable, solid geometry of nature with the changing movements of human characters. To convey both the landscape and associated mood, Hemingway relied on concrete diction arranged in paratactic clauses (clauses joined by "and"). Cézanne's influence on Hemingway is apparent in the following passage, excerpted from the opening of *A Farewell to Arms*:

In the late summer of that year we lived in a house in a village that looked across the river and the plain to the mountains. In the bed of the river there were pebbles and boulders, dry and white in the sun, and the water was clear and swiftly moving and blue in the channels. Troops went by the house and down the road and the dust they raised powdered the leaves of the trees. The trunks of the trees too were dusty and the leaves fell early that year and we saw the troops marching along the road and the dust rising and leaves, stirred by the breeze, falling and the soldiers marching and afterward the road bare and white except for the leaves.

The plain was rich with crops; there were many orchards of fruit trees and beyond the plain the mountains were brown and bare. There was fighting in the mountains and at night we could see the flashes from the artillery. In the dark it was like summer lightning, but the nights were cool and there was not the feeling of a storm coming.

....in the fall when the rains came the leaves all fell from the chestnut trees and the branches were bare and the trunks black with rain. The vineyards were thin and bare branched too and all the country wet and brown and dead with the autumn. There were mists over the river and clouds on the mountain and the trucks splashed mud on the road and the troops were muddy and wet in their capes; their rifles were wet and under their capes the two leather cartridge-boxes on the front of the belts, gray leather boxes heavy with the packs of clips of thin, long 6.5 mm. cartridges, bulged forward under the capes so that the men, passing on the road, marched as though they were six months gone with child....

At the start of the winter came the permanent rain and with the rain came the cholera. But it was checked and in the end only seven thousand died of it in the army.

(3–4)

Like Cézanne, Hemingway portrays form through color. His prose depicts nature as a symbol of stability and endurance, a backdrop against which he reveals the changing circumstances of his characters. As Michael Reynolds has pointed out, the novel's opening chapter is replete with contrasting images. In the beginning, the bare mountains contrast the plain, fruitful with crops and abundant, colorful orchards. The mountains, by contrast, are sterile, brown, and sere. Enforcing this contrast of fertility and sterility are leaves and dust, both of which suggest death, further enforced by the vineyards, "thin and bare-branched...and all the country wet and brown and dead with the autumn" (4).

A contrast between natural and human forces accompanies the life and death of nature. Troops stir up dust; soldiers march in the plains and fire artillery in the mountains; they hide their weapons under capes that make them look like pregnant women. These contrasts Hemingway exploits in his typical matter-of-fact, low-key manner. Nonetheless, the images accumulate an increasingly ominous destructive power, wrought in turn by the artillery in the mountains, by the cholera, which killed "only" seven thousand, and by the dust into which all soldiers eventually subside.

The passage works much like an imagist poem: "in the fall when the rains came the leaves all fell from the chestnut trees and the branches were bare and the trunks black with rain." The predominant image of rain—mist, wet, damp, fog—is accompanied by images of desolation and by a tone of unremitting bleakness that is never dissipated, whatever temporary respite the characters may experience.

It is not so much that we can't understand Hemingway's fiction without knowledge of Mantegna's paintings, Goya's etchings, Cézanne's landscapes, or Christian prayer. It is, rather, that knowledge of political and art history, and of Christian faith, clarifies Hemingway's intent and artistry. That knowledge underscores the thematic finality of death; it helps us better comprehend the despair and hopelessness of Hemingway's characters. Understanding how Hemingway uses art and religion—how he deploys his knowledge in his works—increases our appreciation of his literary achievement.

10 Interrupted Reading—Kate Chopin
"The Story of an Hour"

Even though we may read stories and novels line by line, sentence by sentence, and page by page, these forms of linearity belie what happens mentally as we read. Our mental action in reading literature is cyclical rather than linear. We project ahead, and we glance back; we remember and we predict. Doing so enables us to follow a story and make sense of it in the first place and to see more in it on subsequent readings.

To exemplify the actual *process* of reading a short work of fiction, I have chunked, or divided, Kate Chopin's "The Story of an Hour" into six segments. Between the sections I have interpolated comments and questions to reflect the actual process of one reader's reading. They highlight the *experience* of reading literature; they demonstrate how we read toward an *interpretation* of a literary work; and they consider various *values* Chopin's story embodies—especially social, cultural, and sexual values.

One of the benefits of the interrupted reading is that we can see how a writer prepares readers to connect and relate particular bits of description and dialogue. We can also gain experience in seeing how a story develops and progresses, and how writers direct readers' attention to key elements of plot, character, imagery, setting, point of view, and other fictional elements.

> Knowing that Mrs. Mallard was afflicted with a heart trouble, great care was taken to break to her as gently as possible the news of her husband's death.
>
> It was her sister Josephine who told her, in broken sentences; veiled hints that revealed in half concealing. Her husband's friend Richards was there, too, near her. It was he who had been in the newspaper office when intelligence of the rail-road disaster was received, with Brently Mallard's name leading the list of "killed." He had only taken the time to assure himself of its truth by a second telegram, and had hastened to forestall any less careful, less tender friend in bearing the sad message.
>
> She did not hear the story as many women have heard the same, with a paralyzed inability to accept its significance. She wept at once, with sudden, wild abandonment, in her sister's arms. When the storm of grief had spent itself she went away to her room alone. She would have no one follow her.

Comments

The comments that follow each segment of the story include both observations and questions. The observations are designed to point to details to consider, relate to one another, and ultimately use as a basis for understanding of the story.

The opening action is presented quickly and economically. We are not given Mrs. Mallard's first name. And we might wonder if there is any significance in the name "Mallard." Do we hear something suggestive in the description of Mrs. Mallard's ailment as "a heart trouble"? A literal heart problem, or a metaphorical one? Perhaps both? More important than these details is the announcement of her husband's death. Mrs. Mallard is contrasted with other women who sit paralyzed by such news—women who refuse, initially at least, to accept the significance and finality of such an announcement. We notice that Mrs. Mallard weeps with "sudden, wild abandonment," after which she wishes to be alone in her room. What kind of weeping is this? And what might it signify?

The story continues:

> There stood, facing the open window, a comfortable, roomy armchair. Into this she sank, pressed down by a physical exhaustion that haunted her body and seemed to reach into her soul.
>
> She could see in the open square before her house the tops of trees that were all aquiver with the new spring life. The delicious breath of rain was in the air. In the street below a peddler was crying his wares. The notes of a distant song which some one was singing reached her faintly, and countless sparrows were twittering in the eaves.
>
> There were patches of blue sky showing here and there through the clouds that had met and piled one above the other in the west facing her window.
>
> She sat with her head thrown back upon the cushion of the chair, quite motionless, except when a sob came up into her throat and shook her, as a child who has cried itself to sleep continues to sob in its dreams.

Comments

The setting for the middle section of the story is Mrs. Mallard's room. She looks out through an open window. What is the significance of the things she notices—trees, birds, rain, patches of blue sky, peddler, and song—and what do they have in common? To what extent is Mrs. Mallard's noticing of these things important? The narrator compares Mrs. Mallard to a child who sobs in its dreams. We may wonder about the implications of this comparison.

Here is the next segment of the story:

> She was young, with a fair, calm face, whose lines bespoke repression and even a certain strength. But now there was a dull stare in her eyes, whose

gaze was fixed away off yonder on one of those patches of blue sky. It was not a glance of reflection, but rather indicated a suspension of intelligent thought.

There was something coming to her and she was waiting for it, fearfully. What was it? She did not know; it was too subtle and elusive to name. But she felt it, creeping out of the sky, reaching toward her through the sounds, the scents, the color that filled the air.

Now her bosom rose and fell tumultuously. She was beginning to recognize this thing that was approaching to possess her, and she was striving to beat it back with her will—as powerless as her two white slender hands would have been.

When she abandoned herself a little whispered word escaped her slightly parted lips. She said it over and over under her breath: "free, free, free!" The vacant stare and the look of terror that had followed it went from her eyes. They stayed keen and bright. Her pulses beat fast, and the coursing blood warmed and relaxed every inch of her body.

Comments

These paragraphs alter slightly the story's pace and tone. We are not told what Mrs. Mallard is waiting for. Whatever it is, however, she feels it; she senses it coming as she looks out the window. And we see her resisting it—but powerlessly. Do we perhaps also hear sexual overtones in the description of what is "approaching to possess" her? Or do we wish to assign psychological or religious significance to this imminent possession and her apparently ambivalent feelings about it? We notice, too, that Mrs. Mallard is described as not conscious of what is happening to her. Chopin's narrator says that there is "a suspension of intelligent thought." Mrs. Mallard, at this point in the story's action, seems to *feel* rather than to think.

At last, Mrs. Mallard abandons herself to what comes to possess her. The word "abandoned" echoes the earlier description of Mrs. Mallard's "wild abandonment" when she hears of her husband's death. Her repetition of the word "free" signals her excitement, an emotional excitement rendered in physical imagery: her pulse beats fast, and her blood courses through her body—both signs of awakening feeling.

The story continues:

> She did not stop to ask if it were or were not a monstrous joy that held her. A clear and exalted perception enabled her to dismiss the suggestion as trivial.
>
> She knew that she would weep again when she saw the kind, tender hands folded in death; the face that had never looked save with love upon her, fixed and gray and dead. But she saw beyond that bitter moment a long procession of years to come that would belong to her absolutely. And she opened and spread her arms out to them in welcome.

There would be no one to live for her during those coming years; she would live for herself. There would be no powerful will bending hers in that blind persistence with which men and women believe they have a right to impose a private will upon a fellow-creature. A kind intention or a cruel intention made the act seem no less a crime as she looked upon it in that brief moment of illumination.

And yet she had loved him—sometimes. Often she had not. What did it matter! What could love, the unsolved mystery, count for in face of this possession of self-assertion which she suddenly recognized as the strongest impulse of her being!

Comments

We pause over the words "monstrous joy." Clearly Mrs. Mallard is overjoyed. And from one perspective, her joy, however honestly and robustly felt, is monstrous. She is happy—exultantly happy—that her husband is dead and that she is free of him. But the author indicates that Mrs. Mallard does not think about what she is feeling. The first paragraph of this segment underscores Mrs. Mallard's clear-sighted confidence. We may wonder if her husband had treated her cruelly, but the text answers that he was kind, which makes Mrs. Mallard's welcoming of the coming years monstrous indeed. In the second paragraph Chopin does not exactly condemn Mrs. Mallard, for even though her husband had been kind, Mrs. Mallard had to bend her will to his. Kind or not, he controlled her; loving wife or not, she resented it.

Chopin here seems to move beyond the case of a particularly unhappy wife to the larger issue of the bonds of marriage, using language that strongly condemns the husband's dominance of the wife. We hear it in words and phrases such as "powerful will bending hers," "blind persistence," "impose," and "crime." This language is balanced by a lyrical evocation of Mrs. Mallard, in the years to come, living for herself rather than under the control of her husband. The moment is described as "that brief moment of illumination," building on the earlier description of her eyes as "keen and bright." Mrs. Mallard is possessed by a new sense of herself and a new self-confidence, as she envisions her future solo life. This turning point, a moment of insight and recognition, makes her previous life with Brently Mallard pale into insignificance.

The next paragraphs could end the story (though they don't):

"Free! Body and soul free!" she kept whispering.

Josephine was kneeling before the closed door with her lips to the keyhole, imploring for admission. "Louise, open the door! I beg; open the door—you will make yourself ill. What are you doing, Louise? For heaven's sake open the door."

"Go away. I am not making myself ill." No; she was drinking in a very elixir of life through that open window.

Her fancy was running riot along those days ahead of her. Spring days, and summer days, and all sorts of days that would be her own. She breathed a quick prayer that life might be long. It was only yesterday she had thought with a shudder that life might be long.

She arose at length and opened the door to her sister's importunities. There was a feverish triumph in her eyes, and she carried herself unwittingly like a goddess of Victory. She clasped her sister's waist, and together they descended the stairs. Richards stood waiting for them at the bottom.

Comments

The discrepancy between why Josephine thinks Mrs. Mallard keeps herself locked in her room and our knowledge of the real reason is ironic. Irony inheres, too, in Mrs. Mallard's praying for a long life, since only the day before she had shuddered at the thought of a long life with her husband. The language of these paragraphs is charged with feeling, extending and intensifying Mrs. Mallard's highly emotional state. She drinks in the "elixir of life," has a "feverish triumph in her eyes," and comports herself like a "goddess of Victory." Those paragraphs could end the story, but they don't because Chopin has a final surprise—both for us and for Mrs. Mallard:

Someone was opening the front door with a latchkey. It was Brently Mallard who entered, a little travel-stained, composedly carrying his grip-sack and umbrella. He had been far from the scene of the accident, and did not even know there had been one. He stood amazed at Josephine's piercing cry; at Richards' quick motion to screen him from the view of his wife.

But Richards was too late.

When the doctors came they said she had died of heart disease—of joy that kills.

Comments

The surprise is too much for Mrs. Mallard. It kills her. Does she die of shock, of despair? Something else? And what do we make of a "joy that kills"? We are left with the impression that Josephine, Richards, and the doctor do not understand that Mrs. Mallard dies not of shock at seeing her husband alive, not out of joy at his presence, but out of something like despair. Why does the narrator suggest that none of them realize the truth that we readers see?

Some interesting questions are left unresolved by this ending. Is Mrs. Mallard being punished for harboring a desire to be free of her husband and for exulting at the news of his death? Or is Mrs. Mallard a symbol of repressed womanhood yearning to be free of male bondage? Does the story transcend the sexual identity of its protagonist? Could we imagine a man in Mrs.

Mallard's position, tethered to a wife from whom he would prefer to escape and similarly seem to exult at the thought of her death? Such are the kinds of questions stories can leave us with. Such are the provocations to thought fiction can provide. These forms of intellectual stimulation are among fiction's many and diverse pleasures.

Interlude II
The Novel and Novella

In reading a novel, it's important to take pains with its opening. Whether we are being introduced to a fog-obscured world of London in Dickens's *Bleak House*; different forms of family disarray in Tolstoy's *Anna Karenina* and Dostoevsky's *The Brothers Karamazov*; strange worlds where clocks strike thirteen in Orwell's *1984*; creatures called hobbits, who live in their hobbit holes in Tolkien's *The Hobbit*, each of these novels draws us into its unique world and establishes its special tone. It's worth taking time to absorb such novelistic elements, becoming familiar with what's distinctive about each work. In doing so we also become acquainted with a novel's major themes and preoccupations. And, in addition, with its prevailing tone.

Tone is a writer's attitude toward his or her subject. One form of engagement, and one of the most important kinds of tone to recognize in literary works, is irony. Irony is less a fictional element than a pervasive aspect in it. Irony may appear in a work's style, it its plot, or in its point of view. Writers use verbal irony to convey a character's limited understanding—often to indicate a gap between the author's knowledge and the narrator's, as for example that between Mark Twain as author and Huckleberry Finn as narrator. Writers use irony of situation to reveal discrepancies between what appears to be the case and what is actually the case, or between what is expected to happen and what actually happens. Writers use dramatic irony to show the difference between what a character knows and what readers know.

When a number of these aspects of irony work together throughout a novel, as for example in Jane Austen's *Pride and Prejudice* and in Flannery O'Connor's (and Edgar Allan Poe's) short fiction, we can speak of an ironic vision. In the case of Austen and O'Connor their ironic visions span their body of work. Their novels and stories are steeped in irony.

We can see how irony functions in the following passage—the beginning of Austen's *Pride and Prejudice*, which we considered earlier from the perspective of its dialogue—its voices. Here, we revisit the opening of Austen's novel, this time to consider the writer's tone.

> It is a truth universally acknowledged, that a single man in possession of a good fortune, must be in want of a wife.

However little known the feelings or views of such a man may be on his first entering a neighborhood, this truth is so well fixed in the minds of the surrounding families, that he is considered as the rightful property of some one or other of their daughters.

"My dear Mr. Bennet," said his lady to him one day, "have you heard that Netherfield Park is let at last?"

Mr. Bennet replied that he had not.

"But it is," returned she; "for Mrs. Long has just been here, and she told me all about it."

Mr. Bennet made no answer.

"Do not you want to know who has taken it?" cried his wife impatiently.

"You want to tell me, and I have no objection to hearing it."

This was invitation enough.

"Why, my dear, you must know, Mrs. Long says that Netherfield is taken by a young man of large fortune from the north of England; that he came down on Monday in a chaise and four to see the place, and was so much delighted with it that he agreed with Mr. Morris immediately; that he is to take possession before Michaelmas, and some of his servants are to be in the house by the end of next week."

"What is his name?"

"Bingley."

"Is he married or single?"

"Oh! Single, my dear, to be sure! A single man of large fortune; four or five thousand a year. What a fine thing for our girls!"

"How so? How can it affect them?"

"My dear Mr. Bennet," replied his wife, "how can you be so tiresome! You must know that I am thinking of his marrying one of them."

To get at the multiple ironies in this passage, we need to begin with a fundamental question: Is it a truth—that is, do we accept as fact what the opening sentence seems to assert: that a single man of means must be looking for a wife? Do we believe that this search for a wife is a phenomenon universally acknowledged, recognized around the world in other times and places and not merely in those of Austen's novel? Is it possible that Jane Austen's sentence means the opposite of what it purports to suggest: that single men of means more often than not are not in search of wives at all? How would we go about determining whether the sentence is ironic—that what it says explicitly and what it covertly implies are at odds, discrepant—and thus should not be taken at face value?

We can feel confident about the ironic tone of Austen's first sentence when we consider it in relation to the sentence that follows it. There we are told that the feelings and views of the eligible bachelor mean little or nothing. Clearly, however, the man's feelings and views should be a prime concern. That they are unknown suggests they are of no consequence to the families intent on marrying off one of their daughters to the gentleman. This, of course, is ironic, the opposite of what might be expected in such a situation. A further irony is that marriageable eligibility is determined by wealth alone, with character, intelligence, wisdom, virtue, and other admirable and presumably desirable qualities in a spouse ignored entirely. In this world, marriage matters; money matters; status and rank matter. Kindness, generosity, goodness are ignored. Or so it appears, at least among the Bennet parents.

Portraying characters whose view of marriage is so mercenary, Austen distances herself from them and from their mercantile values. She does this through the comments of her narrator. This ironic distance is enforced when the author describes the misconceptions of her characters about single men, along with their reversal of the common notion then that a wife is a man's property. For these and other reasons, as the chapter and the novel develop, Austen displays an ironic tone that she uses to satirize Mr. and Mrs. Bennet, as well as a number of other characters who make their appearance later. In this opening segment of her novel, and throughout the remainder of its brief opening chapter, Austen helps us perceive her ironic tone with her narrator's brief comments inserted between the characters' dialogue. Once alerted from the start to Austen's irony, we can be carefully attentive to it as the novel progresses.

Short Novel

The short novel, sometimes called the novella, shares characteristics with both the short story and the novel. Like the short story, the novella relies on glimpses of understanding, flashes of insight, quick turns of action that solidify theme and reveal character. Like the novel, the short novel accumulates incidents and illustrates character over time in ways the short story cannot because of its limited scope.

Unlike the short story, which must unfold quickly, the short novel allows for a slower unfolding of incident, character, and idea, or theme. The brevity of the short story demands a single snapshot of time rather than the collage or mosaic than can be created in the short novel, or novella. Nonetheless, the quick flash of revelation, the momentary shock of recognition, the surprise twist of an ending, however, can be found in both the short story and the short novel.

What distinguishes the short novel from its longer full-length counterpart is its sharper focus, concentration, and efficiency. Lacking time and space that the novel affords to accumulate incident, develop character, and reveal theme, the short novel works within a narrower compass, disavowing the novel's amplitude and more panoramic sweep. The result for the novella is a compression of effect that are hallmarks of the form.

Henry James, an American master of the novella, called it a "blessed form." Vladimir Nabokov, the modern Russian writer best known for his novel *Lolita*, has suggested that "by diminishing large things and enlarging small ones" the short novel is an "intrinsically artistic" form. The American critic Irving Howe has noted that in masterpieces of the short novel genre "the action forms a harmonious equivalent to the motivating idea." Such is the case with the following examples.

Henry James's *Daisy Miller* is one of the best known and loved works in the genre. It tells the story of an American girl from Schenectady, New York, as she is sojourning in Europe, in Vevey, Switzerland and in Rome. She is traveling with her mother and younger brother, as part of what a certain class of Americans were expected to do as part of their cultural education—to visit Europe and soak up the culture.

Daisy is an American innocent; her name itself reflects her freshness and naivete. As a rich American heiress, she is prey for some European gigolo gold-digger, who will see her as an easy mark and an equally easy ticket to a life of ease and affluence.

James presents Daisy to us through the lens of an onlooker and participating character, a Mr. Winterbourne, who befriends Daisy and her family. Winterbourne is a transplanted American, somewhat Europeanized, as he has lived abroad for some time and picked up the cultural norms of Europe, while losing his Americanness. For Winterbourne, who is himself said to be involved with a sophistical European lady in Switzerland, Daisy is a breath of fresh air, by turns charming and perplexing, as she "misbehaves" according to the customs of Europe.

James often places Europeans in America and Americans in Europe to display the various ways customs and cultures clash in large and small ways. He plays these cultural contrasts for their comedic implications, but he also shows how cultural misunderstanding can lead to far more serious, even tragic consequences, as this novella demonstrates.

Part of the pleasure of reading *Daisy Miller* is trying to figure out just what we should understand about the title character. James doesn't make it easy for us, as various characters have different views of her. He keeps us guessing about Daisy right up until the end, as she navigates the social norms and censors that surround her. We wonder about the extent to which she might be, on the one hand, naive and innocent, and on the other, deceptive and manipulative. By presenting multiple views of Daisy and filtering them through the consciousness of Winterbourne (whose name, like Daisy's, is suggestive of an aspect of his character), James generates ambiguities galore to challenge and complicate our understanding of his title character.

Another masterful novella is a more modern work, Franz Kafka's *The Metamorphosis*. Among the many glories of this short novel is its opening sentence: "When Gregor Samsa awoke one morning, he found himself transformed into a giant insect." The story unfolds uncannily and seemingly inevitably from this surprising beginning. Gregor, a traveling salesman, is somewhat disconcerted about his newly discovered metamorphosis, but he appears to take it in his stride, as he struggles to turn over in bed and get himself up and about so he can get to work on time. Such is the beginning of what will prove to be a series of misadventures for Gregor, as he is unable to easily adjust to his cumbersome body with its numerous waving legs and to his new highly pitched voice, which is not understood by his mother to whom he speaks through his locked bedroom door.

Kafka makes a subtle and nuanced comedy out of Gregor's plight, while he simultaneously provokes his readers to consider just what this far-fetched story of Gregor's transformation might mean. Among the various approaches to interpreting *The Metamorphosis* are the sociological, which considers how Gregor has become a mere cog in the machine of the business world, as he slaves away for a company that undervalues his work and contribution. Gregor is overwhelmed by life, and unable to cope well with the responsibilities it presses upon him. Allied with this social perspective is a psychological one, in which Gregor is considered a mere "bug," someone small and unimportant, the lowest of the low. One question of the novella is the extent to which he sees himself this way, with his metamorphosis a symbolic outward manifestation of this inward, psychological state of mind.

This short novel can be approached productively from a number of interpretive angles. One of the pleasures of reading Kafka's novella is enjoying the odd and unpredictable ways its plot unfolds, while simultaneously thinking about its social and psychological significance. Among the additional pleasures *The Metamorphosis* offers is an evocation of a world that is both funny and sad, comical yet pathetic, where strange developments occur in the most familiar of settings among the most ordinary people. It's a world that has come to be known as "Kafkaesque."

Whether novel or novella, these longer fictional forms bring us into new worlds of experience—larger worlds, of course, with bigger, more expansive novels. These longer fictional forms also introduce us to varied ways of portraying the complexities of human experience, social, psychological, and cultural. Novels and novellas constitute, in and of themselves, as Dean Flower has suggested, "modes of knowing, even of revelation." What more might we ask of fiction than such splendid benefits?

Part III
Reading Drama—Five Ways In

Prelude III
The Pleasures of Drama

In *The Life of the Drama*, Eric Bentley asks whether a play is complete without an actual performance (148). Is the script of Sophocles' *Antigone* or Ibsen's *The Master Builder*, for example, complete in itself, or does it require staging? We might respond that, yes, as a work of literature, Sophocles' and Ibsen's plays are complete in and of themselves. And through being realized as dramatic performances in the theater, they are complete in another way— as dramatic actions, or, in multiple ways, in different performances.

Although we may read plays far more often than we see them staged, plays are written to be performed; with few exceptions, plays are designed to be seen, to be experienced as works of theater and not only read as works of literature. In seeing drama performed in the theater, we share our experience of plays with others. As John Sutherland notes in *A Little History of Literature*, drama is "community literature" (39); ideally, we experience it in company, publicly, unlike the way we read a novel in solitary quietude. We respond to theater and modern genres, such as film, that have evolved from it, as social creatures. Though rituals of live theater differ somewhat from rituals in movie theaters, resemblances exist because of the communal experience common to both genres. We grow silent, for example, as a play or film gets underway. We laugh together, or experience fear and excitement at the same moments other audience members do, and we applaud together at the end of a play's performance.

Much of our pleasure in drama arises from the way the language of a play's script comes alive in the speech of living actors. Part of our pleasure involves watching (or imagining) actors dramatically enacting the characters they portray. We enjoy the way the actors/characters walk and talk, the way they interact with other characters, the way they communicate through facial expressions and bodily gestures. Even the smallest gesture, such as a raised or lowered hand, or the slightest facial expression, such as a downturned lip, can contribute to our sense of a play's dramatic human experience.

These are some of the pleasures of experiencing plays. But there are others, as well. Among them is that drama is a *mimetic* art, one that imitates or represents human life and experience. A large part of the pleasure drama generates results from its ability to reveal aspects of human life meaningfully dramatized, vividly actualized.

Drama is also an *active* art in which actors portraying characters serve as agents, doers, who make things happen through speech and bodily action. Actors perform the scripts of plays. They enact those scripts, bringing them to life.

In addition, drama is an *immediate* art, one that represents action that occurs in the play's present. Our experience of drama is one of watching events *as* they occur. We are firsthand witnesses of present-tense action rather than auditors who simply hear about events from a narrator at secondhand after the fact.

As Wendy Lesser notes in *Why I Read*, what we witness in watching a performance of a play are people like us standing on a stage, "representing actions and emotions that cry out for our sympathy, our hatred, our anxiety, our laughter, our distress" (64). We know, of course, that the people on stage are "actors," and that they play assigned roles that have been scripted by the dramatist. We engage, as Samuel Taylor Coleridge has written, in a "willing suspension of disbelief" in them (8). It is interesting, however, that for the hours that we watch actors perform, we give them life, and in doing so they enable us to feel our own emotions.

Drama is also an *interactive* art. The action of a play involves *interplay* between and among characters. Dramatic characters respond and relate to one another through dialogue and action. Such character interaction is the heart of drama: it is the spring of plot, the source of meaning, and the central reason for our pleasure in theatrical experience.

It's what makes drama, *drama*.

Drama is interactive, however, in yet another way, for drama is a *composite* art—one that makes use of many other arts. Painting and architecture are used to design and create stage sets; they are implicated in how actors are lighted or kept in shadow. Music and other sound effects suggest feelings, build tension, and create mood and atmosphere. Sculpture and dance indicate the way characters are positioned on stage and their movements around it.

Drama, thus, is a complex art that involves a dynamic interaction of many visual and aural elements. Given the nature of drama as theater, we need to ask ourselves two key questions: (1) how can we appreciate the theatrical elements of plays we may never see performed; (2) how can we enjoy drama when we are limited to reading a play's script without the benefit of performance?

In reading plays, we can emphasize their theatrical elements. In doing so we can become alert to all that a play can convey. Although the devices on which we read and view plays are always changing, the human experiences plays dramatize—love and hate, ambition and competition, greed and generosity, vengeance and forgiveness—remain constant across time and language and culture. And that those experiences, dramatized through language, are available to our understanding, appreciation, and enjoyment. To enable those kinds of experiences reading plays, we need to imagine our minds as mental theaters.

Mental Theater

When we read a play rather than see it performed, it is important to imagine how its script might be enacted on a stage. Reading a play *imaginatively*, as if we were watching it, can enhance our appreciation of a play's theatrical qualities, the dramatically enacted aspects of its script.

But what does it mean to read a play imaginatively? It means, essentially, translating a play's script into a *mental performance*. By attending to the performance implications of the words on the page, we can imagine how those words might be brought to life on stage. We envision how the play's dialogue might be spoken—for example, sweetly or sarcastically, slowly or swiftly, loudly or softly, with a smile or a sneer. We imagine what small gestures such as a broad grin or a raised eyebrow, for example, and larger ones, such as a raised fist or a welcoming embrace, would accompany the dialogue, and how the actors playing their roles might react to those gestures. A playwright's stage directions sometimes guide actors in these matters, and in the process make it easier for readers to imagine how speech and action might be synchronized in performance.

We imagine, too, where a play's characters are positioned relative to one another on stage, how close or far apart. We can envision their ways of walking, the subtle ways they vary their voices and alter their body postures and positions. These details, coupled with characters' costumes, the play's scenery, music, and sound effects, all contribute to the richness of our imagined reenactment of a play. The more concretely we can envision such elements, the better we will absorb the atmosphere and feeling of a play, and the more our reading experience of drama will approach a theatrical experience of a play. And so, our goal in reading a play is to use our imagination to bring it to vivid theatrical life.

11 Mental Theater—August Strindberg
The Stronger

One effective way to read a play when you can't attend a performance is to approach it conceptually as a form of "mental theater." To accomplish this kind of imaginary dramatic thinking you might read the play aloud alone, perhaps playing the various roles with alterations of your voice. Another is to read the play with a partner or a small group. Best of all, however, is to do a dramatic reading with others, each with an assigned role—not a full-out "performance," but rather a read-aloud that allows us to hear the voices of the plays' characters, to slow down and attend to its details of description, dialogue, imagery, and action.

Read the following brief one-act play *The Stronger*. As you read, imagine how the play might be performed on stage. Consider how the actors should be dressed, where they should stand in relation to one another, how they should talk and listen to one another—in what tone of voice, as well as what gestures and expressions they might use with one another.

CHARACTERS

MME. X., an actress, married
MLLE. Y., an actress, unmarried

[SCENE—The corner of a ladies' cafe. Two little iron tables, a red velvet sofa, several chairs. Enter Mme. X., dressed in winter clothes, carrying a Japanese basket on her arm.]

[Mlle. Y. sits with a half-empty beer bottle before her, reading an illustrated paper, which she changes later for another.]

MME. X. Good afternoon, Amelie. You're sitting here alone on Christmas eve like a poor bachelor!

MLLE. Y. [Looks up, nods, and resumes her reading.]

MME. X. Do you know it really hurts me to see you like this, alone, in a cafe, and on Christmas eve, too. It makes me feel as I did one time when I saw a bridal party in a Paris restaurant, and the bride sat reading a comic paper, while the groom played billiards with the witnesses. Huh, thought I, with such a beginning, what will follow, and what will be the end? He played billiards on his wedding eve! [Mlle. Y. starts to speak.]

And she read a comic paper, you mean? Well, they are not altogether the same thing.

MME. X. You know what, Amelie! I believe you would have done better to have kept him! Do you remember, I was the first to say "Forgive him?"

Do you remember that? You would be married now and have a home. Remember that Christmas when you went out to visit your fiancé's parents in the country? How you gloried in the happiness of home life and really longed to quit the theatre forever? Yes, Amelie dear, home is the best of all, the theatre next and children—well, you don't understand that.

MLLE. Y. [Looks up scornfully.]

[Mme. X. sips a few spoonfuls out of the cup, then opens her basket and shows Christmas presents.]

MME. X. Now you shall see what I bought for my piggywigs. [Takes up a doll.] Look at this! This is for Lisa, ha! Do you see how she can roll her eyes and turn her head, eh? And here is Maja's popgun. [Loads it and shoots at Mlle. Y.]

MLLE. Y. [Makes a startled gesture.]

MME. X. Did I frighten you? Do you think I would like to shoot you, eh? On my soul, if I don't think you did! If you wanted to shoot me it wouldn't be so surprising, because I stood in your way—and I know you can never forget that—although I was absolutely innocent. You still believe I intrigued and got you out of the Stora theatre, but I didn't. I didn't do that, although you think so. Well, it doesn't make any difference what I say to you. You still believe I did it. [Takes up a pair of embroidered slippers.] And these are for my better half. I embroidered them myself—I can't bear tulips, but he wants tulips on everything.

MLLE. Y. [Looks up ironically and curiously.]

MME. X. [Putting a hand in each slipper.] What little feet Bob has! What? And you should see what a splendid stride he has! You've never seen him in slippers! [Mlle. Y. laughs aloud.] Look! [She makes the slippers walk on the table. Mlle. Y. laughs loudly.] And when he is grumpy he stamps like this with his foot. "What! damn those servants who can never learn to make coffee. Oh, now those creatures haven't trimmed the lamp wick properly!" And then there are draughts on the floor and his feet are cold. "Ugh, how cold it is; the stupid idiots can never keep the fire going." [She rubs the slippers together, one sole over the other.]

MLLE. Y. [Shrieks with laughter.]

MME. X. And then he comes home and has to hunt for his slippers which Marie has stuck under the chiffonier—oh, but it's sinful to sit here and make fun of one's husband this way when he is kind and a good little man. You ought to have had such a husband, Amelie. What are you laughing at? What? What? And you see he's true to me. Yes, I'm sure of that, because he told me himself—what are you laughing at? —that when I was touring in Norway that brazen Frédérique came and wanted to seduce him! Can you fancy anything so infamous? [Pause.] I'd have torn her eyes out if she had come to see him when I was at home. [Pause.] It was lucky that Bob told me about it himself and that it didn't reach me through gossip. [Pause.] But would you believe it, Frédérique wasn't the only one! I don't know why, but the women are crazy about my husband. They must think he has influence about getting them theatrical engagements, because he is connected with the government. Perhaps you were after him yourself. I didn't use to trust you any too much. But now I know he never bothered his head about you, and you always seemed to have a grudge against him someway.

[Pause. They look at each other in a puzzled way.]

MME. X. Come and see us this evening, Amelie, and show us that you're not put out with us,—not put out with me at any rate. I don't know, but I think it would be uncomfortable to have you for an enemy. Perhaps it's because I stood in your way [*rallentando*] or—I really—don't know why—in particular.

[Pause. Mlle. Y. stares at Mme. X curiously.]

MME. X. [Thoughtfully.] Our acquaintance has been so queer. When I saw you for the first time I was afraid of you, so afraid that I didn't dare let you out of my sight; no matter when or where, I always found myself near you—I didn't dare have you for an enemy, so I became your friend. But there was always discord when you came to our house, because I saw that my husband couldn't endure you, and the whole thing seemed as awry to me as an ill-fitting gown—and I did all I could to make him friendly toward you, but with no success until you became engaged. Then came a violent friendship between you, so that it looked all at once as though you both dared show your real feelings only when you were secure—and then—how was it later? I didn't get jealous—strange to say! And I remember at the christening, when you acted as godmother, I made him kiss you—he did so, and you became so confused—as it were; I didn't notice it then—didn't think about it later, either—have never thought about it until—now! [Rises suddenly.] Why are you silent? You haven't said a word this whole time, but you have let me go on talking! You have sat there, and your eyes have reeled out of me all these thoughts which lay like raw silk in its cocoon—thoughts—suspicious thoughts, perhaps.

Let me see—why did you break your engagement? Why do you never come to our house any more? Why won't you come to see us tonight?

[Mlle. Y. appears as if about to speak.]

MME. X. Hush, you needn't speak—I understand it all! It was because—and because—and because! Yes, yes! Now all the accounts balance. That's it. Fie, I won't sit at the same table with you. [Moves her things to another table.] That's the reason I had to embroider tulips—which I hate—on his slippers, because you are fond of tulips; that's why [Throws slippers on the floor] we go to Lake Mälarn in the summer, because you don't like salt water; that's why my boy is named Eskil—because it's your father's name; that's why I wear your colors, read your authors, eat your favorite dishes, drink your drinks—chocolate, for instance; that's why—oh—my God—it's terrible, when I think about it; it's terrible. Everything, everything came from you to me, even your passions. Your soul crept into mine, like a worm into an apple, ate and ate, bored and bored, until nothing was left but the rind and a little black dust within. I wanted to get away from you, but I couldn't; you lay like a snake and charmed me with your black eyes; I felt that when I lifted my wings they only dragged me down; I lay in the water with bound feet, and the stronger I strove to keep up the deeper I worked myself down, down, until I sank to the bottom, where you lay like a giant crab to clutch me in your claws—and there I am lying now.

I hate you, hate you, hate you! And you only sit there silent—silent and indifferent; indifferent whether it's new moon or waning moon, Christmas or New Year's, whether others are happy or unhappy; without power to hate or to love; as quiet as a stork by a rat hole—you couldn't scent your prey and capture it, but you could lie in wait for it! You sit here in your corner of the café—did you know it's called "The Rat Trap" for you? —and read the papers to see if misfortune hasn't befallen some one, to see if some one hasn't been given notice at the theatre, perhaps; you sit here and calculate about your next victim and reckon on your chances of recompense like a pilot in a shipwreck.

Poor Amelie, I pity you, nevertheless, because I know you are unhappy, unhappy like one who has been wounded, and angry because you are wounded. I can't be angry with you, no matter how much I want to be—because you come out the weaker one. Yes, all that with Bob doesn't trouble me. What is that to me, after all? And what difference does it make whether I learned to drink chocolate from you or someone else.

[Sips a spoonful from her cup.]

Besides, chocolate is very healthful. And if you taught me how to dress—*tant mieux*!—that has only made me more attractive to my husband; so you lost and I won there. Well, judging by certain signs, I believe you have already lost him; and you certainly intended that I should leave him—do as you did with your fiancé and regret as you now regret; but, you see, I don't do that—we mustn't be too exacting. And why should I take only what no one else wants?

Perhaps, take it all in all, I am at this moment the stronger one. You received nothing from me, but you gave me much. And now I seem like a thief since you have awakened and find I possess what is your loss. How could it be otherwise when everything is worthless and sterile in your hands? You can never keep a man's love with your tulips and your passions—but I can keep it. You can't learn how to live from your authors, as I have learned. You have no little Eskil to cherish, even if your father's name was Eskil. And why are you always silent, silent, silent? I thought that was strength, but perhaps it is because you have nothing to say! Because you never think about anything! [Rises and picks up slippers.]

Now I'm going home—and take the tulips with me—your_ tulips! You are unable to learn from another; you can't bend—therefore, you broke like a dry stalk. But I won't break! Thank you, Amelie, for all your good lessons. Thanks for teaching my husband how to love. Now I'm going home to love him. [Goes.]

Questions

1 What do you learn about each of the characters? How do you learn it? Why doesn't Mlle. Y say anything? How do the characters relate to each other?
2 Besides the play's two characters, Mme. X and Mlle. Y, there is a third individual mentioned—Mr. X. What is his relationship with each of the women characters?

3. To what extent do you think Mme. X excuses her husband's behavior in a form of self-deception? And why might she want or need to do this? Do you think she, at any point, faces the presumed truth about him and his relationship with Mlle. Y?
4. What is the effect of making Mlle. Y a silent character? What is the effect of never bringing Mr. X onstage? What is the effect of naming the characters with letters rather than names?
5. Who do you consider to be the "stronger" of the two women? Why? Do you think a case might be made for the other woman as the stronger? Why or why not?
6. Explain what directions you would give the actors who perform the two characters' roles. What do you tell each of them?
7. What elements of the play's setting would you emphasize in its staging? What sound effects might you include? How would you stage when Mlle. Y is about to speak?
8. Why do you think August Strindberg wrote this play? Do you think *The Stronger* suggests a particular message or lesson? If so, what is it, and where do you find evidence to support your interpretation?
9. To what extent does *The Stronger* seem to confirm or conflict with your personal beliefs and values? To what extent do your beliefs and values influence your interpretation of and your response to *The Stronger*?
10. What additional observations can you make about Strindberg's play? What questions do you have? What connections can you make, or what relationships establish, between your response to and understanding of *The Stronger* and other works of literature that you have read—or other films or works of art in other genres with which you are familiar?

12 Subtext—Wendy Wasserstein
Tender Offer

We often speak of "reading between the lines"—of considering what the words on the page suggest or imply. You can read "beneath" the text—another way of getting at, essentially, the same kind of attention to textual implications. Often a play's subtext concerns emotion, feelings a character possesses that are not explicitly acknowledged.

To interpret characters and their objectives accurately, we frequently need to look beneath the surface of a play's dialogue and consider its *subtext*. Russian director and teacher Konstantin Stanislavski considered the subtext the innermost essential reason for any character's speech.

Frequently in life and on stage, people and characters do not say precisely or specifically what they mean. For many reasons, they often prefer to hint or to speak indirectly, hoping that the listener will grasp their meaning through implication, through the subtext of what their overt speech suggests. Of course, there is always a danger that the intent of indirect speech will be missed, that a speaker will be misunderstood.

In the theater, actors help us understand subtext through gesture and intonation. The playwright supplies the text, the actor the subtext. This, unsurprisingly, is more challenging when we are reading the text of a play rather than seeing it enacted on a stage in a live performance. Even so, however, we can become attentive to subtext and become alert to the implications of dialogue in this way.

Consider the following lines from Wendy Wasserstein's one-act play *Tender Offer*, as the teenage Lisa is engaged in conversation with her father, Paul:

LISA: ... Talia Robbins told me she's much happier living without her father in the house. Her father used to come home late and go to sleep early.
PAUL: Lis, stop it. Let's go.
LISA: I can't find my leg warmers.
PAUL: Forget your leg warmers.
LISA: Daddy.
PAUL: What is it?
LISA: I saw this show on television, I think it was WPIX Channel 11. Well, the father was crying about his daughter.

DOI: 10.4324/9781003620280-21

PAUL: Why was he crying? Was she sick?
LISA: No. She was at school. And he was at business. And he just missed her, so he started to cry.
PAUL: What was the name of the show
LISA: I don't know. I came in the middle.

Comments

What Lisa is trying to communicate to her father has little to do with the actual words she speaks to him. She is angry with her father for missing her dance recital. When she mentions Talia Robbins, whose situation she cares little about, she is posing a veiled threat to her father that she is too timid to press directly. Her subtext might be put this way: "For all the attention you give me, you might as well never come home. At least I won't be so hurt and disappointed when you fail to keep a promise to me."

Her father is tired and wants to go home. And so he tries to ignore this subtext and his daughter's hurt feelings. Lisa, however, attempts a delaying tactic—using the leg warmers as a way to prevent Paul from leaving. We suspect she has not really misplaced her leg warmers; she simply uses that as a way to keep her father with her a while longer.

Her one-word line "Daddy" signals, on one hand, her tenderness toward her father, and on the other, her exasperation with his lack of attentiveness toward her. What tone do imagine that she uses in saying "Daddy"?

Lisa wants him to know how she feels, but she is not comfortable confronting her feelings directly. Besides, she wishes he would see that for himself—take the hint of her subtext. She tries to make him feel guilty by her references to a likely imaginary TV program.

Considering the emotional subtext of the dialogue in plays allows us to better understand dramatic characters. In this case, an understanding of the depth of Lisa's emotions—her pain, frustration, desperation, love, and longing for her father.

13 Language and Style—William Shakespeare
Othello

In a play, words do many things. They convey feelings and attitudes. They reveal character. They initiate events and effect action. We consider, next, how language—dialogue, specifically—does all these things simultaneously. Our text is an excerpt from Act IV, Scene iii of Shakespeare's *Othello*. Listen to the following conversation between Othello's wife Desdemona and Iago's wife Emilia about adultery.

DESDEMONA: Dost thou in conscience think, tell me, Emilia,
  That there be women do abuse their husbands
  In such gross kind?
EMILIA: There be some such, no question.
DESDEMONA: Wouldst thou do such a deed for all the world?
EMILIA: Why, would not you?
DESDEMONA: No, by this heavenly light!
EMILIA: Nor I either by this heavenly light.
  I might do't as well i' the dark.
DESDEMONA: Wouldst thou do such a deed for all the world?
EMILIA: The world's a huge think; it's a great price for a small vice.
DESDEMONA: In troth, I think thou woulds't not.
EMILIA: In troth, I think I should; and undo't when I had done. Marry, I would not do such a thing for a joint-ring, nor for measures of lawn, nor gowns, petticoats, nor caps, or any petty exhibition, but for all the whole world? Why, who would not make her husband a cuckold to make a monarch? I should venture purgatory for't.
DESDEMONA: Beshrew me if I would do such a wrong for the whole world.
EMILIA: Why, the wrong is but a wrong i' the' world; and having the world for your labor, 'tis a wrong in your own world, and you might quickly make it right.
DESDEMONA: I do not think there is any such woman.

Comments

About this conversation we need to see and hear not only evidence of a radical difference of values, but also of a striking difference of character.

Desdemona's innocence is underscored by her unwillingness to imagine being unfaithful to her husband, her naiveté, her inability to believe in any woman's infidelity. Emilia, on the other hand, is clearly willing to compromise her virtue. Her joking tone and bluntness also contrast with Desdemona's seriousness, as well as with her inability to even speak the word "adultery."

We listen next to Iago working on Desdemona's father Brabantio in Act I, scene i, as he tells Brabantio about his daughter's elopement with Othello:

IAGO: Zounds, sir y'are robbed! For shame. Put on your gown!
Your heart is burst, you have lost half your soul.
Even now, now, very now, an old black ram
Is tupping your white ewe. Arise, arise!
Awake the snorting citizens with the bell,
Or else the devil will make a grandsire of you.
...
I am one sir, that comes to tell you your daughter
and the Moor are making the beast with two backs.

Comments

Notice how Iago's language reveals his coarseness; how he crudely reduces sexual intimacy and love to animal copulation. His language also demonstrates his ability to make things happen, as he infuriates Brabantio with this description. The remainder of the play's opening scene shows the consequences of Iago's speech, especially its power to incite others to action, which follows from it. Iago is thus revealed as both an instigator and a man of gross sensibilities.

Iago's language is cast in a similar mold in Act II, scene i, when he tries to convince Roderigo, Desdemona's rejected suitor, that she will tire of Othello and turn to someone else for sexual satisfaction. Again Iago's language stresses the carnality of sex, while revealing his violent imagination:

IAGO: ...Her eye must be fed. And what delight shall she have to look on the devil? When the blood is made dull with the act of sport, there should be a game to inflame it and to give satiety a fresh appetite, loveliness in favor, sympathy in years, manners, and beauties; all which the Moor is defective in. Now for want of these required conveniences, her delicate tenderness will find itself abused, begin to heave the gorge, disrelish and abhor the Moor. Very nature will instruct her in it and compel her to some second choice....

Comments

Iago's language indicates the crudeness of his character—consistently so from the beginning of the play to its final act. Shakespeare does something different, however, with the language he gives Othello, whose early speeches and gestures are elegant and formal, a formality and exaltation that give way to a downward slope of degradation. Here is Othello early in the play, in Act I, scene ii, responding to a search party out to find him (after Iago's rousing of Brabantio during the night):

OTHELLO: Hold your hands,
    Both you of my inclining and the rest,
    Were it my cue to fight, I should have known it
    Without a prompter. Whither will you that I go
    To answer your charge?

Comments

Othello's speech here is formal, stately, measured. It bespeaks a man in command of himself, one who assumes authority easily and naturally. Othello's language in large part accounts for our sympathetic response to him, for our admiration of his poise and equanimity.

By the middle of Act III, however, this view of Othello is no longer tenable. Iago reduces Othello to incoherent babbler, a man at odds with himself who has completely lost his equilibrium. A bit later, in Act IV, we see Iago's effect on Othello, as he suggests that Desdemona has been unchaste with his lieutenant, Michael Cassio. Iago spares no lubricious detail.

OTHELLO: Lie with her?—We say lie on her when they belie her—Lie with her! Zounds, that's fulsome. Handkerchief—confession—handkerchief—. To confess, and be hanged for his labor—first to be hanged, and then to confess! I tremble at it....It is not words that shake me thus.—Pish! Noses, ears, and lips? Is 't possible?—Confess?—Handkerchief?—O devil.

Comments

In the language of both Iago and Othello we see meaning enacted as well as expressed. The verbal dimension of their dialogue is reinforced by movement, gesture, action. We can observe in these brief excerpts and throughout the play not only how language reveals character and advances action, but how it also makes things happen, and itself becomes action. Shakespeare's play abounds in such revelations.

14 Scene and Sound—William Shakespeare

Macbeth

Another "way in" to plays is to attend to a playwright's use of sound effects in a scene. Shakespeare uses sounds other than dialogue and speech to convey all manner of things, but especially atmosphere, mood, and emotion. One of his best-known uses of sound straddles two scenes in Macbeth, starting at the end of one scene and continuing into the beginning of the next.

The sound is a knocking at the gate of Macbeth's castle, just after Macbeth has murdered the king, Duncan.

MACBETH: Whence is that knocking?
How is 't with me, when every noise appalls me?
What hands are here? Ha! They pluck out mine eyes!
Will all great Neptune's ocean wash this blood
Clean from my hand? No; this my hand will rather
The multitudinous seas incarnadine,
Making the green one red.

Enter **Lady Macbeth**.

LADY MACBETH: My hands are of your color, but I shame
To wear a heart so white. (*Knock*.) I hear a knocking
At the south entry. Retire we to our chamber.
A little water clears us of this deed:
How easy is it then! Your constancy
Hath left you unattended. (*Knock*.) Hark! More knocking.
Get on your nightgown, lest occasion calls us
And show us to be watchers. Be not lost
So poorly in your thoughts.
MACBETH: To know my deed, 'twere best not know myself.
(*Knock*.)
Wake Duncan with thy knocking! I would thou couldst!

Exeunt (They leave the stage.)

Enter a **Porter**. *Knocking within.*

PORTER: Here's a knocking indeed! If a man were porter of hell gate, he should have old turning the key. (*Knock.*) Knock, knock, knock! Who's there, i' th' name of Beelzebub! Here's a farmer, that hanged himself on th' expectation of plenty. Come in time! Have napkins enough about you; here you'll sweat for 't. (*Knock.*) Knock, knock! Who's there in th' other devil's name? Faith, here's an equivocator, that could swear in both the scales against either scale; who committed treason enough for God's sake, yet could not equivocate to heaven. O, come in, equivocator. (*Knock.*) Knock, knock, knock! Who's there? Faith, here's an English tailor come hither for stealing out of a French hose: Come in tailor. Here you may roast your goose. (*Knock.*) Knock, knock; never at quiet! What are you? But this place is too cold for hell. I'll devil-porter it no further. I had thought to have let in some of all professions that go the primrose way to th' everlasting bonfire. (*Knock.*) Anon, anon! (*Opens an entrance.*) I pray you, remember the porter.

Comments

What can we say about all this knocking, both the insistent knocking at the gate and the repeated references to it by Macbeth, Lady Macbeth, and the Porter? First, of course, the knocking means something different to Macbeth from what it does to the Porter, who makes a game of talking about the knocking while he goes to answer it. The knocking provides comic relief after the accumulating tension during and after the scene of the murder. Thematically, the Porter's references to hell link up with Macbeth's guilt at what he's done and the eternal damnation he incurs. Dramatically, the knocking scene increases suspense as the audience waits to find out who's knocking and why. Symbolically, the repeated knocks echo the pounding of Macbeth's heart.

The knocking at the gate also represents the matter-of-fact, everyday world intruding upon Macbeth's wild imaginings of bloodying the seas and having his eyes plucked out. Macbeth wishes he could undo the murder, imagining that the knocking at the gate would then waken Duncan. Finally, the knocking in these contiguous scenes exhibits a dramatic structure that builds to a climax and then falls off. As such, it is part of a larger dramatic movement in the play that prepares for the eventual arousal from sleep of the people in the castle and their discovery of the murdered king, signaled later by a clanging bell that shatters the nocturnal silence.

15 Interrupted Reading—George Bernard Shaw

Arms and the Man

We can acquire a sense of the process of reading drama by attending closely to the following excerpt from Act II of George Bernard Shaw's satirical comedy *Arms and the Man*. In the first excerpt, we meet the play's two main characters, Raina, the fiancée of Sergius, a military leader. Raina is alone with him for the first time since his return from a recent successful battle. The scene is presented here in segments interspersed with commentary. In addition to dialogue between the lovers, there are also, a bit later, conversations between Sergius and a servant girl, Louka.

My interspersed comments suggest the kinds of thinking we do in the process of reading a play. Those comments focus on details of language, gesture, and behavior that we might observe in viewing a performance, and which we need to imagine while reading the play in lieu of seeing it on stage or screen. Patiently working through segments of a play's early scenes, noticing dramatic elements, enhances our understanding of a play's unfolding action. This process also enables us to follow a playwright's hints and suggestions, implications about its characters and the attitude taken toward them, as well as helping us gain a sense of the play's thematic preoccupations.

Here is the first segment of the play, followed by a bit of commentary:

RAINA: (*placing her hands on his shoulders as she looks up at him with admiration and worship*) My hero! My king!
SERGIUS: My queen! (*He kisses her on the forehead.*)
RAINA: How I have envied you, Sergius! You have been out in the world, on the field of battle, able to prove yourself there worthy of any woman in the world; whilst I have had to sit at home inactive—dreaming useless—doing nothing that could give me the right to call myself worthy of any man.
SERGIUS: Dearest: all my deeds have been yours. You inspired me. I have gone through the war like a knight in a tournament with his lady looking down at him!
RAINA: And you have never been absent from my thoughts for a moment. (*Very solemnly.*) Sergius, I think we two have found the higher love. When I think of you, I feel that I could never do a base deed, or think an ignoble thought.
SERGIUS: My lady and my saint! (*He clasps her reverently.*)
RAINA: (*returning his embrace*) My lord and my –

DOI: 10.4324/9781003620280-24

SERGIUS: Sh-sh! Let me be the worshipper, dear. You little know how unworthy even the best man is of a girl's pure passion!

Comments

What are we to make of such grand language and such exaggerated gestures? Do we see them as heroic? Do we see the characters as impressive? Or do we take those characters with less seriousness than they take themselves? Their style of speech and their manner are suitable for heroic melodrama, familiar to Shaw's nineteenth-century audience. But this play is not melodrama; it is comedy, something that quickly becomes evident.

Consider Raina's elevation of Sergius to royal heights ("My hero! My king!"), and Sergius's reciprocal coronation of Raina ("My queen!"). Their language is exaggerated and their behavior stilted, making them objects of Shaw's satire. Raina's speech is clichéd and Sergius's is filled with heroic posturing. We see through these exaggerations and laugh at the attitudes toward romantic love and military glory Raina and Sergius represent.

Shaw pokes fun at their romanticized exaltation of each other, seeing it as a game they play with and for each other. Sergius, however, comes close to honesty when he remarks that a man is not worthy of his fiancée's pure passion. The ambiguity of his remark leaves us wondering to what extent he is aware that he is suggesting that men are incapable of the "higher" spiritual love he and Raina have been discussing.

Sergius's attitude becomes clear in the next part of the scene:

RAINA: I trust you. I love you. You will never disappoint me, Sergius. (*Louka is heard singing within the house. They quickly release each other.*) I can't pretend to talk indifferently before her: my heart is too full. (*Louka comes from the house with her tray. She goes to the table, and begins to clear it, with her back turned to them.*) I will get my hat; and then we can go out until lunch time. Wouldn't you like that?

SERGIUS: Be quick. If you are away five minutes, it will seem five hours. (*Raina runs to the top of the steps, and turns there to exchange looks with him and wave him a kiss with both hands. He looks after her with emotion for a moment; then turns slowly away, his face radiant with the loftiest exaltation. The movement shifts his field of vision into the corner of which there now comes the tail of Louka's double apron. His attention is arrested at once. He takes a stealthy look at her, and begins to twirl his moustache mischievously, with his left hand akimbo on his hip. Finally, striking the ground with his heels in something of a cavalry swagger, he strolls over to the other side of the table, opposite her, and says*) Louka: do you know what the higher love is?

LOUKA: (*astonished*) No, sir.

SERGIUS: Very fatiguing thing to keep up for any length of time, Louka. One feels the need of some relief after it.

LOUKA: (*innocently*) Perhaps you would like some coffee, sir? (*She stretches her hand across the table for the coffee pot.*)
SERGIUS: (*taking her hand*) Thank you, Louka.
LOUKA: (*pretending to pull*) Oh, sir, you know I didn't mean that. I'm surprised at you!
SERGIUS: (*coming clear of the table and drawing her with him*) I am surprised at myself, Louka. What would Sergius, the hero of Slivnitza, say if he saw me now? What would Sergius, the apostle of the higher love, say if he saw me now? What would the half dozen Sergiuses who keep popping in and out of this handsome figure of mine say if they caught us here? (*Letting go her hand and slipping his arm dexterously round her waist.*) Do you consider my figure handsome, Louka?
LOUKA: Let me go, sir. I shall be disgraced. (*She struggles: he holds her inexorably.*) Oh, will you let go?
SERGIUS: (*looking straight into her eyes*) No.
LOUKA: Then stand back where we can't be seen. Have you no common sense?
SERGIUS: Ah! That's reasonable. (*He takes her into the stable yard gateway, where they are hidden from the house.*)

Comments

We notice, in this segment, a profusion of stage directions, as Shaw indicates explicitly what he wants the actors to do, which makes it easy for readers of the play to "see" what's going on. Ironies emerge, as well, beginning with Raina's comment that she can't pretend in front of the servant girl, Louka. She means, of course, that she won't be able to conceal her emotion, but we quickly deduce another implication of the pretense and concealment that will be evident. Sergius's pretense becomes apparent as he approaches Louka, who is too smart to be taken in by their act; her more realistic view of romance differs from their idealistic one. Louka sings as a warning to the lovers that she is approaching and she keeps her back to them as well—part of her pretense that she does not know what is going on between them.

The crux of this part of the scene, however, is Sergius's abrupt change of behavior. His mischievous, swaggering gestures and his dialogue with Louka puncture the bubble of the "higher" love he had been blowing up moments before with Raina. Notice, too, Louka's gestures. She is also playing a part, especially by feigning surprise at the turn of events. Her acquiescence, after a cursory struggle, parallels the change in Sergius's behavior.

Here is the next segment of the scene, in which Shaw keeps the surprises coming:

LOUKA: (*plaintively*) I may have been seen from the windows: Miss Raina is sure to by spying about after you.
SERGIUS: (*stunned: letting her go*) Take care, Louka. I may be worthless enough to betray the higher love; but do not you insult it.

LOUKA: (*demurely*) Not for the world, sir, I'm sure. May I go on with my work, please, now?

SERGIUS: (*again putting his arm round her*) You are a provoking little witch, Louka. If you were in love with me, would you spy out of windows on me?

LOUKA: Well, you see, sir, since you say you are half a dozen different gentlemen all at once, I should have a great deal to look after.

SERGIUS: (*charmed*) Witty as well as pretty. (*He tries to kiss her.*)

LOUKA: (*avoiding him*) No: I don't want your kisses. Gentlefolk are all alike: you making love to me behind Miss Raina's back; and she doing the same behind yours.

SERGIUS: (*recoiling a step*) Louka!

LOUKA: It shews how little you really care.

SERGIUS: (*dropping his familiarity, and speaking with freezing politeness*) If our conversation is to continue, Louka, you will please remember that a gentleman does not discuss the conduct of the lady he is engaged to with her maid.

LOUKA: It's so hard to know what a gentleman considers right. I thought from your trying to kiss me that you had given up being so particular.

SERGIUS: (*turning from her and striking his forehead as he comes back into the garden from the gateway*) Devil! Devil!

LOUKA: Ha! Ha! I expect one of the six of you is very like me, sir; though I am only Miss Raina's maid. (*She goes back to her work at the table, taking no further notice of him.*)

SERGIUS: (*speaking to himself*) Which of the six is the real man? That's the question that torments me. One of them is a hero, another a buffoon, another a humbug, another perhaps a bit of a blackguard. (*He pauses, and looks furtively at Louka as he adds, with deep bitterness*) And one, at least, is a coward: jealous, like all cowards. (*He goes to the table.*) Louka.

LOUKA: Yes?

SERGIUS: Who is my rival?

LOUKA: You shall never get that out of me, for love or money.

SERGIUS: Why?

LOUKA: Never mind why. Besides, you would tell that I told you; and I should lose my place.

SERGIUS: (*holding out his right hand in affirmation*) No! on the honor of a—(*He checks himself; and his hand drops, nerveless, as he concludes sardonically*)— of a man capable of behaving as I have been behaving for the last five minutes. Who is he?

LOUKA: I don't know. I never saw him. I only heard his voice through the door of her room.

SERGIUS: Damnation! How dare you?

LOUKA: (*retreating*) Oh, I mean no harm: you've no right to take up my words like that. The mistress knows all about it. And I tell you that if that gentleman ever comes here again, Miss Raina will marry him, whether he likes it or not. I know the difference between the sort of manner you and she put on before one another and the real manner.

Comments

Just as we have adjusted to the amorous play between Sergius and Louka, Sergius shifts ground to defend the honor of his insulted lady in response to Louka's suggestion that Raina is spying on him. (We subsequently discover that she *was* spying on him, a fact that affects our response to her claim that she trusts Sergius.) Shaw continues the repartee of dialogue and action, as Sergius advances on Louka and then retreats, feigning wounded pride. Louka comes across as shrewd, quick-witted, and capable of taking care of herself. She knows the difference between real and counterfeit passion. In her suspicion of Sergius's mannered artifice, she voices a realistic rather than a romantic view of love. She uses Sergius's words against him, making him look foolish, which he acknowledges by calling himself a buffoon and a humbug. In accepting Louka's accusation so readily, he assents to a view of Raina, of himself, and of the nature of love radically at odds with what he and Raina had declared earlier.

Here is the final segment of the excerpt:

(*Sergius shivers as if she had stabbed him. Then, setting his face like iron, he strides grimly to her, and grips her above the elbows with both hands.*)
SERGIUS: Now listen you to me.
LOUKA: (*wincing*) Not so tight: you're hurting me.
SERGIUS: That doesn't matter. You have stained my honor by making me a party to your eavesdropping. And you have betrayed your mistress.
LOUKA: (*writhing*) Please—
SERGIUS: That shews that you are an abominable little clod of common clay, with the soul of a servant. (*He lets her go as if she were an unclean thing, and turns away, dusting his hands of her, to the bench by the wall, where he sits down with averted head, meditating gloomily.*)
LOUKA: (*whimpering angrily with her hands up her sleeves, feeling her bruised arms*) You know how to hurt with your tongue as well as with your hands. But I don't care, now I've found out that whatever clay I'm made of, you're made of the same. As for her, she's a liar; and her fine airs are a cheat; and I'm worth six of her. (*She shakes the pain off hardily; tosses her head; and sets to work to put the things on the tray.*)
    (*He looks doubtfully at her. She finishes packing the tray, and laps the cloth over the edges, so as to carry all out together. As she stoops to lift it, he rises.*)
SERGIUS: Louka! (*She stops and looks defiantly at him.*) A gentleman has no right to hurt a woman under any circumstances. (*With profound humility, uncovering his head.*) I beg your pardon.
LOUKA: That sort of apology may satisfy a lady. Of what use is it to a servant?
SERGIUS: (*rudely crossed in his chivalry, throws it off with a bitter laugh, and says slightingly*) Oh! You wish to be paid for the hurt! (*He puts on his shako, and takes some money from his pocket.*)

LOUKA: (*her eyes filling with tears in spite of herself*) No: I want my hurt made well.

SERGIUS: (*sobered by her tone*) How?

(*She rolls up her left sleeve; clasps her arm with the thumb and fingers of her right hand; and looks down at the bruise. Then she raises her head and looks straight at him. Finally, with a superb gesture, she presents her arm to be kissed. Amazed, he looks at her; at the arm; at her again; hesitates; and then, with shuddering intensity, exclaims Never! And gets away as far as possible from her.*

Her arm drops. Without a word, and with unaffected dignity, she takes her tray, and is approaching the house when Raina returns, wearing a hat and jacket in the height of the Vienna fashion of the previous year, 1885. Louka makes way proudly for her, and then goes into the house.)

RAINA: I'm ready. What's the matter? (*Gaily.*) Have you been flirting with Louka?

SERGIUS: (*hastily*) No, no. How can you think such a thing?

RAINA: (*ashamed of herself*) Forgive me, dear: it was only a jest. I am so happy today.

Comments

Louka's forthright declaration angers Sergius to the point of hurting her. But Louka insists that although she may be "clay," so is Sergius; she asserts that he and Raina are no better and no "higher" than she is. The scene ends with Sergius frustrated, Louka resentful, and Raina lighthearted, as she teases Sergius about his flirtation. At this point, we wonder where Shaw will take Sergius, Raina, and Louka, and when we will meet Sergius's competition for Raina's hand.

By attending carefully to details of dialogue, description and action, and by imagining the action through the playwright's stage directions, we can gain a good sense of how this scene might be acted, and with what comic effects. In the process of reading the scene imaginatively, we also begin to think about Shaw's larger thematic intentions—and just what this scene might imply in terms of a dramatic idea. For that, of course, we would need to read the entire work and see how this set of excerpts fits into the larger picture and concept of the play overall.

Interlude III
Types of Drama

Some plays evoke laughter, others elicit tears. Some are comic, others tragic, still others a blend of both. The comic view celebrates and affirms life; it is typically joyous and festive. The tragic view stresses life's sorrows; it is typically brooding and solemn. Comedies usually end happily, often with a celebration such as a marriage; tragic plays end unhappily, often with the death of the hero. Both comedy and tragedy contain changes of fortune, with the fortunes of comic characters turning from bad to better and those of tragic figures from good to bad, or even bad to worse.

These two major dramatic modes have been represented traditionally by contrasting masks, one sorrowful the other joyful. Actors once wore such masks, which represented more than these different types of plays. They also stood for contrasting or opposing ways of viewing the world, aptly summarized by Horace Walpole's remark, "the world is a comedy to those who think and a tragedy to those who feel."

In his *Poetics*, Aristotle described tragedy as "an imitation of an action that is serious, complete in itself, and of a certain magnitude." This definition suggests that tragedies concern grave human actions and their consequences, with a tragic play's action complete—possessing a discernible beginning, middle, and end. Also in the *Poetics*, Aristotle notes that the incidents of a tragedy must be causally connected. That is, the play's events have to be logically related, one following naturally, even inevitably, from another. Each of a tragic drama's events leads, in part, to the inevitable catastrophe, usually the downfall of the hero.

Some readers of tragedy have suggested that the catastrophe results from a flaw in the hero's character. Others have contended that the hero's tragic flaw results from fate, or coincidence, from circumstances beyond the hero's control. A third view posits that tragedy results from an error of judgment committed by the hero, one that may or may not have its source in a weakness of character.

Typically, tragic protagonists misjudge other characters, misinterpret events, and confuse appearances with reality. Shakespeare's Othello, for example, mistakes Iago for an honest, loving friend when, in reality, Iago deceives Othello in an attempt to destroy him. Sophocles' Oedipus mistakes

DOI: 10.4324/9781003620280-25

his own identity and misconstrues his destiny. The misfortunes and catastrophic events of tragedy are frequently precipitated by such errors of judgment and discernment.

Tragic heroes such as Oedipus and Othello are usually grand, noble figures. They are men, as Aristotle says, "of high estate," who enjoy "great reputation and prosperity." Tragic heroes tend to be privileged, exalted personages who have earned their high repute and status by heroic exploit (Othello), by intelligence (Oedipus), or by their inherent nobility of character (both Oedipus and Othello).

The fall of the tragic hero affects other characters as well. Othello's tragedy includes his wife Desdemona, whom he slays, and his faithful lieutenant Cassio, whom he mistakenly believes has cuckolded him. The tragedy of Oedipus extends to his entire family, his mother/wife, his two sons, his two daughters, his brother-in-law, and his brother-in-law's family. Greek tragedy, typically, involves the destruction and downfall of an entire generation—or more—of a family. The catastrophes of Shakespearean tragedy are not always as extensive and pervasive, though they can be no less horrifying.

An essential element of the tragic hero's experience is a recognition of what has happened to him, however his downfall was occasioned. This often involves the hero discovering something previously unknown or something he knew about but did not correctly understand. According to Aristotle, the tragic hero's recognition or discovery is typically aligned with a reversal of his expectations. Such an ironic reversal occurs in *Oedipus the King* when a messenger's information, designed to reassure Oedipus about his identity, unsettles him instead. Once a tragedy's reversal or discovery occurs, the tragic plot moves swiftly to its catastrophic conclusion.

Some of the same dramatic elements we find in tragedy also occur in comedy. Scenes of discovery, recognitions, and reversals of fortune occur in comedy, as do misrepresentations of truth, errors of judgment, and exhibitions of human weakness and failure. In comedy, however, the reversals and errors lead not to calamity, but instead to prosperity and happiness.

Comic heroes, unlike their tragic counterparts, are usually ordinary people of modest circumstances. Comic heroes and other comic characters are often one-dimensional, and they tend to represent stereotypical figures such as the braggart, the hypocrite, the hypochondriac, the swaggering liar, the know-it-all, the ardent young lover, and more.

If comic characters are frequently predictable in their behavior, comic plots are not; they thrive on surprise and the unexpected, on various types of improbability. Cinderella stories, for example, are a staple of comedy; an impoverished student inherits a fortune; a beggar turns out to be a prince; a wife or husband or child, presumed dead, winds up alive and well; a dispute between families is resolved, the two sides reconciled, and in all these situations everybody lives happily after.

And yet the happy endings of comedies are not always so for all their characters. This marks a difference between romantic comedies, described up till now, and satiric comedies, or satires. Satire criticizes human misconduct, exposes human folly, and aims to correct it. While ridiculing the weaknesses of human beings, satiric comedy reveals the low level to which human behavior can sink.

Romantic comedy, on the other hand, portrays its characters more gently, even generously; its spirit is more tolerant and its tone more genial. Whatever adversities romantic heroes and heroines undergo, they are treated without bitterness or rancor. The humor of romantic comedy is more sympathetic and indulgent than critical and corrective. It intends to entertain more than instruct, to delight than to ridicule. Romantic comedies may also contain elements of satire, and satiric comedies may contain elements of romance.

Tragicomedy

Many modern plays mix not modes of comedy, but elements of comedy with tragedy. These bi-genre works are difficult to classify—except as tragicomic plays. It's often less important to categorize a work as predominantly tragic or comic than to acknowledge its mixture of dramatic modes and simply to respond to the characters and situations such plays dramatize. Some twentieth-century playwrights have found tragicomedy more suitable for representing a complex, uncertain, and often confusing world than either comedy or tragedy alone.

Realism and the Absurd

Throughout the history of drama and theater, plays through the centuries have represented human life in very different ways. Human character has been portrayed both realistically and unrealistically in the plays of the ancient Greek and Roman dramatists, in those of medieval and Renaissance playwrights, including Shakespeare, and in plays written during the Neoclassical era (eighteenth century) and the Romantic period (nineteenth century) and on into the modern period of the twentieth century and after.

We'll consider briefly both realism and an alternative, the theater of the absurd. A few words about each.

Realism can be defined as the representation of everyday life in literature. Considered with the average, the commonplace, the ordinary, realist dramatists, such as Henrik Ibsen in tragedy, and George Bernard Shaw in comedy, employ theatrical conventions to create the illusion of everyday life (in the various times in which their plays were set). With realistic drama came the depiction of subjects close to the lives of middle-class people, especially work, love and marriage, and family life.

From this standpoint, Ibsen's *A Doll's House* and Arthur Miller's *Death of a Salesman* are more realistic than Shakespeare's *Othello* and *Macbeth*, which, in turn, possess greater realism than does Sophocles' *Oedipus the King*. Although each of these very different plays creates something of a true-to-life quality, each operates according to differing theatrical conventions. Royal personages, gods, military heroes, and exalted language are absent from realist plays of modern drama, which also create a sense of realism through their settings. Other conventions of realism in drama include use of a three-walled room with an open fourth "wall" into which the audience peers to view the play's dramatic action.

Dialogue in realist plays approximates the idiom of everyday speech, polished to be sure, but designed to sound like spoken discourse rather than exalted language, including poetry. The plots, too, turn on subjects closer to home rather than being taken from myth or history.

One of the most noteworthy developments in drama after the rise of realism in the mid-nineteenth century was the emergence of the theatre of the absurd. Absurdist drama is nonrealistic, even anti-realistic. Absurdist playwrights reject the conventions of realism, substituting storyless plots for well-contrived ones and replacing realism's believable characters with understandable psychologically motivated behavior, with barely recognized figures who often behave bizarrely. The dialogue in absurdist plays often seems rambling and disconnected, even incoherent, compared to the grandly eloquent speeches and witty repartée found in Greek and Shakespearean plays. Two prominent representatives of absurdist theater are Samuel Beckett and Eugène Ionesco.

Why such a theatrical about-face? Why such a rejection of realist theatrical conventions? Primarily because ways of perceiving reality in the twentieth century changed so radically that those conventions were considered both inaccurate and inadequate. Absurdist dramatists rejected the assumptions that underlie realistic theatrical conventions, as for example that characters should be understood, or plots rationally ordered. According to absurdism, people are enigmas to both themselves and one another, and life is disorderly and chaotic to the point of meaninglessness. Absurdist dramatists see human beings as irrational, pathetic figures, helpless against life's forces. They view people as deracinated, rootless, cut off from their historical context, dispossessed of religious certainty, alienated from their physical and social environments, and unable to communicate effectively with one other. This sense of being out of tune, out of sync with life, for the absurdist writers, thwarts people's hopes, deprives them of happiness, and robs their lives of purpose and meaning.

Part IV
Reading the Essay—Five Ways In

Prelude IV
The Pleasures of the Essay

Essays have long had an uncertain status as literature, having been considered the distant and less elegant cousin, the poor relation, of the dominant literary genres—drama, fiction, and poetry, both lyric and epic. The essay arrived later in the history of literature. Its uses mostly were practical—to inform and persuade rather than to entertain and move. Its province was more factual than imaginative; hence its second-class status.

In contrast to the imaginative representations of reality we expect in drama, fiction, and poetry, the usual purpose of the essay is to explain a set of circumstances, to explore a topic, and persuade readers of a particular view of them. Instead of ambiguity often associated with the other genres, we associate the essay with the direct and the explicit. If it contains narrative or figurative language, these are used to illustrate, dramatize, or otherwise support an idea, and are, thus, subordinate to its exposition.

To acknowledge the primacy of idea in the essay, however, is not to deny that essays can be imaginative, visionary, even literary. Reading essays with attention only to ideas and information, while ignoring their styles and voices, is to miss a full experience of what the genre offers. Like the other literary genres, the essay invites and gratifies active, deliberative reading; it rewards attention to its literary elements of voice and tone, style and structure, language and form. Although we may read essays to extract information and to acquire knowledge, we also read them for the literary pleasures they provide.

The essay possesses its own pleasures, engages in its own forms of seduction.

Essays come in many styles and flavors, reflect a wide variety of visions, and sound a chorus of varied voices. An essay can be about anything—from taking a nap to analyzing the state of the world economy, from everyday matters like hating an enemy and living with your pets to complex philosophical and scientific concepts like evolution and string theory. Identity is a frequent topic of essayists; so, too, are related issues of gender, race, and culture. Essayists are fond of writing about the natural world as well as the human race. Politics and religion afford many essayists opportunities for explanation, exploration, reflection, and debate.

Essays invite and reward considered and thoughtful reading. Reading essays, in fact, is a lot like reading other forms of literature. Some essays are

DOI: 10.4324/9781003620280-27

much like short stories because these essays tell stories; they use narrative structures, though the stories these essays narrate are more factual than fictional. Langston Hughes's "Salvation" and Zora Neale Hurston's "How It Feels to Be Colored Me" are two noteworthy examples. Narrative essays, such as these, and others, including George Orwell's "Shooting an Elephant," lay out their ideas explicitly, unlike fictional stories, which work largely by implication and suggestion rather than through direct statement and explanation.

Essays can also be like poems in their use of highly charged language, especially figurative language, including imagery, simile, and metaphor. This affiliation, however, is only approximate, as poets typically write about one thing in terms of another, whereas essayists are generally more literal about conveying a sense of their subjects and ideas. Essayists tend to use figurative language to clarify and explain ideas. Their main intent is to explain and persuade.

The Essay Spectrum

We can classify essays as expository, exploratory, analytical, and argumentative. We situate essays on a spectrum with exploratory pieces based on writers' personal experience on one end and academic argumentative essays on the other. Narrative essays feature anecdote and personal experience; formal arguments rely on syllogistic reasoning and other logical strategies.

Expository essays explain ideas. Analytical essays dissect ideas and texts. Argumentative essays make claims and support them with evidence. Exploratory essays are less direct than expository, analytical, or argumentative essays. Exploratory essays typically inquire into ideas, considering their implications rather than making an argument or providing a direct explanation.

Expository essays explain ideas more straightforwardly, much as do analytical essays, which as their name suggests provide analysis and interpretation. Argumentative essays focus on persuasion, typically employing logical thinking, using both deductive and inductive reasoning. It is less important to classify essays, however, than to understand how the most interesting of them modulate between and among these varied possibilities.

Regardless of where they appear on the essay spectrum, nearer the personal/narrative pole or nearer the analytical/argumentative pole, all essays, to some extent, attempt to persuade. Essayists don't all persuade in the same way; they write to make their readers see something their way—at the very least to weight and consider what they are saying and suggesting.

Some essays are more descriptive than explanatory and some convey ideas obliquely rather than directly, through suggestion and implication. Exploratory and expository essays can be analytical, speculative, or argumentative—sometimes all of these together. As thoughtful readers we need to be aware of the complex range of purposes essays pursue and provide.

The Essay and Thinking

The essay relishes and enshrines thinking. We read essays and write them to discover what others think so we can better see what we think ourselves. We read essays for the intellectual stimulation they provide. We write essays to experience what we think in a recursive, deep-rooted process of slow, playful (and sometimes painful) discovery. The essay genre involves exploration, inquiry, invitation, and provocation toward considered and deliberative thinking.

The word "essay" (from the French "essayer," to try or attempt) is an attempt to explore an idea, to discover its implications, and to convey something of the thinking process and the resulting idea to readers. In *A Literary Education*, Joseph Epstein, a committed essayist, describes the personal essay as a form of discovery, in which the essayist finds out where they stand on complex issues by testing their thinking through the process of writing the essay (381). As David Mikics notes in *Slow Reading in a Hurried Age*, "essays drift, turn sharply this way or that, run up a blind alley and stay there for a while" (291). He notes, further, how essays develop and rely upon a "partnership" (291) between readers and essay writers. We follow essayists' meanderings because, at their best, essays engage us, entertain us, surprise us, enlighten us.

Larger goals for reading essays with understanding include recognizing a writer's purpose, comprehending an essay's central idea, identifying its tone, evaluating evidence and reasoning, and recognizing a writer's (or narrator's) perspective, position, and bias. We attempt to see what a writer (or narrator) says through how it is said, our goal to consider how well a writer's evidence supports an essay's claims (if, indeed, it makes any explicit claims).

To do this analytical work well, however, we need to overcome any initial resistance to a text we might harbor, any impulse to contradict, counter, or otherwise challenge it. We need to remain open to what a text offers, responsive to a writer's aims and goals, and to how any essay is designed to achieve them. We can voice our questions and qualifications later, after we have given the essayist the benefit of the doubt.

The challenge for readers, in the words of Thomas Newkirk, is "to attune themselves to texts, to align themselves with [their] generative energy" (*Minds* 14). Attending carefully, being fully present and focused while reading, are among the most important things we can do as we read any literary works, essays included. Among the ways such attunement and alignment can be achieved is through the slow, patient, responsible work of active, analytical reading. Some ways to do that kind of reading I presented earlier for reading poems, stories, and plays. Others follow here for reading essays, each tied to a specific essay or essay excerpt.

Reading Essays as Conversation

When we most engage an essayist and essay, we make our reading a kind of conversation with writer and text. We listen to what's being "said"; we consider and evaluate it. Sometimes we remain silent; other times we talk back. We speculate and wonder beyond what's being given us as we engage in our mental conversation with the author. Such imagined conversations stimulate our critical thinking faculty and our capacity for creative thinking as well.

When can identify a number of different kinds of conversations we have while reading essays in this dialogic way:

- Our conversation with the text—our response, interpretation, evaluation of it.
- Our conversation with the author, who is both beyond the text yet embodied in it.
- Our imagined sense of the writer, including the writer's aim and purpose.
- Our conversation with ourselves—including our changes of mind, shifts of response to what we're reading, and reconsideration of the essay's idea.
- Our conversation with others about what we've read and are reading.

Besides our conversations in these ways, we can also consider various conversations the writer has: conversations with her subject; conversations with her readers, actual and imagined; conversations with her reading; conversations with herself at various times.

16 Annotation—Francis Bacon
"Of Youth and Age"

One way to read an essay closely and productively is by annotating it to better follow an author's thinking. Annotating an essay can help us identify significant aspects of its style and structure—how an essay is organized and progresses, as well as what it seems to say and suggest, what it illustrates, explains, argues.

We can demonstrate with annotations for the following essay by Francis Bacon. We begin with a question: What does the title of Bacon's essay suggest for you? What do you imagine or expect will come in his essay?

A man that is young in years, may be old in hours, if he have lost no time. But that happeneth rarely. Generally, youth is like the first cogitations, not so wise as the second. For there is a youth in thoughts, as well as in ages. And yet the invention of young men, is more lively than that of old; and imaginations stream into their minds better, and, as it were, more divinely. Natures that have much heat, and great and violent desires and perturbations, are not ripe for action, till they have passed the meridian of their years; as it was with Julius Caesar and Septimius Severus. Of the latter, of whom it is said, *Juventutem egit erroribus, imo furoribus, plenam.* And yet he was the ablest emperor, almost, of all the list. But reposed natures may do well in youth. As it is seen in Augustus Caesar, Cosmus Duke of Florence, Gaston de Foix, and others. On the other side, heat and vivacity in age, is an excellent composition for business. Young men are fitter to invent, than to judge; fitter for execution, than for counsel; and fitter for new projects, than for settled business. For the experience of age, in things that fall within the compass of it, directeth them; but in new things, abuseth them.

The errors of young men, are the ruin of business; but the errors of aged men, amount but to this, that more might have been done, or sooner. Young men, in the conduct and manage of actions, embrace more than they can hold; stir more than they can quiet; fly to the end, without consideration of the means and degrees; pursue some few principles, which they have chanced upon absurdly; care not to innovate, which draws unknown inconveniences; use extreme remedies at first; and, that

DOI: 10.4324/9781003620280-28

which doubleth all errors, will not acknowledge or retract them; like an unready horse, that will neither stop nor turn. Men of age object too much, consult too long, adventure too little, repent too soon, and seldom drive business home to the full period, but content themselves with a mediocrity of success. Certainly it is good to compound employments of both; for that will be good for the present, because the virtues of either age, may correct the defects of both; and good for succession, that young men may be learners, while men in age are actors; and, lastly, good for extern accidents, because authority followeth old men, and favor and popularity, youth. But for the moral part, perhaps youth will have the pre-eminence, as age hath for the politic. A certain rabbin, upon the text, Your young men shall see visions, and your old men shall dream dreams, inferreth that young men, are admitted nearer to God than old, because vision, is a clearer revelation, than a dream. And certainly, the more a man drinketh of the world, the more it intoxicateth; and age doth profit rather in the powers of understanding, than in the virtues of the will and affections. There be some, have an over-early ripeness in their years, which fadeth betimes. These are, first, such as have brittle wits, the edge whereof is soon turned; such as was Hermogenes the rhetorician, whose books are exceeding subtle; who afterwards waxed stupid. A second sort, is of those that have some natural dispositions which have better grace in youth, than in age; such as is a fluent and luxuriant speech; which becomes youth well, but not age: so Tully saith of Hortensius, *Idem manebat, neque idem decebat.* The third is of such, as take too high a strain at the first, and are magnanimous, more than tract of years can uphold. As was Scipio Africanus, of whom Livy saith in effect, *Ultima primis cedebant.*

Here is a sample set of annotations for Bacon's essay followed by notes that identify references and allusions, and that translate its Latin quotations.

Annotations (in Script)

Left Margin

Bacon opens with talk of mind and thought.
Should youth not act till middle age?
"But," "yet," "if," "on the other side"—lots of shifts of viewpoint.
A catalogue of youth's faults.
Youth imagined as horse—compare earlier image of ripeness for the aged.
Biblical reference—distinction valid or just clever?
Ends with examples of youthful success.
Three types of youth fading into age. Implies a judgment?
Does Bacon celebrate age over youth? The opposite?

Right margin

Title suggests comparison and contrast.
Youth and age not matters of time/chronology.
Bacon qualifies, avoids oversimplifications.
Suggests young men better suited to some things than others.
A shorter list of shortcomings of age.
An old man's understanding does not always result in virtuous behavior.
Essay stops abruptly.
What does Bacon leave us thinking about?

Notes

Julius Caesar (100 BCE–44 BCE), Roman general, statesman, and author.
Septimus Severus (145–211), Roman soldier and emperor CE 193–CE 211.
Juventutem egit erroribus, imo furoribus, plenam. Latin for: He spent a youth full of errors and madness.
Augustus Caesar (63 BCE–14 CE), first Roman Emperor, ruled 27 BCE–14 BCE.
Cosmus, Cosimo de Medici (1389–1464), Duke of Florence 1537–1574, also reigned as Duke of Tuscany 1569–1574.
Gaston de Foix (1489–1512), French nobleman and military commander.
Hermogenes, a Greek philosopher who flourished around 400 BCE.
Hortensius (114 BCE–50 BCE), Roman orator.
Idem manebat, neque idem decebat. Latin for: He continued the same when the same was not appropriate.
Tully, Marcus Tullius Cicero (106 BCE–43 BCE), a Roman orator, senator, and author.
Scipio Africanus (286 BCE–183 BCE), general and statesman of the Roman Republic.
Livy, Titus Livius Patinus (59 BCE–17 CE), Roman historian.
Ultima primis cedebant. Latin for: His last actions did not equal his first.

The following exercise and ancillary comments can take you more deeply into the essay's language, structure, and ideas.

Considerations

1   To what extent does Bacon seem to favor youth over age or age over youth? Or does he balance their merits and faults equally so as not to favor one over the other?
2   Divide the essay into three or four paragraphs. Where would you make the paragraph breaks, and why?
3   What is the effect of the Latin quotations Bacon introduces?
4   Why do you think Bacon includes other references, primarily allusions to figures of historical, political, military, and authorial significance?

5   Do you think Bacon's ideas about youth and age remain relevant today? Why or why not?

Comments

Bacon's essay is more than a simple comparison and contrast between youth and age. For even though Bacon oscillates between the advantages of age over youth and of youth over age, "Of Youth and Age" does not provide a clearly articulated thesis, or argumentative claim, typical of standard expository essays. Nor does Bacon's essay conform to a clear-cut pattern of organization. Instead, Bacon swerves rapidly and repeatedly between observations on youth and observations about age, without providing transitions from one aspect of his discussion to another. Our experience in reading the essay, consequently, is quite different from what it would be had it been organized in a more conventional manner—in a simple two-part structure, with comments about youth preceding others about age.

Bacon makes our experience in reading "Of Youth and Age" an exercise in uncertainty, in qualification, in thinking. Bacon qualifies his praise of youth and of age with criticism and his criticism with praise. As we read, we have to keep adjusting our sense of what Bacon seems to think. He seems more interested in disturbing our comfortable certainties about youth and age than in arguing strongly for the merits of one stage of life over the other. In the process, he undermines our desire for closure and for a conclusive answer to which part of life he prefers. Yes, he seems to suggest, there are specific assets and liabilities, advantages and drawbacks to youth as there are to age. Young readers may see the essay favoring the merits of youth, whereas older readers may incline more favorably towards the values of age. Bacon himself remains noncommittal.

In "The Uncommon Reader," George Steiner argues that reading responsibly requires that we be "answerable to the text" (6). Answerability includes both response and responsibility; it requires an "answerable reciprocity" (7), such that active, analytical, critical engagement with a text results in a form of commerce with it. This kind of reading requires a dialogue between text and reader, the kind of dialogue created with textual annotation, the kind of dialogue Bacon has with his readers, the kind of dialogue Bacon has with himself. And the kind of dialogue we have with Francis Bacon and with ourselves as we read and think about his essay.

Through annotation we attempt to elucidate the text for ourselves, to understand it, comprehend it. Following Steiner, we can introduce the complementary practice of writing marginalia, which allow readers to talk back to the text, replying to it rather than representing it. In writing marginalia, we augment the author's text, perhaps disputing aspects of it, perhaps extending its significance through arguing with it, and through relating it to other texts we have read and other experiences we have had. The process is dynamic, collaborative, re-creative. It involves pulling apart and piecing together, thereby making something of and from the texts we read.

We can begin our critical, analytical reading with annotation, jotting brief observations about the text—what we notice. We can then extend our thinking with writing marginalia—commenting, questioning, connecting, and further elucidating what we are reading, as we clarify and deepen our thinking—thinking that we might then develop and elaborate in an essay of our own, analyzing, elucidating, exploring the implications of Bacon's "Of Youth and Age."

17 Style and Tone—Mary Wollstonecraft
A Vindication of the Rights of Woman

As we noted in our discussions of both poetry and fiction, tone is one of the most difficult aspects of writing to understand and explain. Learning to discern a writer's tone takes practice with many kinds of texts across genres, and within the essay genre with a variety of essay examples. We consider here a passage about women's rights from 1792 by Mary Wollstonecraft:

1 My own sex, I hope, will excuse me, if I treat them like rational creatures, instead of flattering their *fascinating* graces, and viewing them as if they were in a state of perpetual childhood, unable to stand alone. I earnestly wish to point out in what true dignity and human happiness consists—I wish to persuade women to endeavour to acquire strength, both of mind and body, and to convince them, that the soft phrases, susceptibility of heart, delicacy of sentiment, and refinement of taste, are almost synonymous with epithets of weakness, and that those beings who are only the objects of pity and that kind of love, which has been termed its sister, will soon become objects of contempt.

2 Dismissing then those pretty feminine phrases, which the men condescendingly use to soften our slavish dependence, and despising that weak elegancy of mind, exquisite sensibility, and sweet docility of manners, supposed to be the sexual characteristics of the weaker vessel, I wish to show that elegance is inferior to virtue, that the first object of laudable ambition is to obtain a character as a human being, regardless of the distinction of sex; and that secondary views should be brought to this simple touchstone.

3 This is a rough sketch of my plan; and should I express my conviction with the energetic emotions that I feel whenever I think of the subject, the dictates of experience and reflection will be felt by some of my readers. Animated by this important object, I shall disdain to cull my phrases or polish my style—I aim at being useful, and sincerity will render me unaffected; for wishing rather to persuade by the force of my arguments, than dazzle by the elegance of my language, I shall not waste my time in rounding periods, nor in fabricating the turgid bombast of artificial

feelings, which, coming from the head, never reach the heart. I shall be employed about things, not words! and, anxious to render my sex more respectable members of society, I shall try to avoid that flowery diction which has slided from essays into novels, and from novels into familiar letters and conversation.

4 These pretty nothings, these caricatures of the real beauty of sensibility, dropping glibly from the tongue, vitiate the taste, and create a kind of sickly delicacy that turns away from simple unadorned truth; and a deluge of false sentiments and over-stretched feelings, stifling the natural emotions of the heart, render the domestic pleasures insipid, that ought to sweeten the exercise of those severe duties, which educate a rational and immortal being for a nobler field of action.

In order to describe and explain Wollstonecraft's tone, we need to consider her language—diction, syntax, and tone—as well as her examples, and details, especially. We can tackle the passage one paragraph at a time. I encourage you to make notes in the margins; to underline phrases, circle words, and mark the passage in other ways with your observations about diction, syntax, and tone.

Here are a few questions to get you started.

1. What does Wollstonecraft condemn in her first paragraph? Why?
2. In her second paragraph, what does she suggest should replace what she condemns in her first paragraph?
3. Notice that in her third paragraph, Wollstonecraft shifts her focus to matters of style—her writing style. What does she say about *how* she intends to express her ideas about this important subject of women and their rights? What, for example, does she say that she will avoid? What will she not do in terms of her writing style?
4. The fourth paragraph recapitulates, or summarizes, what Wollstonecraft has said in the first three paragraphs. She develops a set of contrasting terms to drive home her central idea. Identify those contrasting terms—what she condemns and what she admires.
5. What is Mary Wollstonecraft's attitude toward her subject—that is, what is her tone?

Comments

Once you have done this analytical work, we can elaborate and further extend what you have noticed. Wollstonecraft begins her first paragraph with a tone of apparent apology—women, she says, will "excuse" her if she engages their intellects—treating them as "rational creatures" instead of as "children" (whose rational faculties—knowledge and intelligences) are still in development. From the start, the tone here is complex. When Wollstonecraft indicates that she will not be "flattering their *fascinating* graces" (with *fascinating* in italics), we detect that she disapproves of this aspect of the feminine. We detect a sense of criticism of women for playing this game, for allowing themselves to be perceived this way, and for letting men treat them as "children."

And that's just the first sentence. In the second sentence, Wollstonecraft tells us directly what her purpose is: "to persuade women" and to "convince" them and also to "point out" something important to her. We can ask ourselves: What does she want to point out to women? Of what does she aim to persuade and convince them? Although the sentence is long, it breaks down into these three goals: to point, persuade, and convince.

But we might pause, in that sentence, over the phrase "epithets of weakness." What are they? Weakness we know; but "epithets"? By looking at the phrase in context, we can get an idea of its meaning. We can then ask ourselves what words are nearly the same as, or are associated with, "epithets of weakness"; the answer: "soft phrases, susceptibility of heart, delicacy of sentiment, and refinement of taste."

We need to discern the opening paragraph's ironic, critical tone. And we need to understand the writer's purpose—to persuade and convince women that they should abandon their traditional feminine "fascinating graces." But what should women put in place of "soft phrases" and the rest? For that we need to analyze her second paragraph, which consists of a single long sentence.

We should notice how the second paragraph begins with the same kinds of things the writer has already condemned: "pretty feminine phrases," "weak elegancy of mind," "sweet docility of manners," all of which contribute to women's "slavish dependence." That's a strong condemnation. And so we might add to the ironic tone of the first paragraph the strong tone of condemnation of the second.

We notice that all those phrases occur in the first half of the sentence, and that Wollstonecraft is "[d]ismissing" them. But in favor of what? She wants women to acquire "virtue" and "a character as a human being." "Elegance," she writes, is "inferior to virtue"; and women's first "object" should be to "obtain" a "character" as a "human being." Each of these word choices matters. "Virtue" means both morally appropriate behavior and also a type of strength. "Character" refers to something individual, personal, meaningful, and substantial. And "human being" suggests an equality with men.

In the third paragraph, Wollstonecraft claims that she will not pay much attention to her writing style—that instead she will focus on her arguments. She will avoid what she calls "flowery diction"; she will not bother to "polish" her style. She will, instead, attend to "things" and to actions rather than to "dazzle by the elegance of [her] language." We might note, however, that in this paragraph, as in the other three, the writing is actually quite polished. So, it is ironic that she claims not to be concerned about her language and style, which she manages with care and skill and grace.

We conclude, here, with a quick look at Wollstonecraft's fourth and final paragraph. We see how the phrases "pretty nothings," "false sentiments," and "over-stretched feelings" tie in with the attitudes and behaviors she condemned earlier—those "soft phrases," "delicacy of sentiment," "exquisite sensibility," and "sweet docility," to choose a few earlier examples. And we notice as well how her language continues to be critical and judgmental: "dropping glibly," "vitiate the taste," "sickly delicacy." Her criticism of all these things is consistent with what she says from the start. The alternative Wollstonecraft sees for women is expressed clearly and forcefully at the end of the passage: to "educate a rational and immortal being for a nobler field of action." This goal ties in directly to what she says earlier about "true dignity and human happiness," about women acquiring "strength, both of mind and body," and of acquiring "virtue" and "character."

Learning to detect a writer's tone and understanding how writers achieve varying kinds of tone in their work is one of the most challenging demands of reading essays. It's especially important, especially when a writer's tone verges on or strongly embodies irony.

18 Slow Reading—Leslie Jamison
"A Street Full of Splendid Strangers"

We can reap the rewards that reading literature provides, including essays, by reading slowly and deliberatively. Yes, I am advocating slowing reading down and not speeding it up. Why? Because slow reading brings rewards of insight and of pleasure, of understanding, of experience, of wisdom.

I invite you to test my claim by reading along with me the opening paragraphs of a recent essay, "A Street Full of Splendid Strangers," by Leslie Jamison, originally published in *The Atlantic*, and reprinted in *The Best American Essays 2020*. Here is how Jamison begins her essay:

> When I was young, the beauty of church always belonged to other people: the believers. They saw the same stained glass I saw, but when its jeweled light cut their skin into kaleidoscopic colors, they somehow belonged in that light in a way I never would. They could feel the lilt and soar of the hymns as truth, as collective yearning, as a tin-can telephone connecting them to God. That's what I told myself. I told myself I was alien to that beauty—I'd never be anything but an interloper lurking just outside its grace.

Let's begin with a few observations about the writer's opening sentence, which immediately places us in church. Jamison suggests that being in church can be uplifting for people—a beautiful experience—but that this experience is one she does not share. She emphasizes this point with the last four words of that initial sentence and with her use of the colon. This experience of beauty, Jamison insists, belongs to "other people: the believers." She herself feels somehow shut out from that experience. That's a striking admission for jump-starting an essay. We wonder why that might be the case. Jamison answers our question later, but first she tells us what the experience is like for those "others," providing us with vivid details so that we can imagine what "believers" see and hear of beauty in church.

Ironically, Jamison notes that she sees the same stained glass they see, describing vividly its "jeweled light" and "kaleidoscopic colors." In doing so, however, she separates herself from those other believers: "they somehow belonged," Jamison writes, "in a way I never would." Here, again, we may wonder why she doesn't belong, and perhaps why she suggests that she not only does not belong now, but that she doesn't see herself as ever belonging, as ever being able to experience the beauty of church as believers do. We may surmise that it has something to do with belief—with faith—and that it is religious faith that separates Jamison from the believers and their more deeply emotional experience of the beauty they experience in church. We don't know that, of course, but we might infer it, given the way Jamison distinguishes herself from the congregation of believers. But that surmise can be tested only by reading further—and doing some additional thinking about what Jamison is saying and suggesting.

So far, we have been reading slowly through the first two sentences of Jamison's opening paragraph, taking us about halfway through that paragraph. Slowing down this way to notice and wonder—to ask some questions really—gets us thinking, very likely, not only about Jamison's church experience, but also about our own. Jamison's details—first visual, then aural—(which we'll get to momentarily)—should evoke the sights and sounds (and perhaps the tastes and smells) of our own remembered church experiences. In doing so we connect our reading with our lives, with our past experience, perhaps sharing in the experiences Jamison imagines for the believers she describes, perhaps sharing, as well, Jamison's experience of self-exclusion. Perhaps our reflections about this passage and the questions that arise in our minds as we read take us in other directions. That would not be unusual.

But let's continue with Leslie Jamison's paragraph. One of the most striking sentences in her first paragraph is the third, the sentence about sounds, where she notes that those other believers could "feel the lilt and soar of the hymns." The hymns, she imagines, evoke feeling, emotion, for the believers though not for Jamison, as she once again separates herself from the "truth" and the "collective yearning" she presumes that believers experience. Her sentence about sounds and what they evoke in church, however, has something more in it—another detail: the "telephone connecting them to God." Did you notice and wonder about Jamison's use of the word "tin-can" to describe the telephone? What image does she conjure for you with that adjective? What tone do you hear in Jamison's use of that word? A bit of disdain, perhaps?

What we are doing with these opening sentences of Jamison's essay is noticing textual details and raising questions about them, as we slow our reading down and re-read her sentences, some of them aloud. This deliberative process of reading leads to our discovering moments of exhilaration that we experience while reading her essay.

The last two sentences of the opening paragraph pivot to "what she told [her]self."

Jamison uses that phrase twice, for emphasis. And what she tells herself is that she is an "interloper," an "alien" presence who does not, cannot, and will never share the experience of beauty that believers do, noting that she lurks "just outside its grace."

And what a word that is, "grace," to conclude a paragraph about the beauty experienced in church. It's a loaded word, an exhilarating one appropriate in the context of religious belief and churchgoing, and one that captures well what Jamison is missing—how she lacks the benevolent gift of grace.

As we read this concluding sentence, and as we mull over the significance of what Jamison suggests in her first paragraph, we may wonder where she will go next with her essay. We might wonder whether there may be some other form of grace available to her.

Here is how Jamison continues with her essay's second paragraph.

> Some version of that girl I'd been in church—with legs too long for her denim overalls, and palms covered with half-moon crescents where she'd dug her nails into her skin—was summoned for a different rapture, years later, by the photography of Garry Winogrand. Some version of that girl was told: *This is beauty you belong in.* The first time I entered the Brooklyn Museum's 2019 exhibit of his color photography, part of its force was this immediate sense of invitation, as if a door had been carved in a wall, leading to some new world, and now I could cross into it—or perhaps simply see more clearly that I'd been living in that miraculous world all along. It had only disguised itself as something familiar, or banal.

Let's note, first, the splendid details of that long first sentence, the vivid description sandwiched between the double dashes, which make those details stand out. Let's observe, too, how Jamison takes herself and us to another place—to the Brooklyn Museum of Art, a different kind of sublime space, one in which she, and we, can experience beauty unconnected to church and religious faith. Let's remark, as well, on Jamison's diction—on her choice of the word "summoned" to something she can't resist, and her choice of "rapture," a word rich in connotation, with both spiritual and sensual associations. What might it mean to be "summoned" to "rapture"; with what kind of "force" we wonder with anticipation as we read?

Jamison feels that some form of rapture, a special but different kind of grace, can be hers, a transcendent experience of beauty and its attendant emotion occasioned by an exhibition of color photographs (an echo of the colored stained glass?) by Garry Winogrand, whose works create "[a kind of] beauty" that Jamison tells herself that she "belong[s] in." We, thus, discover that Jamison can, indeed, experience moments of exhilaration and of rapture, but that these moments occur, for her, not in churches, but in secular spaces, including museums.

Jamison reserves, for the last part of her second paragraph, a series of striking images that capture the sense of splendor and grandeur she experiences upon viewing Winogrand's photographs. For her, a "door" opens into a new world, one into which she "crosses," entering a different extraordinary space where she experiences transcendence—a sublime beauty that she feels includes her, a beauty she relishes, cherishes, and feels as rightfully hers.

Jamison concludes this paragraph with the stunning idea that the "miraculous world" Winogrand's photographs create has been there all along—in the everyday world that she—and we—inhabit. It's just that she, and we, have somehow missed its beauty, and that it takes an artist like Garry Winogrand to open our eyes and minds and hearts to its hidden-in-plain-sight glory. A final irony is that the miraculous beauty Winogrand captures and that Jamison describes not only has been available all along, but that it is "familiar," even "banal." Beauty lurks where we least expect to find it. Glory reveals itself to us in seemingly ordinary moments—if we know where to find it and how to see, in those moments, its astonishing, luminous radiance. That's a notion to reckon with, to deliberate about, to experience with exhilaration.

Are you curious as to what Jamison saw at the exhibition of Garry Winogrand's photography? Here is a small sampling of the pictures she describes in her essay:

> A woman propped on her elbows on her beach towel, a messy mickey stick-and-poke tattoo on her arm, cat's-eye sunglasses hiding her mood. A man lying on his back, with his blue-canvas sneakers tucked beside him and the sunlight pouring across his body, the cigar in his mouth pointed straight up toward the sky....a family having a picnic against a backdrop of rolling white sand dunes; street clowns at a parade beneath a sign advertising Dallas' finest hamburgers; flight attendants in their powder-blue suits, clustered on an asphalt divider, shadowed by palm trees and boxy, off-white airport hotels.

What's especially interesting about the Winogrand photography exhibit is that his pictures were slides—horizontal images that rotated every eight seconds and vertical images every thirteen seconds. Viewers observed them more than once, a little at a time, and always in relation to different images appearing on the museum walls. Jamison characterizes her experience of the moving images as "a tutorial in the proximity of the sacred," a phrase that takes us back to the notion of "grace" with which she begins her essay. Her "tutorial" invites us to think about what "grace" and the "sacred" might mean for us and how they might manifest themselves in our lives in churches and museums and other less exalted places and spaces.

Reading with this degree of attention and care brings benefits beyond compare. We read literary works, including Jamison's essay, for some of the reasons she reads and celebrates Garry Winogrand's photographs. We read them for the shared feelings they evoke; for a sense of other people's humanity; for a sense of what others care about; for a glimpse of what they do and make and love.

Reading literature disciplines us and strengthens our powers of focus, aids our capacity for noticing, prompts our inclination to ask questions and to make connections. Reading slowly, carefully, deliberately, a work like Jamison's essay—as she herself reads Winogrand's photographs—enables us to participate in a provocative and engaging conversation that leads our thinking in directions we could not have imagined when we began reading her essay.

19 Reading Framework—Jamaica Kincaid
"On Seeing England for the First Time"

In reading essays, as with the reading of literary works in other genres, everything hinges on observation—on what we notice about the text. I have been illustrating the process of analysis and interpretation throughout the book. Here I step back and recount the stages of that process: making observations; connecting them; from those connections making inferences; considering values embodied in the text, from that work, developing a provisional interpretation. And so, I provide them and explanation of its components, followed by an application to an essay excerpt.

Making Observations

All interpretation begins with observation. We can't say about a text more than we can see in it. This is true whether we are observing a poem or a person, a movie or a monument, an artifact or an architectural structure, a laboratory experiment, a mathematical proof, a musical performance, a theatrical production, an athletic feat, or an essay. Seeing and saying are reciprocal and mutually reinforcing. Deep noticing, recursively practiced, is fundamental to successful critical reading and writing. We can't say more than we can see. Seeing more, we have more to think about, and more to say about what we see.

Establishing Connections

Observing textual details, however, is not enough. To read well, we need to make connections among those details—two kinds of connections: (1) connections among textual details; (2) connections between the writer's text and their lives and ours, as well. The order in which we make these connections is arbitrary and individual. The sequence in which these kinds of connections are made is less important than the range of connections made.

Such connections move us toward the making of meaning; they provide the basis for our preliminary thinking about implications—about what the observed details might suggest, signify, mean. Establishing and understanding relationships between and among details, and then between and among parts of a text, object, or process, deepens and enriches the interpretive process.

DOI: 10.4324/9781003620280-31

Making Inferences

All disciplinary study requires making sound inferences. Scientists are expert inference makers. They base their theories upon their observations, which they test and confirm or disconfirm. Those theories are inference-based extrapolations into the unknown from the observed data. The iconic physicist Richard Feynman, who identified the problem that caused the space shuttle *Challenger* catastrophe, calls them good guesses that have held up as true so far. Those good-guess inferences that determine the theory could be proven inadequate; they might be shown to be slightly or even totally wrong in the future. But they are the best inferences that can be made at the time—and thus they constitute current scientific knowledge.

Historical investigation follows an analogous process, mostly using primary and secondary source documents rather than experiments as evidence upon which to develop conclusions through reasoning inductively about particular instances and arriving at general principles. The particular details of history—historical facts, data, documents, and other forms of information—provide the evidence for developing inferences and theories of historical explanation.

Both scientific experimentation and historical analysis, however, may begin and often do begin with a theory or an idea—that is, with a generalization the investigator sets out to test, by finding evidence that either supports it or falsifies it. In this case, the process of thought moves from a general idea or concept to specific supporting evidence. Thus, thinking, including scientific and historical thinking, typically involves interplay between inductive and deductive reasoning, moving back and forth between them repeatedly in a looping recursive process.

Evaluating—Considering Values

It's necessary to distinguish between the two distinctly different ways of thinking of *evaluation* with respect to literary works. In evaluating a story, poem, play, or essay, we do, largely, two things: (1) we assess its literary quality; (2) we consider the values it embodies, whether or not those values seem to be endorsed, questioned, or challenged in or by the work.

An evaluation is essentially a judgment, an opinion about a work formulated as a conclusion. In thinking about Leslie Jamison's essay, we may agree or disagree with the author's ideas about what people experience in churches or museums, or about her views of "grace." But however we evaluate Jamison's views, we invariably measure the work's values against our own.

In evaluating any literary work, we appraise it according to our own special combination of social, cultural, moral, and aesthetic values. Our social and cultural values derive from our lives as members of families, communities, and larger social entities. These values are linked with our moral values and our ethical norms—what we believe to be right and wrong, good and evil. Our aesthetic values reflect what we consider to be beautiful or ugly, well or ill made. Over time, with experience and education, our values often change.

Our aesthetic evaluations are often affected by the informed responses of others, who likely have had different experiences with life and literature than we have had. Eventually, through the experience of living and reading literature, we develop a form of literary tact—an ability to distinguish between good and bad writing, successful and unsuccessful works, a kind of balanced judgment informed by thoughtful reflection. There are no shortcuts to developing this kind of aesthetic understanding and appreciation of literature. And even if and when we do develop literary tact, we will find that others do not necessarily see, experience, or value any particular work of literature as we do.

Thinking about textual inferences and values leads toward interpretation, which is always tentative and provisional. Like scientific theories and historical models, any textual interpretation is subject to revision. It can change as a result of re-reading a text and thinking more about it; it can change based on conversations we have with others or from reading what others have written about it. Interpretations of texts are subject to revision in the same way as our evaluations of texts can change.

We can demonstrate the process of responsible, reflective critical reading—using the framework of observation, connection, inference, evaluation, and conclusion—with a look at the first few paragraphs of an essay about England by Jamaica Kincaid.

> When I saw England for the first time, I was a child in school sitting at a desk. The England I was looking at was laid out on a map gently, beautifully, delicately, a very special jewel: it lay on a bed of sky blue—the background of the map....she said, "This is England"—and she said it with authority, seriousness, and adoration, and we all sat up. It was as if she had said, "This is Jerusalem, the place you will go to when you die but only if you have been good." We understood then—we were meant to understand then—that England was to be our source of myth and the source from which we got our sense of reality, our sense of what was meaningful, our sense of what was meaningless—and much about our own lives and much about the very idea of us headed that last list.
>
> I was already very familiar with the greatness of it. Each morning before I left for school...I ate breakfast, half a grapefruit, a bowl of oat porridge, bread and butter and a slice of cheese, and a cup of cocoa. The can of cocoa was often left on the table in front of me. It had written on it..."Made in England." Those words, "Made in England," were written on the box the oats came in too. They would also have been written on the box the shoes I was wearing came in:...The shoes I wore were made in England; so were my socks and cotton undergarments and the satin ribbons I wore tied at the end of two plaits of my hair. The shoes [my father] wore to work would have been made in England, as were his khaki shirt and brown felt hat. Felt was not the proper material from which a hat that was expected to provide shade from the hot sun should be made, but my father must have seen and admired a picture of an

Englishman wearing such a hat in England, and this picture that he saw must have been so compelling that it caused him to wear the wrong hat for a hot climate most of his long life....[T]his breakfast business was Made in England like almost everything else that surrounded us, the exceptions being the sea, the sky, and the air we breathed.

Observations

There are many things worth noticing about this excerpt from Kincaid's essay on England. Perhaps the first is the simplicity and directness of her opening sentence, which she follows with an intricate, meandering sentence complex in both syntax and tone. The opening sentence also presents an image, a young child sitting at a school desk. And it announces a key theme of the essay: seeing England, which will become an increasingly complicated problem for the author, and an important center of focus and interpretive significance for the reader.

We begin to get a sense of that complication—what the author sees of and in England—in her second sentence, which is rich with ambivalence. England is a jewel, a myth, and a reality, a myth that for the author and her Antiguan compatriots is their reality; the English people are meaningful; the author and her kind, by contrast and implication, are not, she seems to suggest. The writer's complex, ambivalent attitude toward England begins to emerge early.

Connections

These observations about the beginning of Kincaid's essay bleed over into connections—relationships between and among details. We might couch the overarching observations about the essay's first two paragraphs as presenting a double perspective about England: admiring and critical; proud and ashamed; submissive and resistant. Kincaid begins her second paragraph by reprising the image of the essay's opening sentence; she extends that image, however, by highlighting England's "greatness" in her opening paragraph, in terms of its imperial dominion.

The contrasts Kincaid establishes in her opening paragraph, she continues and develops further in her second. She fills this next paragraph with details about food and clothes. She and her Antiguan counterparts eat English food—the big English breakfast of eggs and porridge and cocoa especially—eating with knife and fork rather than their bare hands (which the young Kincaid much prefers, as her food tastes better, she says later, eaten that way). They wear clothes from England: the author's school uniform, her socks and underwear, her hair ribbons and her shoes; her father's shoes and shirt, and most strikingly his felt hat, all wrong for the hot island climate, but which, for her father, symbolize both his character and his aspirations toward all things English.

These hyper-English details extend the implied idea of Kincaid's opening paragraph about England's domination of her and her island nation. "Made in England" is stamped literally on Kincaid's and her father's clothes; it is also stamped metaphorically on their minds, as well. The upper-case letters add emphasis, as if any were needed.

And yet, even with England's dominance, Kincaid reveals, through her carefully chosen diction and details, an element of defiance against what England represents. For England may claim dominion over her food and clothes, but there remains an important exception: the sea and sky and air Kincaid breathes on her island home. Kincaid cherishes these distinctive, unforgettable natural elements of her island home, which contrast irrevocably and irreconcilably with the air and sky and water of England.

Inferences

At this point we should be ready to make some inferences based on our observations and on the connections (contrasts mostly in these paragraphs) between and among them. What might we infer, given what's been said so far about Kincaid's excerpted paragraphs? What is her attitude toward England?

One thing, certainly, is her critical defiance of the colonial power. She doesn't like England. Rather than submit to its influence on her life and aspirations, she resists, pushes back, rebels. She refuses to accept the myth of England as her reality, regardless of what her father might do and think and believe.

It's important to make inferences, to go out on the inferential limb, to make the inferential leap—based on Kincaid's choices of diction and her selection of detail. Those inferences must, of course, derive from textual evidence, in this case, on how Kincaid piles up details about England's cultural dominance. A bit later in her essay she will present a less glorious, even uglier side to how England presents and represents itself, including England as a jewel that only English people can wear; and with squiggly red lines on a map, suggestive of the blood shed in England's global wars, including England's colonizing in places it should never have gone, Antigua, by implication, among them.

Kincaid's outward submission masks an inner rebelliousness. These opening paragraphs provide a foundation for an increasingly critical view of England and all things English, which Kincaid develops through more extensive descriptions of incidents in her essay that are too long to include here.

Values and Provisional Interpretations

I touched on the notion of values in Kincaid's opening paragraphs. We might add, however, something of the implied celebration of a life in Antigua more in tune with the island's climate and weather, a way of living more relaxed and easy than how the English live. Kincaid suggests Antiguans' cultural values through her comments about clothing and food, that overbearing

English breakfast both culturally and physically oppressive, making her feel heavy and sleepy, exactly the wrong kind of breakfast for people living in a warm climate.

What Kincaid values and what she implies Antiguans, generally, value is "the sea, the sky, and the air [they] breath[e]," which are not "Made in England," and which can be neither conscripted nor adapted to the English way of doing things. That sea and sky and air are the outward and natural manifestations of Kincaid's inward and cultural resistance to England and what it stands for. Later in the essay, Kincaid accumulates details from English history, including the naming of English kings, which culminates in a set of contrasts between England and Antigua that show how deeply alien England and the English are to her, how, as she writes, "their world was theirs not mine; everything told me so." In another passage Kincaid expresses her hatred of England, rendering a judgment so harsh that she wonders what she would do if she had the power to destroy England and everything it stands for—everything that she herself is not, can never be, as she differs radically from what England has come to represent for her. The "myth" of England, with which Kincaid begins her essay, is displaced by a much grimmer reality, Kincaid having traversed the "wide space" between "the idea of something and its reality," when in a kind of epiphany, she comes to see England for the first time as the horrible place it is for her and not the myth she long accepted.

20 Interrupted Reading—George Orwell
"A Hanging"

As in the ways in to poetry, fiction, and drama, I provide here an interrupted reading, this time of George Orwell's essay "A Hanging." As with the other genres' interrupted readings, Orwell's essay is presented in segments, mostly of one or two paragraphs. What's different about the interspersed comments this time, though, is that they are questions—questions inviting you to consider the details of "A Hanging" and also the individual reader's experience of the essay.

1 It was in Burma, a sodden morning of the rains. A sickly light, like yellow tinfoil, was slanting over the high walls into the jail yard. We were waiting outside the condemned cells, a row of sheds fronted with double bars, like small animal cages. Each cell measured about ten feet by ten and was quite bare within except for a plank bed and a pot of drinking water. In some of them brown silent men were squatting at the inner bars, with their blankets draped round them. These were the condemned men, due to be hanged within the next week or two.

Questions: What do you know once you've read this opening paragraph? What is its purpose? What details stand out? What associations do you bring personally, if any, to those details? What do you expect will come next in the essay?

2 One prisoner had been brought out of his cell. He was a Hindu, a puny wisp of a man, with a shaven head and vague liquid eyes. He had a thick, sprouting moustache, absurdly too big for his body, rather like the moustache of a comic man on the films. Six tall Indian warders were guarding him and getting him ready for the gallows. Two of them stood by with rifles and fixed bayonets, while the others handcuffed him, passed a chain through his handcuffs and fixed it to their belts, and lashed his arms tight to his sides. They crowded very close about him, with their hands always on him in a careful, caressing grip, as though all the while feeling him to make sure he was there. It was like men handling a fish which is still alive and may jump back into the water. But he stood quite unresisting, yielding his arms limply to the ropes, as though he hardly noticed what was happening.

Questions: Does this second paragraph provide what you expected it would? To what extent does it seem a natural follow-up to the opening paragraph? What is its center of interest? What impression of the prisoner do you gain from it? What details lead you to that impression? What does the comparison with the fish suggest? What is your response to the precautions taken by the six guards—and why so many of them?

> 3 Eight o'clock struck and a bugle call, desolately thin in the wet air, floated from the distant barracks. The superintendent of the jail, who was standing apart from the rest of us, moodily prodding the gravel with his stick, raised his head at the sound. He was an army doctor, with a grey toothbrush moustache and a gruff voice. "For God's sake hurry up, Francis," he said irritably. "The man ought to have been dead by this time. Aren't you ready yet?"
>
> 4 Francis, the head jailer, a fat Dravidian in a white drill suit and gold spectacles, waved his black hand. "Yes sir, yes sir," he bubbled. "All iss satisfactorily prepared. The hangman iss waiting. We shall proceed."
>
> 5 "Well, quick march, then. The prisoners can't get their breakfast till this job's over."

Questions: We meet two new characters in this section, Francis and the superintendent. What impression do you have of each? What do their comments reveal about them?

> 6 We set out for the gallows. Two warders marched on either side of the prisoner, with their rifles at the slope; two others marched close against him, gripping him by arm and shoulder, as though at once pushing and supporting him. The rest of us, magistrates and the like, followed behind. Suddenly, when we had gone ten yards, the procession stopped short without any order or warning. A dreadful thing had happened—a dog, come goodness knows whence, had appeared in the yard. It came bounding among us with a loud volley of barks, and leapt round us wagging its whole body, wild with glee at finding so many human beings together. It was a large woolly dog, half Airedale, half pariah. For a moment it pranced round us, and then, before anyone could stop it, it had made a dash for the prisoner, and jumping up tried to lick his face. Everyone stood aghast, too taken aback even to grab at the dog.

Questions: The march to the scaffold begins in this paragraph and is stopped almost as soon as it starts—by a barking, bounding dog. What is the relationship between the dog's action and the actions of the men? Why do you think Orwell included the dog? By now you have been forming an impression of the narrator. What sort of person is this narrator? To what extent do you like or dislike him? Why?

Interrupted Reading—George Orwell   137

7 "Who let that bloody brute in here?" said the superintendent angrily. "Catch it, someone!"

8 A warder, detached from the escort, charged clumsily after the dog, but it danced and gambolled just out of his reach, taking everything as part of the game. A young Eurasian jailer picked up a handful of gravel and tried to stone the dog away, but it dodged the stones and came after us again. Its yaps echoed from the jail wails. The prisoner, in the grasp of the two warders, looked on incuriously, as though this was another formality of the hanging. It was several minutes before someone managed to catch the dog. Then we put my handkerchief through its collar and moved off once more, with the dog still straining and whimpering.

Questions: How does the dog respond to the exertions of the men? What is its view of things? What is the effect of the dog's gamboling about and its not being caught right away?

9 It was about forty yards to the gallows. I watched the bare brown back of the prisoner marching in front of me. He walked clumsily with his bound arms, but quite steadily, with that bobbing gait of the Indian who never straightens his knees. At each step his muscles slid neatly into place, the lock of hair on his scalp danced up and down, his feet printed themselves on the wet gravel. And once, in spite of the men who gripped him by each shoulder, he stepped slightly aside to avoid a puddle on the path.

Questions: Orwell describes the prisoner as he walks to the gallows—his muscles sliding into place, his hair dancing on his scalp, his feet imprinting the wet gravel. What effect do those details create—what is their cumulative impact? How do you feel about the prisoner at this point in the essay? What do you make of his stepping aside to avoid a puddle? Why do you think Orwell may have included that detail?

10 It is curious, but till that moment I had never realized what it means to destroy a healthy, conscious man. When I saw the prisoner step aside to avoid the puddle, I saw the mystery, the unspeakable wrongness, of cutting a life short when it is in full tide. This man was not dying, he was alive just as we were alive. All the organs of his body were working—bowels digesting food, skin renewing itself, nails growing, tissues forming—all toiling away in solemn foolery. His nails would still be growing when he stood on the drop, when he was falling through the air with a tenth of a second to live. His eyes saw the yellow gravel and the grey walls, and his brain still remembered, foresaw, reasoned—reasoned even about puddles. He and we were a party of men walking together, seeing, hearing, feeling, understanding the same world; and in two minutes, with a sudden snap, one of us would be gone—one mind less, one world less.

Questions: What's different about paragraph 10? What does Orwell do in it that he has not done previously in the essay? What is the relationship between paragraph 10 and what goes before it, in particular its relationship to paragraph 9? What is the effect of Orwell's use of the words "we" and "us"? What is the effect of his use of "ing" verbs—present participles? What conclusion do you think Orwell might want his readers to make after reading this paragraph?

> 11 The gallows stood in a small yard, separate from the main grounds of the prison, and overgrown with tall prickly weeds. It was a brick erection like three sides of a shed, with planking on top, and above that two beams and a crossbar with the rope dangling. The hangman, a grey-haired convict in the white uniform of the prison, was waiting beside his machine. He greeted us with a servile crouch as we entered. At a word from Francis the two warders, gripping the prisoner more closely than ever, half led, half pushed him to the gallows and helped him clumsily up the ladder. Then the hangman climbed up and fixed the rope round the prisoner's neck.

Questions: How does paragraph 11 connect with paragraph 9; how does it differ from paragraph 10? What do the details of paragraph 11 reveal about the hangman and about the warders?

> 12 We stood waiting, five yards away. The warders had formed in a rough circle round the gallows. And then, when the noose was fixed, the prisoner began crying out on his god. It was a high, reiterated cry of "Ram! Ram! Ram! Ram!", not urgent and fearful like a prayer or a cry for help, but steady, rhythmical, almost like the tolling of a bell. The dog answered the sound with a whine. The hangman, still standing on the gallows, produced a small cotton bag like a flour bag and drew it down over the prisoner's face. But the sound, muffled by the cloth, still persisted, over and over again: "Ram! Ram! Ram! Ram! Ram!"

> 13 The hangman climbed down and stood ready, holding the lever. Minutes seemed to pass. The steady, muffled crying from the prisoner went on and on, "Ram! Ram! Ram!" never faltering for an instant. The superintendent, his head on his chest, was slowly poking the ground with his stick; perhaps he was counting the cries, allowing the prisoner a fixed number—fifty, perhaps, or a hundred. Everyone had changed colour. The Indians had gone grey like bad coffee, and one or two of the bayonets were wavering. We looked at the lashed, hooded man on the drop, and listened to his cries—each cry another second of life; the same thought was in all our minds: oh, kill him quickly, get it over, stop that abominable noise!

Questions: How do you respond to the prisoner's cries of "Ram! Ram! Ram!"? What other sounds are mentioned, and what do they contribute to the paragraph's tone and effect? What is the effect of repeating the word "Ram" a dozen times? How many uses and with what effect do you find for the verb "to cry"?

14 Suddenly the superintendent made up his mind. Throwing up his head he made a swift motion with his stick. "Chalo!" he shouted almost fiercely.

Questions: Why do you think Orwell made this paragraph so brief? What's the effect of that brevity?

15 There was a clanking noise, and then dead silence. The prisoner had vanished, and the rope was twisting on itself. I let go of the dog, and it galloped immediately to the back of the gallows; but when it got there it stopped short, barked, and then retreated into a corner of the yard, where it stood among the weeds, looking timorously out at us. We went round the gallows to inspect the prisoner's body. He was dangling with his toes pointed straight downwards, very slowly revolving, as dead as a stone.

Questions: To what details does Orwell direct our attention in this paragraph? With what effects?

16 The superintendent reached out with his stick and poked the bare body; it oscillated, slightly. "*He*'s all right," said the superintendent. He backed out from under the gallows, and blew out a deep breath. The moody look had gone out of his face quite suddenly. He glanced at his wrist-watch. "Eight minutes past eight. Well, that's all for this morning, thank God."

Questions: Why does the superintendent poke the body? What does he mean by saying "*He*'s all right"? Why does he exhale? How much time has elapsed during the full extent of the action? And what is the effect of his remark: "Well, that's all for this morning, thank God?"

17 The warders unfixed bayonets and marched away. The dog, sobered and conscious of having misbehaved itself, slipped after them. We walked out of the gallows yard, past the condemned cells with their waiting prisoners, into the big central yard of the prison. The convicts, under the command of warders armed with lathis, were already receiving their breakfast. They squatted in long rows, each man holding a tin pannikin, while two warders with buckets marched round ladling out rice; it seemed quite a homely, jolly scene, after the hanging. An enormous relief had come upon us now that the job was done. One felt an impulse to sing, to break into a run, to snigger. All at once everyone began chattering gaily.

Questions: What contrast does paragraph 17 highlight? How are the contrasted groups compared? Why is everyone chatting "gaily"? Is their response to the hanging plausible? Why or why not?

18 The Eurasian boy walking beside me nodded towards the way we had come, with a knowing smile: "Do you know, sir, our friend (he meant the dead man), when he heard his appeal had been dismissed, he pissed on the floor of his cell. From fright.—Kindly take one of my cigarettes, sir. Do you not admire my new silver case, sir? From the boxwallah, two rupees eight annas. Classy European style."

19 Several people laughed—at what, nobody seemed certain.

20 Francis was walking by the superintendent, talking garrulously. "Well, sir, all hass passed off with the utmost satisfactoriness. It wass all finished—flick! like that. It iss not always so—oah, no! I have known cases where the doctor wass obliged to go beneath the gallows and pull the prisoner's legs to ensure decease. Most disagreeable!"

21 "Wriggling about, eh? That's bad," said the superintendent.

22 "Ach, sir, it iss worse when they become refractory! One man, I recall, clung to the bars of hiss cage when we went to take him out. You will scarcely credit, sir, that it took six warders to dislodge him, three pulling at each leg. We reasoned with him. 'My dear fellow,' we said, 'think of all the pain and trouble you are causing to us!' But no, he would not listen! Ach, he wass very troublesome!"

23 I found that I was laughing quite loudly. Everyone was laughing. Even the superintendent grinned in a tolerant way. "You'd better all come out and have a drink," he said quite genially. "I've got a bottle of whisky in the car. We could do with it."

24 We went through the big double gates of the prison, into the road. "Pulling at his legs!" exclaimed a Burmese magistrate suddenly, and burst into a loud chuckling. We all began laughing again. At that moment Francis's anecdote seemed extraordinarily funny. We all had a drink together, native and European alike, quite amicably. The dead man was a hundred yards away.

Questions: What is the point of each of the remarks made after the hanging is over? What do you make of the essay's final sentence? What would be lost if it were omitted?

Interlude IV
The Video Essay

Analogous to the written essay, a literary work, is the video essay, a documentary film of varying length. The video essay derives from documentary films that focus on biographies of notable figures, now often referred to as "biopics." Documentary film has long been a movie category included among other film categories in the Oscar award ceremonies. Among the more notable film documentaries of the past are Robert Flaherty's *Nanook of the North* (1922), a silent predecessor to modern documentary films. Flaherty spent a year following an Inuit man, Nanook, and his family. His film conveys how indigenous people of northern Quebec province survive resourcefully their harsh climate, including building their igloo home and creating and using the tools they need to hunt and fish for their food.

Early documentaries were often characterized by a focus on exploration and anthropology, providing viewers with glimpses into different cultures and ways of life. The Great Depression of the 1930s marked a turning point for documentary filmmaking, with government-sponsored projects like the Works Progress Administration's documentary unit employing filmmakers to capture the struggles of the American people.

One form of teaching and learning that became highly popular in the last quarter of the twentieth century and after (though it had begun decades earlier) is documentary film for television. TV documentaries, especially those incorporating multiple episodes—documentary series—have long been a mainstay of mainstream television. Among the best known and received of such documentary series are those of Ken Burns, whose documentary films span a wide range of subjects, including the American Civil War, World War II, the Vietnam War, the American Revolution, jazz, baseball, prohibition, country music, Leonardo da Vinci, and more. Absent from the subjects of Burns's documentary reach has been science, which was the focus of documentaries by Carl Sagan (*Cosmos*, 1980), a complete science course, encompassing cosmology, chemistry, physics, biology, and the history of human discovery; and of David Attenborough (*Life on Earth*, 1979 and *The Living Planet*, 2002), among others.

Different forms widen the account of the literary in the twenty-first century. Among the interesting forms the essay has taken is the video essay, which has

DOI: 10.4324/9781003620280-33

been a significant part of documentary filmmaking and of online cultures in spaces such as YouTube. A video essay is a short documentary film of about 5 to 15 minutes. It is a visual equivalent of the traditional written research paper that students write to present research.

We can make a number of connections between video essays, which include a hybrid form that combines video with written text, and the traditional written essay. Both the older forms of the essay, along the essay spectrum, and newer forms that rely exclusively on visual images, or which integrate images into written text, provide pathways for writers and filmmakers to explain and explore, analyze and synthesize, narrate and persuade—using the tools of verbal and visual language to communicate ideas and feelings, attitudes and perspectives.

A video essay is an essay presented in the format of a video recording or short film rather than a conventional piece of writing; the form often overlaps with other kinds of video entertainment on online platforms such as YouTube. A video essay illustrates a topic, expresses an opinion and develops a thesis statement based on research through editing video, sound, and image. It consists of images (filmed footage and found footage) and sound (music and audio). A video essay allows an author to directly quote from film, video games, music, or other digital media, which is impossible with traditional writing. While many video essays are intended for entertainment, they can also have an academic or political purpose.

Part V
Reading with Literary Elements—Five Takes

Prelude V
The Value of the Literary Elements

In reading literature with attention to literary elements, we focus on one element of a literary work at a time, such as plot or character, and then on another, such as diction or imagery. Different literary genres invite and reward varying degrees of attention to different literary elements. Plot and character, for example, usually require and reward more attention in reading fiction and drama than they do in reading poetry and essay. Diction and imagery, on the other hand, while not unimportant in drama and fiction, typically assume greater importance in poetry, and, on occasion, in our reading of essays as well.

Focusing on literary elements, such as rhythm and meter in reading poetry, provides us with an opportunity to better appreciate the way poems make use of these elements. Calling attention to a poem's metrical patterning and its rhythmic pulse allows us to better experience what the poet has accomplished with these aspects of sound play. Similarly, in reading poems, we might highlight the use of other forms of sound experimentation—rhyme, for example, and assonance (repeated vowel sounds) and alliteration (repeating consonants).

Analogously, in reading plays, we tend generally to listen and look less to aspects of sound and syntax, or sentence structure, and more to the relations between and among characters, along with plot and structure—the shape and development of a play's unfolding action. If in reading poems we attend to their division into stanzas (or other discernible sections), in reading plays, we consider the ways individual scenes and acts are constructed and developed, and how those structural elements of drama contribute to a play's effects—intellectual, emotional, and theatrical.

Whatever genre we are reading, and whichever literary element we may be highlighting, the elements of any literary work need to be considered together—as part of the work as a whole, in its integral unity. The elements of literature do not exist in isolation; they form part of a unified entity, which constitutes the work in its completeness and unique singularity.

This is particularly important with respect to "theme," the element common across poetry, fiction, drama, and essay. Theme is related to the other literary elements more as a consequence than as a parallel literary element. In formulating a theme, we explain what those elements collectively

DOI: 10.4324/9781003620280-35

suggest. A work's theme derives from its details of language and action; a work's theme, thus, is the implied significance of all of its details.

The theme of a literary work largely concerns its implied idea—its meaning, which in works of literature, however brief, is always multiple. When considering theme in a literary work, we need to think beyond a simple, single meaning, and toward its pluri-significance—its multiple meanings. Theme involves a work's resonating implications, which are embodied and reflected in all the combined elements of a literary work as they overlap and intersect.

21 Elements of Lyric Poetry—Gerard Manley Hopkins

"Spring and Fall: *to a young child*"

We begin with the first of our takes using elements of literature as our basis for literary analysis with a poem by the nineteenth-century British Jesuit priest-poet, Gerard Manley Hopkins. For Hopkins's poem, "Spring and Fall: *to a young child*," we consider a traditional set of poetic elements, with comments about each element appearing as observations about the poem, one poetic element at a time, though, of course, those elements exist together as a harmonious whole.

> Márgarét, áre you gríeving
> Over Goldengrove unleaving?
> Leáves, líke the things of man, you
> With your fresh thoughts care for, can you?
> Ah! ás the heart grows older   5
> It will come to such sights colder
> By and by, nor spare a sigh
> Though worlds of wanwood leafmeal lie;
> And yet you will weep and know why.
> Now no matter, child, the name: 10
> Sórrow's springs áre the same.
> Nor mouth had, no nor mind, expressed
> What heart heard of, ghost guessed:
> It ís the blight man was born for,
> It is Margaret you mourn for.

Speaker and Situation

An adult speaks to a child. The child cries and the adult responds to her. The time: autumn; the place: a grove of trees where yellow leaves have fallen. The child weeps over the scene of fallen and falling leaves, and also over something she is only dimly aware of (the fact of mortality—the fate of leaves and of people, herself among them). The dead leaves intimate Margaret's own inevitable death. That's what evokes her sad feeling and precipitates her tears. The speaker's tone mixes gentle consolation with mild reproof. The reader overhears the voice of the speaker.

DOI: 10.4324/9781003620280-36

Diction

A number of unusual verbal coinages appear in "Spring and Fall," the first of which, "Goldengrove," combines the word "grove" with the color of leaves. Immediately following is "unleaving," leaves in the act of falling from their branches. In line 8 we have "wanwood" and "leafmeal." We can split "wanwood" into its constituent words: "wan," meaning "pale" with connotations of sickness and of death, and "wood," woods or forest; thus, woods with trees whose leaves are pale and dying. On the order of "piecemeal," "leafmeal" suggests fallen leaves that have been ground up in mealy fragments; leaves gradually falling apart and becoming mingled with the soil on which they lie. Together these words convey a sense of natural decay, the leaves losing their leafiness, crispness, and color in their crushed, fragmented state.

The word "ghost" in line 13 means spirit or soul. We can consider the connotations of the poem's title and the denotation and connotations of "blight" in line 14. Substituting *cry* or *weep* for "mourn" in line 15 leads to considering what would be lost with those substitutions.

Syntax

The poem is composed of five sentences, two questions and three statements. Once we are clear about the words in line 2, the first sentence should pose no problems for understanding. It's a beautiful sounding interrogative sentence in normal word order. The second sentence, however, is a bit more challenging with its inverted syntax, which requires a bit of parsing. We can reorder its words via this slight summary: "Can you, with your fresh thoughts, care for leaves as you care for the things of man?" Or: "Can you in your innocence be sad over falling leaves with the same sorrow you feel for human loss?"

Another syntactic snag occurs in lines 12–13, which we might paraphrase like this: "You have never said outright, and you have never been consciously aware of what you have known in your heart, known what your spirit or inward soul has sensed intuitively." This prosy summary lacks the power of Hopkins's lines: the compressed strength of "Nor mouth had, no nor mind, expressed," monosyllabic negatives combined with the alliterations of "mouth [and] mind," "heart heard" and "ghost guessed." Hopkins's syntactic tautness strengthens his lines; the alliteration adds to their allure.

Lines 14–15 complete the sense of the previous lines, which conclude with a colon. The colon following line 13 helps set up the final couplet's meaning; it offers an explanation of what the heart and spirit, intuitively, understand— that Margaret, unknowing, weeps for the fate of death that awaits all living things. (As with the colon earlier, following line 10, where it alerts the reader to what is said in line 11, so, too, with the colon after line 13. In both cases punctuation serves as an aid to syntactic clarity.)

Most readers find the final couplet smoother and easier to process than the two lines that precede it, especially if they have worked through the syntax with guided observations and questions like those we've been considering.

Imagery

Visual images appear in the following words: "Goldengrove," "wanwood," "unleaving," "leafmeal," "blight," and "springs." In addition to their denotations and connotations, we should be alert to the words' sensory impressions. Is "colder" (line 6) used in a tactile way—or not? "[W]eep" suggests tears, of course, which are wet, and thus tactile. More important, however, is the emotional feeling each word expresses, especially the implied comparisons in lines 5–6. As we age, we lose our ability to feel things as deeply as we do when we are young. The cold aging heart contrasts the warm wet tears of the child. The casualness of the language that follows—"By and by, nor spare a sigh"—reinforces the inevitability of this kind of loss.

Sound

Hopkins is a master of sound play. We readily note the triple rhyme on long *i* in *sigh, lie, why,* and perhaps how that sound is framed by assonance (repeated vowel sounds) of the same long *i* in the lines before and after: in line 6, *sights* and line 10, *child.* Alliteration (repeated consonants) abounds: lines 1 and 2 with g's; lines 2 and 3 with l's and v's; c's in lines 3 and 4; s's in lines 6 and 7; w's and l's in lines 8 and 9, along with y's; n's in line 10; s's in 11; m's and n's crisscrossing in line 12; h's and g's in line 13; b's in line 14, and m's in line 15.

Line 5, the only line not alliterated, contains assonance on long o ("grows older") that introduces the rhyme in lines 5–6: "older-colder." This line encapsulates the poem's movement from youth to age, from caring to indifference.

The poem's final pair of lines exhibit feminine rhyme, the accent falling on the next-to-last syllable rather than on the final syllable, as most of the other rhyming pairs in the poem—the exception being lines 5–6, rhyming "older/colder," although lines 3–4 contain an apparent ambiguous masculine/feminine rhyme on "man, you" and "can you."

We hear how alliteration highlights the ideas conveyed by the final lines: "blight ... born" "Márgarét ... mourn." We might note for them, too, how the rhythm on "born" and "mourn" collaborates with that on "older" and "colder" to establish a connection between what the words literally say. The rhymes suggest an inevitable, predetermined relationship between birth and sorrow, experience and loss, life and death.

Rhythm and Meter

With regard to the poem's rhythm and meter, Hopkins accents certain syllables, noting visually where particular stresses should fall. He slows the rhythm with the displaced syntax of lines 3 and 4, which is slowed further by the alliteration in the poem's second half and by rhyme and assonance throughout. The poem's repeated vowels and slower pace contribute to its solemn tone. The concluding couplet's parallel syntax and alliteration returns to the feminine rhyme of the first six lines, with the poem's middle (lines 7–13) departing from feminine rhyme. Additionally, caesura and enjambment vary the poem's tempo.

The meter is basically trochaic, moving from accented to unaccented syllables. We can scan the first two lines to follow Hopkins's accentual markings:

>   Már / ga rét are you / grieving
>   Over / Golden / grove un / leaving?

The first line contains an odd number of syllables. Since the trochaic pattern is clear in line 2, we adapt our scansion of line 1 to correspond. Hence, the first foot of line 1 is irregular in lacking a syllable. The remainder of the line is trochaic, the prevailing meter. Line length is also irregular, varying from six syllables to eight. Nonetheless, we hear four stresses or accents per line.

Form

The form of Hopkins's poem can be discerned from its rhymes and its sentences. The pattern of rhyme in "Spring and Fall" includes six couplets along with a triple rhyme that separates those six couplets into two sets of three. Hopkins divides the poem into five sentences, two before and two after the long five-line sentence in the middle, with its three rhyming words: "sigh," "lie," "why." The poem turns on these lines, which assert that as Margaret grows older, she will learn not to weep over such a scene, but for another reason: the fact of human mortality, including her own. Margaret's grief frames the poem, with the first line containing an implied question (Margaret, why are you grieving?) and the last line answering it (It's the blight man was born for). Moreover, the speaker's answer corrects Margaret's sense of why she grieves. The turn, or *volta*, at line 9 suggests that we are reading a sonnet. It is, however, a quasi-sonnet with an extra line and with an unconventional rhyme pattern.

Theme

What might we say about the theme, or implied meaning, of "Spring and Fall: *to a young child*"? The last couplet suggests that Margaret is mourning the loss of innocence she now possesses as a child and the loss of life that eventually awaits her. Sorrow, suffering, grief, and loss are inevitable, inescapable. Growing from childhood to adulthood, we live through the loss of innocence and eventual loss of life.

The "blight" of the last couplet could be the blight of failure, weakness, and death. "Blight" is linked to the "Fall" of the title, which suggests the fall into experience, the fall from grace, perfection, happiness. The "Spring" of the title suggests youth, vitality, innocence, life. Overall, the poem suggests that the values and virtues of innocence don't last; it conveys a sadness at the inevitable end of all living things, the innocent child Margaret among them. We all share in this inevitable loss. We share our mortality with each other and with the natural world.

Putting the poem's thematic implications in these terms makes it sound depressing, its emphasis on mortality without consolation. And yet that's not what the poem's sounds and rhythms convey. Its music captures the sadness of loss, to be sure, but the speaker's gentle tone with the child tempers the poem's sad message. Her sorrow is his sorrow is our sorrow; "Sórrow's springs áre the same" for us all.

22 Elements of Epic Poetry—John Milton
Paradise Lost

One great epic poem in English written as the Baroque era (the seventeenth century) was waning is John Milton's *Paradise Lost*, which many consider the greatest of all English poems. Milton was blind when he composed *Paradise Lost*. He dictated the epic, which his daughters took down by hand. The poem comprises 10,565 lines divided into a dozen "books." The poem is dense with theological ideas and biblical, geographical, historical, mythological, and literary allusions, adding complexity to its length.

Milton's poem is once serious in outlook and grand in manner, befitting one who wanted to "leave something so written to aftertimes as they should not willingly let it die." In *Paradise Lost*, Milton attempted, in his words, "to justify the ways of God to man." This idea of justification reflected Milton's blend of Puritan theology and classical humanism. He reinterpreted the events of Genesis—humankind's fall from grace, and its banishment from the Garden of Eden, the poem's subject nothing less than the origins of evil in the world and the future fate of humanity. Milton emphasized the central belief of Christianity: the incarnation of God-as-man in Jesus Christ, who atoned for the sin of humanity's first parents. Christ's sacrifice thus gained for human beings the chance for eternal life—providing they live in accordance with Christian teachings. Here are the poem's opening lines:

> Of man's first disobedience, and the fruit
> Of that forbidden tree whose mortal taste
> Brought death into the world, and all our woe,
> With loss of Eden, till one greater Man
> Restore us, and regain the blissful seat,
> Sing, Heavenly Muse, that, on the secret top
> Of Oreb, or of Sinai, didst inspire
> That shepherd who first taught the chosen seed
> In the beginning how the Heavens and Earth
> Rose out of Chaos: or, if Sion hill
> Delight thee more, and Siloa's brook that flowed
> Blest by the oracle of God, I thence
> Invoke thy aid to my adventurous song,

That with no middle flight intends to soar
Above the Aonian mount, while it pursues
Things unattempted yet in prose or rhyme.

This single long sentence introduces the topic of *Paradise Lost*—the fall of humankind in the Garden of Eden with the loss of paradise. Milton also indicates that he will use the high grand style ("no middle flight") and attempt to do something in epic poetry that had never been done before. And though Milton eschews rhyme, he employs other poetic resources—alliteration, for example in "first" and "fruit," assonance in "loss" and "us," and numerous mythological, religious, and historical references.

Milton's poetic enterprise was ambitious. No poem before or since has been created on such an ambitious plan and such a grand cast of characters. But Milton was up to the task, his goal to bring into view the purpose and importance of human existence. And he did it in blank verse—unrhymed iambic pentameter. Milton chose a poetic meter based on the iambic foot—an unstressed syllable is followed by a stressed syllable, as in the word upON. Milton's poetic line consists of five of these iambs, hence "pentameter," as "penta" is the Greek prefix meaning "five." Iambic pentameter is a poetic meter with five iambic "feet."

Milton also liberated himself from conventional religious ideas, as he wrestled with the conundrum of how to present human beings "free to fall," with unimpeded will, and yet sufficient to have withstood the powerful temptations of the arch-seducer, Satan—all while an omniscient God knows the outcome of human choices, beginning with those of Adam and Eve. Satan overcomes their resistance and gets them to commit the "original sin"—eating the fruit from the tree of good and evil, which God forbade them to do. The stakes could not have been higher; they always were for Milton, as he never shied away from the serious religious, moral, and philosophical issues that mattered most to humanity.

Milton employs long sentences, with his epic's first sentence running on for 16 lines and 122 words. Its structure illustrates a form of Latinate style, in particular, the Ciceronian style, after the Roman orator Cicero. In a Ciceronian sentence, the verb is delayed and the meaning suspended. Milton invokes the Muse, an epic convention in which the poet asks for external help, sometimes for divine inspiration. He requests help from the Muse of poetry, Uranus, invoking her aid in his "adventurous song."

Of particular interest and importance is how Milton characterizes Satan, which he begins to do in the second book of his epic. Book II opens with Satan holding council with his fallen angel comrades, debating the best retaliatory measures to take against the almighty god they betrayed in their rebellion, having been hurled tumbling into the darkness of hell by Michael, the archangel, and his faithful comrade angels.

Commentators point to the rhetorical flourishes and the kinds of arguments made in the debate, and ways in which Milton mimics both his own classical education in rhetoric and English parliamentary debates of his time. Satan employs the kinds of rhetorical techniques Milton learned through his study of Greek and Roman writers, especially his epic poet predecessors, Homer and Virgil.

Milton describes Satan in heroic terms, giving him all the best lines, so much so that William Blake in his *The Marriage of Heaven and Hell* wrote that Milton was "a true Poet and of the Devil's party without knowing it." What readers across the centuries have noticed is that Milton's Hell is more richly detailed than his Heaven, his devils more interesting and engaging than his angels.

And although Milton tended to prefer rebels to courtly officials in life, he takes pains at various points in his epic to counter Satan's overweening ambition and monumental pride. One example occurs when the angel Abdiel, whose name means "Servant of God," challenges the arch-fiend rebel, saying "Shalt thou give Law to God? shalt thou dispute / With Him the points of liberty who made / Thee what thou art?" This verbal challenge to Satan is followed later in the poem by physical assault when, during a combat among the faithful and rebellious angels, Abdiel strikes Satan's helmet and drives him backward.

Even so, there is no denying the energy and force of Milton's Satan, as the following passage indicates. Here, the poet introduces Satan, defiant and unrepentant, addressing his legions of fallen angels:

> "Is this the region, this the soil, the clime,"
> Said then the lost Archangel, "this the seat
> That we must change for Heaven?—this mournful gloom
> For that celestial light? Be it so, since He   245
> Who now is sovran can dispose and bid
> What shall be right: farthest from Him is best,
> Whom reason hath equalled, force hath made supreme
> Above his equals. Farewell, happy fields,
> Where joy forever dwells! Hail, horrors! hail,   250
> Infernal World! and thou, profoundest Hell,
> Receive thy new possessor—one who brings
> A mind not to be changed by place or time.
> The mind is its own place, and in itself
> Can make a Heaven of Hell, a Hell of Heaven.   255
> What matter where, if I be still the same,
> And what I should be, all but less than he
> Whom thunder hath made greater? Here at least
> We shall be free; the Almighty hath not built
> Here for his envy, will not drive us hence: 260
> Here we may reign secure; and, in my choice,
> To reign is worth ambition, though in Hell:
> Better to reign in Hell than serve in Heaven.
> But wherefore let we then our faithful friends,

>   The associates and co-partners of our loss, 265
>   Lie thus astonished on the oblivious pool,
>   And call them not to share with us their part
>   In this unhappy mansion, or once more
>   With rallied arms to try what may be yet
>   Regained in Heaven, or what more lost in Hell?" 270

In this passage, we hear some of the poem's most oft-quoted lines: "The mind is its own place, and in itself / Can make a Heaven of Hell, a Hell of Heaven." And: "Better to reign in Hell than serve in Heaven," which captures Satan's arrogant determination and obstreperous pride. We can also note that the passage is a speech Satan gives to inspire his conspiratorial fallen angels to continue their rebellious ways. A bit later in Book II, Milton continues his portrayal of Satan, including his eloquent rhetoric.

>   "Powers and Dominions, Deities of Heaven!—
>   For, since no deep within her gulf can hold
>   Immortal vigour, though oppressed and fallen,
>   I give not Heaven for lost: from this descent
>   Celestial Virtues rising will appear
>   More glorious and more dread than from no fall,
>   And trust themselves to fear no second fate!—
>   Me though just right, and the fixed laws of Heaven,
>   Did first create your leader—next, free choice
>   With what besides in council or in fight
>   Hath been achieved of merit—yet this loss,
>   Thus far at least recovered, hath much more
>   Established in a safe, unenvied throne,
>   Yielded with full consent. The happier state
>   In Heaven, which follows dignity, might draw
>   Envy from each inferior; but who here
>   Will envy whom the highest place expose
>   Foremost to stand against the Thunderer's aim
>   Your bulwark, and condemns to greatest share
>   Of endless pain? Where there is, then, no good
>   For which to strive, no strife can grow up there
>   From faction: for none sure will claim in Hell
>   Precedence; none whose portion is so small
>   Of present pain that with ambitious mind
>   Will covet more! With this advantage, then,
>   To union, and firm faith, and firm accord,
>   More than can be in Heaven, we now return
>   To claim our just inheritance of old,
>   Surer to prosper than prosperity
>   Could have assured us; and by what best way,

Whether of open war or covert guile,
We now debate. Who can advise may speak."

Here, Satan is anything but contrite and hardly seems defeated, ready to pursue the next battle with his adversaries. The question he sets for debate among his fallen angel comrades is whether to engage in overt or covert military operations. Although Milton refers to Satan's eminence as "bad" and to further war with Heaven as "vain," the dominant impression he conveys of Satan is one more of power and control than of weakness and submission. Motivated by resentment and wounded pride, Satan persuades his fallen angelic forces to rebel against God. And even though Satan exhibits overweening pride in his prowess, he exhibits a talent for persuasion such that his cohorts rally in unison behind.

Satan's rhetorical skill is equally evident in one of the poem's greatest scenes, in which, disguised as a serpent, Satan tempts Eve, the first female human being. We witness Satan's psychologically astute deception of Eve, by flattering her as he praises her beauty:

> His fraudulent temptation thus began.
> Wonder not, sovran Mistress, if perhaps
> Thou canst, who art sole Wonder, much less arm
> Thy looks, the Heav'n of mildness, with disdain,
> Displeas'd that I approach thee thus, and gaze
> Insatiate, I thus single, nor have feard
> Thy awful brow, more awful thus retir'd.
> Fairest resemblance of thy Maker faire,
> Thee all things living gaze on, all things thine
> By gift, and thy Celestial Beautie adore
> With ravishment beheld, there best beheld
> Where universally admir'd; but here
> In this enclosure wild, these Beasts among,
> Beholders rude, and shallow to discerne
> "Half what in thee is fair, one man except,
> Who sees thee? (and what is one?) who shouldst be seen
> A Goddess among Gods, ador'd and serv'd
> By Angels numberless, thy daily Train.
> So gloz'd the Tempter, and his Proem tun'd;
> Into the Heart of Eve his words made way,
> Though at the voice much marveling; ...

Eve is amazed that such a creature can speak the way she and Adam do, giving Satan a chance to explain that though once unable to speak, like other animals, he acquired speech by eating the fruit of a certain tree. Following additional flattery coupled with an explanation of how the fruit enhanced his reasoning powers, Satan leads Eve to the one tree in the Garden of Eden whose fruit God forbade her and Adam to eat. Satan has a ready response to this disconcerting information, an answer that Eve finds persuasive, and which leads her to eat the fruit and then induce Adam, against his better judgment, to do the same. Here is how Satan persuades Eve:

"The Tempter all impassiond thus began.

O Sacred, Wise, and Wisdom-giving Plant,
Mother of Science, Now I feel thy Power
Within me cleere, not onely to discerne
Things in thir Causes, but to trace the wayes
Of highest Agents, deemd however wise.
Queen of this Universe, doe not believe
Those rigid threats of Death; ye shall not Die:
How should ye? by the Fruit? it gives you Life
To Knowledge, By the Threatner, look on mee,
Mee who have touch'd and tasted, yet both live,
And life more perfet have attaind then Fate
Meant mee, by ventring higher then my Lot.
Shall that be shut to Man, which to the Beast
Is open? or will God incense his ire
For such a petty Trespass, and not praise
Rather your dauntless vertue, whom the pain
Of Death denounc't, whatever thing Death be,
Deterrd not from atchieving what might leade
To happier life, knowledge of Good and Evil;
Of good, how just? of evil, if what is evil
Be real, why not known, since easier shunnd?
God therefore cannot hurt ye, and be just;
Not just, not God; not feard then, nor obeyd:
Your feare it self of Death removes[...]"

"Why then was this forbid? Why but to awe,

Why but to keep ye low and ignorant,
His worshippers; he knows that in the day
Ye Eate thereof, your Eyes that seem so cleere,
Yet are but dim, shall perfetly be then
Op'nd and cleerd, and ye shall be as Gods,
Knowing both Good and Evil as they know.
That ye should be as Gods, since I as Man,
Internal Man, is but proportion meet,
I of brute human, yee of human Gods.
"So ye shall die perhaps, by putting off
Human, to put on Gods, death to be wisht,
Though threat'nd, which no worse then this can bring.

> And what are Gods that Man may not become
> As they, participating God-like food?
> The Gods are first, and that advantage use
> On our belief, that all from them proceeds;
> I question it, for this fair Earth I see,
> Warm'd by the Sun, producing every kind,
>
> Them nothing: If they all things, who enclos'd
>
> Knowledge of Good and Evil in this Tree,
> That whoso eats thereof, forthwith attains
> Wisdom without their leave? and wherein lies
> Th' offence, that Man should thus attain to know?
> What can your knowledge hurt him, or this Tree
> Impart against his will if all be his?
> Or is it envie, and can envie dwell
> In Heav'nly brests? these, these and many more
> Causes import your need of this fair Fruit.
> Goddess humane, reach then, and freely taste."

Eve eats the fruit, ravenously gorging on it, her physical appetite as inflamed as her greed for the knowledge Satan fraudulently promises her. Once she prompts Adam's complicity in their shared disobedience, they engage in mutual recriminatory accusations, feeling shame and guilt as they realize that they are naked and that they have made a grievous error. Milton manages all this and more with narrative command and psychological acuity, while also further explaining their action's theological significance.

We should note how persuasive the serpent Satan is. He is a master of rhetoric as a tool for seduction—and he is completely effective in seducing Eve. His logic is seemingly irrefutable; Eve has no chance against him. In context, it seems the only choice that Eve could have made—given her belief in what the serpent tells her.

23 Elements of Fiction—James Joyce "Araby"

One way to appreciate the artistry of James Joyce's short story "Araby" is to analyze it in terms of the elements of fiction. We will consider plot, character, setting, and symbolism, along with the story's thematic implications. First, of course, you need to read this short work of fiction. So here you go:

> North Richmond Street being blind, was a quiet street except at the hour when the Christian Brothers' School set the boys free. An uninhabited house of two storeys stood at the blind end, detached from its neighbours in a square ground. The other houses of the street, conscious of decent lives within them, gazed at one another with brown imperturbable faces.
> The former tenant of our house, a priest, had died in the back drawing-room. Air, musty from having been long enclosed, hung in all the rooms, and the waste room behind the kitchen was littered with old useless papers. Among these I found a few paper-covered books, the pages of which were curled and damp: *The Abbot*, by Walter Scott, *The Devout Communicant* and *The Memoirs of Vidocq*. I liked the last best because its leaves were yellow. The wild garden behind the house contained a central apple-tree and a few straggling bushes under one of which I found the late tenant's rusty bicycle-pump. He had been a very charitable priest; in his will he had left all his money to institutions and the furniture of his house to his sister.
> When the short days of winter came dusk fell before we had well eaten our dinners. When we met in the street the houses had grown sombre. The space of sky above us was the colour of ever-changing violet and towards it the lamps of the street lifted their feeble lanterns. The cold air stung us and we played till our bodies glowed. Our shouts echoed in the silent street. The career of our play brought us through the dark muddy lanes behind the houses where we ran the gauntlet of the rough tribes from the cottages, to the back doors of the dark dripping gardens where odours arose from the ashpits, to the dark odorous stables where a coachman smoothed and combed the horse or shook music from the buckled harness. When we returned to the street light from the kitchen windows had filled the areas. If my uncle was seen turning the corner we

hid in the shadow until we had seen him safely housed. Or if Mangan's sister came out on the doorstep to call her brother in to his tea we watched her from our shadow peer up and down the street. We waited to see whether she would remain or go in and, if she remained, we left our shadow and walked up to Mangan's steps resignedly. She was waiting for us, her figure defined by the light from the half-opened door. Her brother always teased her before he obeyed and I stood by the railings looking at her. Her dress swung as she moved her body and the soft rope of her hair tossed from side to side.

Every morning I lay on the floor in the front parlour watching her door. The blind was pulled down to within an inch of the sash so that I could not be seen. When she came out on the doorstep my heart leaped. I ran to the hall, seized my books and followed her. I kept her brown figure always in my eye and, when we came near the point at which our ways diverged, I quickened my pace and passed her. This happened morning after morning. I had never spoken to her, except for a few casual words, and yet her name was like a summons to all my foolish blood.

Her image accompanied me even in places the most hostile to romance. On Saturday evenings when my aunt went marketing I had to go to carry some of the parcels. We walked through the flaring streets, jostled by drunken men and bargaining women, amid the curses of labourers, the shrill litanies of shop-boys who stood on guard by the barrels of pigs' cheeks, the nasal chanting of street-singers, who sang a come-all-you about O'Donovan Rossa, or a ballad about the troubles in our native land. These noises converged in a single sensation of life for me: I imagined that I bore my chalice safely through a throng of foes. Her name sprang to my lips at moments in strange prayers and praises which I myself did not understand. My eyes were often full of tears (I could not tell why) and at times a flood from my heart seemed to pour itself out into my bosom. I thought little of the future. I did not know whether I would ever speak to her or not or, if I spoke to her, how I could tell her of my confused adoration. But my body was like a harp and her words and gestures were like fingers running upon the wires.

One evening I went into the back drawing-room in which the priest had died. It was a dark rainy evening and there was no sound in the house. Through one of the broken panes I heard the rain impinge upon the earth, the fine incessant needles of water playing in the sodden beds. Some distant lamp or lighted window gleamed below me. I was thankful that I could see so little. All my senses seemed to desire to veil themselves and, feeling that I was about to slip from them, I pressed the palms of my hands together until they trembled, murmuring: "O love! O love!" many times.

At last she spoke to me. When she addressed the first words to me I was so confused that I did not know what to answer. She asked me was I going to Araby. I forgot whether I answered yes or no. It would be a splendid bazaar, she said she would love to go.

"And why can't you?" I asked.

While she spoke she turned a silver bracelet round and round her wrist. She could not go, she said, because there would be a retreat that week in her convent. Her brother and two other boys were fighting for their caps and I was alone at the railings. She held one of the spikes, bowing her head towards me. The light from the lamp opposite our door caught the white curve of her neck, lit up her hair that rested there and, falling, lit up the hand upon the railing. It fell over one side of her dress and caught the white border of a petticoat, just visible as she stood at ease.

"It's well for you," she said.

"If I go," I said, "I will bring you something."

What innumerable follies laid waste my waking and sleeping thoughts after that evening! I wished to annihilate the tedious intervening days. I chafed against the work of school. At night in my bedroom and by day in the classroom her image came between me and the page I strove to read. The syllables of the word Araby were called to me through the silence in which my soul luxuriated and cast an Eastern enchantment over me. I asked for leave to go to the bazaar on Saturday night. My aunt was surprised and hoped it was not some Freemason affair. I answered few questions in class. I watched my master's face pass from amiability to sternness; he hoped I was not beginning to idle. I could not call my wandering thoughts together. I had hardly any patience with the serious work of life which, now that it stood between me and my desire, seemed to me child's play, ugly monotonous child's play.

On Saturday morning I reminded my uncle that I wished to go to the bazaar in the evening. He was fussing at the hallstand, looking for the hat-brush, and answered me curtly:

"Yes, boy, I know."

As he was in the hall I could not go into the front parlour and lie at the window. I left the house in bad humour and walked slowly towards the school. The air was pitilessly raw and already my heart misgave me.

When I came home to dinner my uncle had not yet been home. Still it was early. I sat staring at the clock for some time and, when its ticking began to irritate me, I left the room. I mounted the staircase and gained the upper part of the house. The high cold empty gloomy rooms liberated me and I went from room to room singing. From the front window I saw my companions playing below in the street. Their cries reached me weakened and indistinct and, leaning my forehead against the cool glass, I looked over at the dark house where she lived. I may have stood there for an hour, seeing nothing but the brown-clad figure cast by my imagination, touched discreetly by the lamplight at the curved neck, at the hand upon the railings and at the border below the dress.

When I came downstairs again I found Mrs. Mercer sitting at the fire. She was an old garrulous woman, a pawnbroker's widow, who collected used stamps for some pious purpose. I had to endure the gossip of the tea-table. The meal was prolonged beyond an hour and still my uncle did not come. Mrs. Mercer stood up to go: she was sorry she couldn't wait any longer, but it was after eight o'clock and she did not like to be out late as the night air was bad for her. When she had gone I began to walk up and down the room, clenching my fists. My aunt said:

"I'm afraid you may put off your bazaar for this night of Our Lord."

At nine o'clock I heard my uncle's latchkey in the hall door. I heard him talking to himself and heard the hallstand rocking when it had received the weight of his overcoat. I could interpret these signs. When he was midway through his dinner I asked him to give me the money to go to the bazaar. He had forgotten.

"The people are in bed and after their first sleep now," he said.

He did not smile. My aunt said to him energetically:

"Can't you give him the money and let him go? You've kept him late enough as it is."

My uncle said he was very sorry he had forgotten. He said he believed in the old saying: "All work and no play makes Jack a dull boy." He asked me where I was going and, when I had told him a second time he asked me did I know The Arab's Farewell to his Steed. When I left the kitchen he was about to recite the opening lines of the piece to my aunt.

I held a florin tightly in my hand as I strode down Buckingham Street towards the station. The sight of the streets thronged with buyers and glaring with gas recalled to me the purpose of my journey. I took my seat in a third-class carriage of a deserted train. After an intolerable delay the train moved out of the station slowly. It crept onward among ruinous houses and over the twinkling river. At Westland Row Station a crowd of people pressed to the carriage doors; but the porters moved them back, saying that it was a special train for the bazaar. I remained alone in the bare carriage. In a few minutes the train drew up beside an improvised wooden platform. I passed out on to the road and saw by the lighted dial of a clock that it was ten minutes to ten. In front of me was a large building which displayed the magical name.

I could not find any sixpenny entrance and, fearing that the bazaar would be closed, I passed in quickly through a turnstile, handing a shilling to a weary-looking man. I found myself in a big hall girdled at half its height by a gallery. Nearly all the stalls were closed and the greater part of the hall was in darkness. I recognised a silence like that which pervades a church after a service. I walked into the centre of the bazaar timidly. A few people were gathered about the stalls which were still open. Before a curtain, over which the words Cafe Chantant were written in coloured lamps, two men were counting money on a salver. I listened to the fall of the coins.

Remembering with difficulty why I had come I went over to one of the stalls and examined porcelain vases and flowered tea- sets. At the door of the stall a young lady was talking and laughing with two young gentlemen. I remarked their English accents and listened vaguely to their conversation.

"O, I never said such a thing!"
"O, but you did!"
"O, but I didn't!"
"Didn't she say that?"
"Yes. I heard her."
"O, there's a ... fib!"

Observing me the young lady came over and asked me did I wish to buy anything. The tone of her voice was not encouraging; she seemed to have spoken to me out of a sense of duty. I looked humbly at the great jars that stood like eastern guards at either side of the dark entrance to the stall and murmured:

"No, thank you."

The young lady changed the position of one of the vases and went back to the two young men. They began to talk of the same subject. Once or twice the young lady glanced at me over her shoulder.

I lingered before her stall, though I knew my stay was useless, to make my interest in her wares seem the more real. Then I turned away slowly and walked down the middle of the bazaar. I allowed the two pennies to fall against the sixpence in my pocket. I heard a voice call from one end of the gallery that the light was out. The upper part of the hall was now completely dark.

Gazing up into the darkness I saw myself as a creature driven and derided by vanity; and my eyes burned with anguish and anger.

Plot

A few words of context. "Araby" is one of fourteen stories in Joyce's book *Dubliners*, a series of stories that describe the lives of the Irish city of Dublin at the beginning of the twentieth century. The earlier stories, of which "Araby" is one, focus on youth and adolescence, the middle ones on young adulthood, and the last few on full adult maturity. Together, the stories were the writer's effort to describe the state of the Irish soul under the stultifying influence of the Catholic Church and its repressive teachings.

The story's plot—its sequence of related actions—is simple and easy to follow. The story's unnamed teenage boy narrator is attracted to a slightly older sister of a friend. When she tells him that she is unable to attend a bazaar (Araby) in their village, he promises to bring her something from there, as he plans to go. However, his plan nearly comes to naught when his uncle, who is to give him the money to attend the bazaar, returns home late, having been drinking (a characteristic habit of Irish men in Joyce's day), Joyce himself among them.

And when our narrator does finally get to the bazaar, it's late and ready to shut down for the night. Before it closes, however, the narrator overhears a conversation between a young woman selling her wares and two young men who engage her in conversation. That's all. Nothing else seems to happen; no additional external action is described

And yet a few details delay the story's culminating action, especially the conversation between the women and the two men at the bazaar. And before that important scene, the seemingly interminable days that intervene from when the narrator spoke to his friend's sister and the opening of the bazaar; the protracted dinner on the night of the bazaar, including a talkative friend of his aunt; his uncle's late return home and the boy's anxiety over his lateness; the travel delay as the narrator travels to the bazaar; and his inability to locate the cheap entrance—all these elements contribute to the boy's increasing frustration and suppressed anger, which mounts as he realizes he won't see much of the bazaar and will likely be unable to fulfill his promise to Mangan's sister.

Character

Three character groups appear in each of the story's three segments: the boy-narrator with his aunt and uncle at home; the boy-narrator with his friend's sister and younger brothers at her house; and the narrator with two men attending the bazaar and a woman selling her wares there.

We are not provided with much detail about any of these characters. The most important ones, of course, are the narrator and his friend's sister, with whom we hear him speak once, but which Joyce's authorial voice describes carefully from the point of view of his boy-narrator. Next in importance are the two men and the woman, whom they engage in flirtatious conversation, the import of which is suggestively erotic, its sexual nature hinted at without being explicitly indicated.

From the snapshots of the narrator's aunt and uncle we learn only that they are responsible for his care. The aunt seems solicitous toward the boy, as she encourages her husband to provide him with the money to attend the bazaar. The uncle, though he complies, lacks awareness of what the visit to the bazaar means to the boy, coming home late and a bit tipsy from his implied visit to the local pub. And he is in a talkative mood, further delaying the narrator's escape.

Setting

The setting of the story moves among the home of the narrator's relatives to that of the girl with whom he is infatuated, and then the bazaar. Joyce also describes the street on which the narrator lives—using the word "blind" to indicate literally that it's a dead-end street, choosing the word for its symbolic reverberations suggesting the boy's blindness to his own physical and emotional state. The story's setting—among the three locations described—bears symbolic significance.

In each aspect of the story's setting, Joyce conveys a sense of dissatisfaction, of unrealized hopes, of quiet desperation. He does this largely through emphasizing the darkness of the night and the darkness of the bazaar, its lights going out for its closing. Darkness is also suggested by the word "blind" to describe the street and, further, the boy's blindness to the complexity of his attitude toward and sexual feelings with respect to Mangan's sister.

Symbolism

The story's darkness symbolizes the boy-narrator's lack of understanding of what he is feeling—an unawareness of the sexual nature of his impulses, masked by a romanticized image of the girl he desires and the heroic quest he imagines himself undertaking to bring her back a present from the bazaar. These aspects of the story are highlighted in the language choices Joyce makes in describing the narrator's sense of what he is doing. That language reveals, ironically, the extent to which the boy-narrator lacks an awareness of the complexity of his feelings.

Language and Style

Joyce employs religious language throughout the story, including the words "chalice," "prayers and praises," and "adoration." Those religious terms are used to suggest how the narrator envisions his quest to serve Mangan's sister, his service to her in his mind a kind of spiritual devotion. Joyce reveals the lack of the narrator's awareness of the erotic element in his feelings by describing his adoration of the girl as a "confused adoration," his adoration confounded by his unacknowledged and not understood physical attraction to the girl.

We see better than does the narrator, as Joyce describes "her figure defined by the light from the half-opened door" of her house as her brother and the narrator approach. The narrator also notices how "her dress swung as she moved her body" and how "the soft rope of her hair tossed from side to side." These details arouse the narrator in ways he does not yet understand. Joyce, however, implies that the narrator surmises something of his feelings when he notes that "her name was like a summons to all my foolish blood."

When the narrator finally engages Mangan's sister in a brief conversation, he is so confused he hardly speaks, and when he does, he barely remembers what he has been saying. As he speaks to her, he notices how the lamplight "caught the white curve of her neck, lit up her hair that rested there and, falling, lit up the hand upon the railing. It fell over one side of her dress and caught the white border of a petticoat." These details, which highlight the girl's clothing and physical body, contrast Joyce's earlier use of religious diction for the boy.

Theme

What might we make of Joyce's "Araby"? What does Joyce show and suggest in this brief short story? Whatever ideas and their implications we take from the story derive from the kinds of details we have been considering under the umbrella of the elements previously discussed, especially the story's language. The crux of any interpretation of "Araby" is the story's conclusion—both the dialogue that takes place between the young woman and the dialogue between the two male visitors with whom she converses. Their dialogue is, in itself, silly, flirtatious, vacuous, but significant for the story's thematic implications.

The threesome's irreverent conversation with its sexual overtones further contrasts the boy's romanticized image of his relationship with Mangan's sister when, at the end of the story, he describes how the gallery was darkening, with "The upper part of the hall...completely dark." The darkness represents his ignorance of his sexual feelings, which he begins to sense only via witnessing the conversation between the woman and her two soon-to-be companions.

Joyce puts it like this: "Gazing up into the darkness I saw myself as a creature driven and derided by vanity; and my eyes burned with anguish and anger." Anguish because of his realization at his erotic urgings and his self-deception. Anger at himself for his lack of recognition of his own sexual realities. And perhaps anguish and anger at the scene he witnesses at the bazaar having illuminated his own complex, less than tawdry feeling.

24 Elements of Drama—Isabella Augusta Persse, Lady Gregory

The Rising of the Moon

We turn next, with the elements of drama, to *The Rising of the Moon*, a one-act play first produced in Dublin in 1907. The play was written by Isabella Augusta Persse, Lady Gregory (1852–1932), an Irish playwright who was an influential presence in Irish theater.

Lady Gregory, wife of Sir William Gregory, a former Irish governor of Ceylon, became an important part of the Irish literary revival at the turn of the twentieth century. She was a friend and colleague of Irish writers William Butler Yeats and John Millington Synge, who, with her, founded the Irish National Theatre Society in Dublin.

Lady Gregory wrote Irish folk tales and plays in an attempt to revive native Irish cultural traditions, a number of which celebrate patriotic themes. Although initially some of her plays were attributed to other male writers, they were eventually credited properly to her, having enjoyed great popularity during her lifetime.

The Rising of the Moon

SCENE: *Side of a quay in a seaport town. Some posts and chains. A large barrel. Enter three* **Policemen**. *Moonlight.*

Sergeant, *who is older than the others, crosses the stage to right and looks down steps. The others put down a pastepot and unroll a bundle of placards.*

Policeman B. I think this would be a good place to put up a notice. *(He points to barrel.)*

Policeman X. Better ask him. *(Calls to* **Sergeant**.*)* Will this be a good place for a placard?

No answer.

Policeman B. Will we put up a notice here on the barrel?

No answer.

Sergeant. There's a flight of steps here that leads to the water. This is a place that should be minded well. If he got down here his friends might have a boat to meet him; they might send it in here from outside.

Policeman B. Would the barrel be a good place to put a notice up?

Sergeant. It might; you can put it there.

(They paste the notice up.)

Sergeant. *(Reading it.)* Dark hair dark eyes, smooth face, height five feet five there's not much to take hold of in that it's a pity I had no chance of seeing him before he broke out of gaol. They say he's a wonder, that it's he makes all the plans for the whole organization. There isn't another man in Ireland would have broken gaol the way he did. He must have some friends among the gaolers.

Policeman B. A hundred pounds is little enough for the Government to offer for him. You may be sure any man in the force that takes him will get promotion.

Sergeant. I'll mind this place myself. I wouldn't wonder at all if he came this way. He might come slipping along there *(points to side of quay)*, and his friends might be waiting for him there *(points down steps)*, and once he got away it's little chance we'd have of finding him; it's maybe under a load of kelp he'd be in a fishing boat, and not one to help a married man that wants it to the reward.

Policeman X. And if we get him itself, nothing but abuse on our heads for it from the people, and maybe from our own relations.

Sergeant. Well, we have to do our duty in the force. Haven't we the whole country depending on us to keep law and order? It's those that are down would be up and those that are up would be down, if it wasn't for us. Well, hurry on, you have plenty of other places to placard yet, and come back here then to me. You can take the lantern. Don't be too long now. It's very lonesome here with nothing to be looking at but the moon.

Policeman B. It's a pity we can't stop with you. The Government should have brought more police into the town, with him in gaol, and at assize time too.

Well, good luck to your watch. *(They go out.)*

Sergeant *(walks up and down once or twice and looks at placard).* A hundred pounds and promotion sure. There must be a great deal of spending in a hundred pounds. It's a pity some honest man not to be the better of that.

Elements of Drama—Isabella Augusta Persse, Lady Gregory

*(A ragged **Man** appears at left and tries to slip past. **Sergeant** suddenly turns.)*

Sergeant. Where are you going?

Man. I'm a poor ballad-singer, your honour. I thought to sell some of these *(holds out bundle of ballads)* to the sailors. *(He goes on.)*

Sergeant. Stop! Didn't I tell you to stop? You can't go on there.

Man. Oh, very well. It's a hard thing to be poor. All the world's against the poor.

Sergeant. Who are you?

Man. You'd be as wise as myself if I told you, but I don't mind. I'm one Jimmy Walsh, a ballad-singer.

Sergeant. Jimmy Walsh? I don't know that name.

Man. Ah sure, they know it well enough in Ennis. Were you ever in Ennis, sergeant?

Sergeant. What brought you here?

Man. Sure, it's to the assizes I came, thinking I might make a few shillings here or there. It's in the one train with the judges I came.

Sergeant. Well, if you came so far you may as well go farther, for you'll walk out of this.

Man. I will, I will; I'll just go on where I was going. *(Goes towards steps.)*

Sergeant. Come back from those steps; no one has leave to pass down them to-night.

Man. I'll just sit on the top of the steps till I see will some sailor buy a ballad off me that would give me my supper. They do be late going back to the ship. It's often I saw them in Cork carried down the quay in a hand-cart.

Sergeant. Move on, I tell you. I won't have anyone lingering about the quay to-night.

Man. Well, I'll go. It's the poor have the hard life! Maybe yourself might like one, sergeant. Here's a good sheet now. *(Turns one over.)* "Content and a pipe" that's not much. "Johnny Hart" that's a lovely song.

Sergeant. Move on.

Man. Ah, wait till you hear it.
(Sings)

> *There was a rich farmer's daughter lived near the town of Ross;*
> *She courted a Highland soldier; his name was Johnny Hart;*
> *Says the mother to her daughter, "I'll go distracted mad*
> *If you marry that Highland soldier dressed up in Highland plaid."*

Sergeant. Stop that noise.

(**Man** *wraps up his ballads and shuffles towards the steps.*)

Sergeant. Where are you going?

Man. Sure you told me to be going, and I am going.

Sergeant. Don't be a fool. I didn't tell you to go that way; I told you to go back to the town.

Man. Back to the town, is it?

Sergeant *(taking him by the shoulder and shoving him before him).* Here, I'll show you the way. Be off with you. What are you stopping for?

Man *(who has been keeping his eye on the notice, points to it).* I think I know what you're waiting for, sergeant.

Sergeant. What's that to you?

Man. And I know well the man you're waiting for I know him well I'll be going.

He shuffles on.

Sergeant. You know him? Come back here.

What sort is he?

Man. Come back is it, sergeant? Do you want to have me killed?

Sergeant. Why do you say that?

Man. Never mind. I'm going. I wouldn't be in your shoes if the reward was ten times as much. *(Goes on off stage to left.)* Not if it was ten times as much.

Elements of Drama—Isabella Augusta Persse, Lady Gregory

Sergeant *(rushing after him)*. Come back here, come back. *(Drags him back.)* What sort is he? Where did you see him?

Man. I saw him in my own place, in the County Clare. I tell you wouldn't like to be looking at him. You'd be afraid to be in the one place with him. There isn't a weapon he doesn't know the use of, and as to strength, his muscles are as hard as that board *(slaps barrel)*.

Sergeant. Is he as bad as that?

Man. He is then.

Sergeant. Do you tell me so?

Man. There was a poor man in our place, a sergeant from Ballyvaughan. It was with a lump of stone he did it.

Sergeant. I never heard of that.

Man. And you wouldn't, sergeant. It's not everything that happens gets into the papers. And there was a policeman in plain clothes, too ... It is in Limerick he was ... It was after the time of the attack on the police barrack at Kilmallock ... Moon-light ... just like this ... waterside ... Nothing was known for certain.

Sergeant. Do you say so? It's a terrible country to belong to.

Man. That's so, indeed! You might be standing there, looking out that way, thinking you saw him coming up this side of the quay *(points)*, and he might be coming up this other side *(points)* and he'd be on you before you knew where you were.

Sergeant. It's a whole troop of police they ought to put here to stop a man like that.

Man. But if you'd like me to stop with you I could be looking down this side. I could be sitting up here on this barrel.

Sergeant. And you know him well, too?

Man. I'd know him a mile off, sergeant.

Sergeant. But you wouldn't want to share the reward?

Man. Is it a poor man like me, that has to be going the roads and singing in fairs, to have the name on him that he took a reward? But you don't want me. I'll be safer in the town.

Sergeant. Well, you can stop.

Man *(getting up on barrel).* All right, sergeant. I wonder, now, you're not tired out, sergeant, walking up and down the way you are.

Sergeant. If I'm tired I'm used to it.

Man. You might have hard work before you to-night yet. Take it easy while you can. There's plenty of room up here on the barrel, and you see farther when you're higher up.

Sergeant. Maybe so. *(Gets up beside him on barrel, facing right. They sit back to back, looking different ways.)* You made me feel a bit queer with the way you talked.

Man. Give me a bit of 'baccy, sergeant *(he gives it, and* **Man** *lights pipe)*; smoke yourself, sergeant? It'll settle you down. Wait now till I give you a light, but you needn't turn round. Don't take your eye off the quay for the life of you.

Sergeant. Never fear, I won't. *(Lights pipe. They both smoke.)* Indeed it's a hard thing to be in the force, out at night and no thanks for it, for all the danger we're in.

And it's little we get but abuse from the people, and no choice but to obey our orders, and never asked when a man is sent into danger, if you are a married man with a family.

Man
(Sings)

> As through the hills I walked to view the hills and shamrock plain,
> I stood awhile where nature smiles to view the rocks and streams,
> On a matron I fixed my eyes beneath a fertile vale,
> As she sang her song it was on the wrong of poor old Granuaile.

Sergeant. Stop that; that's no song to be singing in these times.

Man. Ah, sergeant, I was only singing to keep my heart up. It sinks when I think of him. To think of us two sitting here, and he creeping up the quay, maybe, to get to us.

Sergeant. Are you keeping a good look-out?

Man. I am; and for no reward too. Amn't I the foolish man? But when I saw a man in trouble, I never could help trying to get him out of it. What's that? Did something hit me? *(Rubs his heart.)*

Sergeant *(patting him on the shoulder)*. You will get your reward in heaven.

Man. I know that, I know that, sergeant, but life is precious.

Sergeant. Well, you can sing if it gives you more courage.

Man
(Sings)

> Her head was bare, her hands and feet with iron bands were bound,
> Her pensive strain and plaintive wail mingles with the evening gale,
> And the song she sang with mournful air, I am old Granuaile,
> Her lips so sweet that monarchs kissed ...

Sergeant. That's not it ... "Her gown she wore was stained with gore." ... That's it you missed it.

Man. You're right, sergeant, so it is; I missed it. *(Repeats line.)* But to think of a man like you knowing a song like that.

Sergeant. There's many a thing a man knows and has no wish for.

Man. Now, I daresay, sergeant, in your youth, you used to be sitting up on a wall, the way you are sitting up on this barrel now, and the other lads beside you, and you singing "Granuaile"? ...

Sergeant. I did then.

Man. And the "Shan Bhean Bocht"? ...

Sergeant. I did then.

Man. And the "Green on the Cape"?

Sergeant. That was one of them.

Man. And maybe the man you are watching for to-night used to be sitting on the wall, when he was young, and singing those same songs ... It's a queer world ...

Sergeant. Whisht! ... I think I see something coming ... It's only a dog.

Man. And isn't it a queer world? ... Maybe it's one of the boys you used to be singing with that time you will be arresting to-day or to-morrow, and sending into the dock ...

Sergeant. That's true indeed.

Man. And maybe one night, after you had been singing, if the other boys had told you some plan they had, some plan to free the country, you might have joined with them ... and maybe it is you might be in trouble now.

Sergeant. Well, who knows but I might? I had a great spirit in those days.

Man. It's a queer world, sergeant, and it's little any mother knows when she sees her child creeping on the floor what might happen to it before it has gone through its life, or who will be who in the end.

Sergeant. That's a queer thought now, and a true thought. Wait now till I think it out ... If it wasn't for the sense I have, and for my wife and family, and for me joining the force the time I did, it might be myself now would be after breaking gaol and hiding in the dark, and it might be him that's hiding in the dark and that got out of gaol would be sitting up where I am on this barrel ... And it might be myself would be creeping up trying to make my escape from himself, and it might be himself would be keeping the law, and myself would be breaking it, and myself would be trying maybe to put a bullet in his head, or to take up a lump of stone the way you said he did ... no, that myself did ... Oh! (*Gasps. After a pause.*) What's that? (*Grasps* **Man***'s arm.*)

Man (*jumps off barrel and listens, looking out over water*). It's nothing, sergeant.

Sergeant. I thought it might be a boat. I had a notion there might be friends of his coming about the quays with a boat.

Man. Sergeant, I am thinking it was with the people you were, and not with the law you were, when you were a young man.

Sergeant. Well, if I was, I was foolish then. That time's gone.

Man. Maybe, sergeant, it comes into your head sometimes, in spite of your belt and your tunic, that it might have been as well for you to have followed Granuaile.

Sergeant. It's no business of yours what I think.

Man. Maybe, sergeant, you'll be on the side of the country yet.

Sergeant *(gets off barrel).* Don't talk to me like that I have my duties and I know them. *(Looks round.)* That was a boat; I hear the oars. *(Goes to the steps and looks down.)*

Man
(Sings)

> O, then, tell me Shawn O'Farrel
> Where the gathering is to be.
> In the old spot by the river
> Right well known to you and me!

Sergeant. Stop that! Stop that, I tell you!

Man
(Sings louder)

> One word more, for signal token,
> Whistle up the marching tune,
> With your pike upon your shoulder,
> At the Rising of the Moon.

Sergeant. If you don't stop that I'll arrest you. *(A whistle from below answers, repeating the air.)*

Sergeant. That's a signal *(stands between him and steps).* You must not pass this way ... Step farther back ... Who are you? You are no ballad-singer.

Man. You needn't ask who I am; that placard will tell you *(points to placard).*

Sergeant. You are the man I am looking for.

Man *(takes off hat and wig.* **Sergeant** *seizes them).* I am. There's a hundred pounds on my head. There is a friend of mine below in a boat. He knows a safe place to bring me to.

Sergeant *(looking still at hat and wig).* It's a pity! it's a pity. You deceived me. You deceived me well.

Man. I am the friend of Granuaile. There is a hundred pounds on my head.

Sergeant. It's a pity, it's a pity!

Man. Will you let me pass, or must I make you let me?

Sergeant. I am in the force. I will not let you pass.

Man. I thought to do it with my tongue *(puts hand in breast)*. What is that?

(Voice of **Policeman X** *outside.)* Here, this is where we left him.

Sergeant. It's my comrades coming.

Man. You won't betray me ... the friend of Granuaile *(slips behind barrel)*.

(Voice of **Policeman B**.*)* That was the last of the placards.

Policeman X *(as they come in)*. If he makes his escape it won't be unknown he'll make it.

*(***Sergeant** *puts hat and wig behind his back.)*

Policeman B. Did anyone come this way?

Sergeant. No one.

Policeman B. No one at all?

Sergeant. No one at all.

Policeman B. We had no orders to go back to the station; we can stop along with you.

Sergeant. I don't want you. There is nothing for you to do here.

Policeman B. You bade us to come back here and keep watch with you.

Sergeant. I'd sooner be alone. Would any man come this way and you making all that talk? It is better the place to be quiet.

Policeman B. Well, we'll leave you the lantern anyhow. *(Hands it to him.)*

Sergeant. I don't want it. Bring it with you.

Policeman B. You might want it. There are clouds coming up and you have the darkness of the night before you yet. I'll leave it over here on the barrel. *(Goes to barrel.)*

Sergeant. Bring it with you I tell you. No more talk.

Policeman B. Well, I thought it might be a comfort to you. I often think when I have it in my hand and can be flashing it about into every dark corner *(doing so)* that it's the same as being beside the fire at home, and the bits of bogwood blazing up now and again.

(Flashes it about, now on the barrel, now on **Sergeant**.*)*

Sergeant *(furious)*. Be off the two of you, yourselves and your lantern!

(They go out. **Man** *comes from behind barrel. He and* **Sergeant** *stand looking at one another.)*

Sergeant. What are you waiting for?

Man. For my hat, of course, and my wig. You wouldn't wish me to get my death of cold?

(**Sergeant** *gives them.)*

Man *(going towards steps)*. Well, good-night, comrade, and thank you. You did me a good turn to-night, and I'm obliged to you. Maybe I'll be able to do as much for you when the small rise up and the big fall down ... when we all change places at the Rising *(waves his hand and disappears)* of the Moon.

Sergeant *(turning his back to audience and reading placard)*. A hundred pounds reward! A hundred pounds! *(Turns towards audience.)* I wonder now, am I as great a fool as I think I am?

The End.

Elements of Drama

The elements of drama overlap largely with those of fiction and in smaller ways with those of poetry. In addition, a few special elements, though present in other literary genres, lie at the heart of drama. We will consider, in turn, plot and structure; character and conflict; dialogue and monologue; setting and staging; symbolism and irony; thought and theme.

Plot and Structure

The first thing to understand about plot in drama is that a dramatic plot is more than a cluster of occurrences; it is, instead, a carefully arranged series of *causally* related incidents. As with fictional plots, the incidents of a dramatic plot must be connected such that one incident gives rise to another or results directly from another.

As Eric Bentley reminds us, "[e]vents are not dramatic in themselves" (4); they need to reveal some type of conflict to which an audience responds emotionally. Bentley notes, further, how a play's supply of incidents needs to add up to a "story," one that arouses interest and satisfies curiosity by increasing suspense and resulting in surprise, even astonishment (13). In addition, a play's dramatic structure satisfies our need for order and form.

We can alert ourselves to a play's structure by attending to repeating elements of dialogue and description and to recurring details of action and gesture; to shifts in direction of a play's action or tone. Repetition signals important connections and relationships in a play: connections between ideas, relationships between and among characters.

A play's structure can also be signaled by changes in the time and place of its action—by changes of "scene"—and by alterations in a play's language, as that between speech and verse. It can be signaled, too, by shifts from one metaphor to another, as well as in changes in a play's tempo, the action slowing down in one part and speeding up in another.

One of the first things to notice about *The Rising of the Moon* is how quickly Lady Gregory establishes the play's conflict. She generates interest from the first short scene, which ends with the sergeant's comment about the hundred pound reward for capturing the escaped convict and the stage direction describing a ragged man trying to slip unnoticed past the sergeant.

The play's first major incident occurs with the appearance of the ragged man, the ballad-singer. This incident begins the play's rising action, which intensifies as the sergeant learns that the ballad-singer knows the wanted man and that he is dangerous. Additional incidents complicate the rising action as the sergeant reveals his familiarity with revolutionary songs. At that point, the playwright slows things down, which gives the audience time to see how the positions of the two antagonists might have been reversed.

These incidents together create suspense and build toward the play's climax, when the man reveals that he is the criminal the sergeant seeks. At this point the two policemen return, and the sergeant hides the man's hat and wig, the man himself hiding behind the barrel. The falling action is brief—simply the sergeant dismissing the policemen. It remains suspenseful, however, because when the policeman swings the lantern around, he could catch sight of the fugitive and the sergeant holding the hat and wig. The denouement is equally brief, consisting of the sergeant's last conversation with the man, followed by his final question, which concludes the play.

Such a structured account testifies to the plot's unity and economy. It suggests, as well, its tempo: slow, faster and faster and more intense, then slower following the climax. Additional structural details of the plot include repetition of words and phrases, especially the sergeant's "It's a pity," and the repetition of gestures, such as the pointing by both the man and the sergeant. The repeated utterances and gestures reveal connections between the sergeant and the man, as well as inviting considerations of the play's overall meaning and significance.

Character and Conflict

While a great deal can be said (and has been written about literary character and characterization), I emphasize here a few critical aspects. First, character is the companion of plot; the two go together, as the plot of a play involves the actions of its characters. Second, just as a play's plot must be unified, so must its characters be coherent. A character's actions, gestures, speech, dress, movement should together convey a single unified idea (except when a dramatist deliberately portrays an incoherent, fractured character). And third, our sense of a play's characters hinges on their identity and personality, which we derive from four things: their actions, their words, their physical gestures, and their responses to one other.

A dramatic character is a force (Bentley 45), a principle of energy that comes into contact with other fields of force in the form of other characters. Together an ensemble of characters connect, combine, and collide in shifting force-fields of energy. In conflict, characters advance the plot, reveal themselves, and through their interactions, dramatize a play's significance.

Lady Gregory's two policemen are clearly minor characters, necessary primarily as accessories for the plot, though they serve as well to reveal the character of the sergeant, the play's protagonist. In the first scene, for example, we notice that Policemen B and X seem more casual, less concerned about the dangerous situation than does the sergeant, and more concerned with finding places to post the placards. The sergeant is shown to be more experienced at the job and more aware of what's at stake in finding the wanted man. More important, however, is the conflict that develops between the sergeant and the wanted man, his antagonist. As it turns out, neither is what he at first seems. The sergeant does not uphold the law and arrest the man; the wanted man does not live up to his reputation as a dangerous killer. Each has the opportunity to act in accord with an expected role, but neither does. Each surprises the other, and both surprise us and perhaps themselves, as well.

It might be that the conflict occurs within the sergeant himself: one part of him sides with law and order, another part with the poor and oppressed. We may wonder to what extent the sergeant resents the authority he espouses and to what extent he resents the ballad-singer, who brings to the surface his internal conflict.

The most significant moment of character revelation occurs as the sergeant muses about fate. He imagines his life having turned out differently, a reversal of roles in which he pictures himself as a hunted criminal and the fugitive as a policeman hunting him. The sergeant sees the similarities more than the differences between the revolutionary and himself. This perception leads him to a radically different sense of his responsibility toward the man and toward their common countrymen.

In a small way, the sergeant helps to bring about the wanted man's prediction that "the small [will] rise up and the big fall down," partly because the sergeant believes this is what should occur. The sergeant is thus shown to be a more complex figure than he initially appears—though his orthodox, practical side appears with his final question: "I wonder, now, am I as great a fool as I think I am?" We readers are left to ponder this question with him.

We notice that the policemen are identified generically rather than individually. (The ballad-singer's name of "Jimmy Walsh" is, of course, a fabrication.) Generic names extend the play's implications beyond the actions of its individual characters; the characters represent the law and the people, which can be (and in this case are) opposed. In addition, we speculate that by avoiding Irish names, the author expands the significance of her play to include other societies and countries where the conflict of *The Rising of the Moon* occurs.

Dialogue and Monologue

About dialogue, we should listen for tone, the attitude a character's speech conveys by the manner in which the character voices and expresses what is being said. The tone of dramatic dialogue emerges best when sections of a play are read aloud, with parts assigned. And when that's not possible, as in one's silent reading, imagining the differing voices can be a goal.

Words that characters say to each other have power to affect one another and to affect the audience as well. Words in drama are a form of action; they do things, initiate events, effect change. Through his words and song the wanted man in *The Rising of the Moon*, for example, convinces the sergeant not to betray him.

We notice that much of the early dialogue in the play centers on the man's attempt to persuade the sergeant that even though his duty is to the law, his heart is with the people. We notice, too, how the man's voluble talk contrasts the sergeant's brusque speech. The sergeant, for example, curtly dismisses the man's suggestion that the lawman may well have been a follower of Granuaile like himself. We start to see a pattern in the sergeant's denials and dismissals, perhaps inferring from them a suspicion that he sympathizes with the wanted man. When the sergeant says, "It's a pity, it's a pity," we could interpret this to mean a number of things: (1) that it is too bad that the man must be arrested—but the sergeant has his duty to perform; (2) that it's a pity the sergeant is put in this difficult position; (3) that it's a shame that a man the sergeant seems to like has to be on the opposite side; (4) that it's too bad that the sergeant never followed through on his youthful idealism to go with Granuaile. The line "It's a pity" has been spoken in the opening scene by both the sergeant and one of the policemen. Echoing at a climactic moment in the play, "It's a pity" resonates with implication; it reverberates with significance.

Dialogue is an important index of a character's personality and personhood. Lady Gregory's sergeant is forceful, authoritative, even peremptory when talking with his two police subordinates. And he sounds abrupt and dismissive at first in dialogue with the ballad-singer. But the harshness evaporates in another more meditative speech—a mini-soliloquy:

If it wasn't for the sense I have, and for my wife and family, and for me joining the force the time I did, it might be myself now would be after breaking gaol and hiding in the dark, and it might be him that's hiding in the dark and that got out of gaol would be sitting up where I am on this barrel....And it might be myself would be creeping up trying to make my escape from himself, and it might be himself would be keeping the law, and myself would be breaking it, and myself would be trying maybe to put a bullet in his head, or to take up a lump of a stone the way you said he did...nom that myself did....

What the sergeant says here is clear enough: he could picture himself in the other man's shoes. But his manner of saying it—in a long, run-together, meandering, meditative sentence strung out with numerous "ands"—is equally revealing of a man who is sympathetic and understanding, one who is not as predictable and single-minded as his police subordinates. The ongoing quality of the sergeant's sentence simulates the ongoing nature of his thinking. The neat balances of "him" and "I" and of "myself" and "himself" convey the sergeant's understanding that he and the criminal are kin—that they are different doppelgängers, doubles, really.

This concern with characters' language is crucial. Ezra Pound once described drama as "persons moving on a stage using words"—in short, people talking. Listening to their talk attentively in ways I am suggesting helps us hear dramatic characters' distinct and distinctive voices as an index to their character.

And so, dialogue inevitably brings us back to character, drama's human center. And though dialogue functions, typically, in plays in three ways—to advance the plot, establish setting, and reveal character—the greatest of these is the revelation of character.

Setting and Staging

The action of a play, like the action of fictional works, occurs in a particular place and time, the play's *setting*. Some plays are set approximately in the times and places where they were written, whereas others deviate in one or both of those attributes. Lady Gregory's *The Rising of the Moon* approximates the temporal and spatial context of the author's life—Ireland in the late nineteenth century.

More often than not, however, a play's setting may depart significantly from the time and place of its composition. The immediate world of a playwright may not directly reflect the milieu in which his or her play is set. This does not mean, however, that there might not be significant connections between the author's milieu and that of the play. Sometimes, historical events of earlier times reflect social and political circumstances of the playwright's own time; this is often the case in political plays, including those of Shakespeare.

Let's consider for a bit the setting of *The Rising of the Moon*, including the stage directions provided at the beginning of the play:

> SCENE: *Side of a quay in a seaport town. Some posts and chains. A large barrel. Enter three* **Policemen**. *Moonlight.*

Clearly, this is a highly generalized set. We are given a few basic objects and some moonlight, and nothing more. Yet the objects, simple as they are, nonetheless establish the elemental world of the play. It will be a play and a world, this set suggests, in which a rich collection of "things" is not important. Far more important will be a basic human conundrum, seen more clearly and represented more starkly in a sparse, uncluttered setting.

The setting of a play is one element of its *staging*, the spectacle a play presents in performance. Staging, in general, refers to all the visual and aural elements of a play. It includes the positions of actors onstage, along with their postures, gestures, expressions, and movements. It also includes props and costumes, scenic background, lighting, and sound effects. Though some of these details may be referenced in the play's script, decisions about staging are often left to the play's director.

We can illustrate these aspects of staging by considering how they play out in *The Rising of the Moon*. The policemen might be distinguishable from their sergeant by some token of authority he wears, a badge perhaps. The sergeant might be distinguished from the ragged man not only in the poor clothing the wanted man wears, but also by a discrepancy in physical appearance, size perhaps most conspicuously.

The props include the placards the policemen are putting up. These posters are important as much for what they omit as for what they contain. They omit, for example, a picture of the man being sought, and they omit also a description of the man's criminal exploits.

The barrel on which the policemen paste one of the placards is the play's central prop. Its importance stems from two critical actions in which it figures—the sergeant sitting on it back-to-back with the man he seeks; the man hiding behind the barrel upon the return of the two policemen. The barrel would most likely be positioned center stage to accentuate its importance. Finally, and also significant, are the man's hat and wig—his simple disguise, which the sergeant hides behind his back when dismissing his two police subordinates.

The positions of the characters onstage, along with their postures and gestures, are not always specifically indicated in a play's stage directions and script. Occasionally, however, they are, as when the sergeant "crosses the stage to right and looks down steps." The sergeant is also specifically directed to take the man's shoulder and shove him. Later, the sergeant and the ragged man echo each other's actions visually when they point down to the water.

Such movements and gestures not only advance the plot; they also direct readers to the play's central concerns, and suggest aspects of its meaning. We noted earlier how their pointing reinforces the connections between the sergeant and the man, which is established in the sergeant's speech about the possibility of each of them being in the other's place.

We should also call attention to a play's lighting. The quality of the lighting indicated by "moonlight" suggest literally a shadowy light from a distance. Its effect should be to increase suspense in the nocturnal atmosphere.

Sound, too, is significant. The sound of the policemen's talk as they return is accentuated by the sparseness of the setting and the late hour. The sound of a boat being rowed—heard by both the man and the sergeant—precipitates the play's climax. The whistle the man's friends use signal their approach to the quay. And the sound of singing both advances the plot and highlights one of the play's central issues. We notice, for example, how the songs are ballads about Irish nationalist heroes and when the ballad-singer omits a line from one ballad, the sergeant supplies it, indicating still another way in which he, the man, and the common people are united.

Symbolism and Irony

In the previous discussion of the play's staging and in our observation about its dialogue and conflicts, we touched implicitly on two additional important aspects of drama: *symbolism and irony*. One of the caveats I have about symbols is that it's easy to get carried away and begin to identify symbols everywhere. And so, while we need to be aware of symbolism in drama as well as in other literary genres, we should make claims for symbolic interpretations judiciously. We also need to explain the literal function of an object, or the literal sense of a dialogic exchange before advocating for any symbolic implications.

Here are three questions to guide your thinking about symbolism:

1 Is the object, action, gesture, or dialogue important to the play? Is it described in detail? Does it occur more than once; does it occur at a climactic or otherwise significant moment in the play?
2 Does the play appear to warrant our granting its details more significance than their literal immediate meaning? If so, why?
3 Does a symbolic interpretation make sense? Does it account for the literal details without either ignoring or distorting them? And does it extend or deepen our understanding of the play?

There will be occasions when we are uncertain whether or not a symbolic interpretation is justified and can be adequately supported. And there will be times when, though we can be fairly confident that we are dealing with a symbol, we may yet remain uncertain about its significance. Interpretation is an art, not a science; it's a skill developed over time with increasing experience of reading, analyzing, and discussing literature. Moreover, interpretive uncertainty reflects the complexity and variability of literary works themselves; most complex literary symbols resist definitive explanation.

We might consider, for example, the symbolic force of the revolutionary songs the ballad-singer sings in *The Rising of the Moon*. At the end of the play he sings a song about "the rising of the moon." We need to consider what the moon's rising stands for in the context of the play. To begin, we can link the fact of the moon's rising with moments in the play when reference is made to groups of people whose fortunes will rise or fall—and generally to images of rising and falling that appear elsewhere in the play.

We can also consider the symbolic importance of the scene in which the sergeant and ballad-singer sit back-to-back on the barrel, looking out in opposite directions. We can ask to what extent this action symbolizes their differences or similarities of attitude, situation, and belief. And when they jump together off the barrel, we can ask whether this action might be construed as a symbolic representation of their decision to overlook their differences.

The heart of the play resides in the conflict between the opposed values represented by the sergeant and the ballad-singer. The ballad-singer embodies a revolutionary freedom for Ireland from the yoke of England; the sergeant embodies the order of law that would prevent revolutionary upheaval in society.

Irony presents other challenges, as readers can completely misunderstand a work when they miss an author's ironic tone or stance. Irony is grounded in contrast and discrepancy between what is said and what is meant, between what happens and what is expected to happen. Irony appears in plays in three ways: in their language, in their incidents, and in their point of view.

At the end of *The Rising of the Moon*, after the sergeant has let the ballad-singer escape, he asks himself whether he was a fool for doing so. The sergeant's question is subtly ironic since once we accept his action and understand the sympathy that motivates it, we do not expect him to express self-doubt. Earlier we were probably surprised to see that the sergeant even considered befriending the ballad-singer, allying himself with what the ballad-singer stands for. The ironic actions in the play multiply.

This last example includes both *irony of incident* and *irony of language*, as the sergeant's question about his being a fool can be taken to mean that he is anything but—that he is wise in deciding and acting as he does. Besides these two kinds of irony—of language and of action—we have *irony of circumstance, or irony of situation*, in which a playwright creates a discrepancy between what characters think is the case and what we readers (or viewers) know is the case. Irony of circumstance appears forcefully in *The Rising of the Moon* when the ballad-singer, instead of resorting to force or violence, persuades the sergeant to relent through his speech and his song. Irony of circumstance is also illustrated in that the two men who seem to have little in common turn out to have much in common.

We should also identify an additional, related form of irony, *dramatic irony*, which involves a discrepancy between what characters know and what readers and viewers know. Playwrights often let us know things their characters do not. We know, for example, that the ballad-singer is the man the sergeant seeks even though for a while the sergeant does not know this. And we know that the ballad-singer is hiding behind a barrel while the sergeant dismisses his two police assistants. Our ironic knowledge of these things increases our pleasure in the play's situation and action while enhancing our appreciation of the dramatist's skill and art.

Thought and Theme

We need to be careful not to reduce the complexity of a play's vision and values to a simple declarative statement of theme. While it may be true to some extent that theme can be explained as a play's main idea cast in the form of a generalization, we should be aware of the limitations of doing so. Abstracting a central general idea from a play moves us away from what gives it life—its details of plot and character, of monologue and dialogue, of setting and staging—and of our experience of reading (or seeing) it.

Here are a few additional suggestions regarding consideration of a play's theme. First, distinguish the ideas that may appear *in* a play from the idea *of* a play. The meaning of a play—its central, governing, animating idea—is rarely identifiable as an explicit social, political, or philosophical idea manifested in its dialogue. A play's idea is almost always implicit, bound up with and derivable from the play's structure, character interactions, dialogue, imagery, and staging.

One of the dangers of reading plays without attending to their theatrical dimension is that we may overgeneralize to an oversimplified single idea. Because the theme of a play grows out of the relationships among its concrete and specific details, any statement of theme that omits significant aspects of a play's dramatic elements will inevitably represent a too severe limitation, perhaps even a distortion of its meaning. Any statement of theme necessarily approximates rather than fully captures a play's meaning. Even when we may speak of multiple themes or thematic strands in a play, we remain concerned with only one aspect of meaning—the intellectual—which ignores its emotional impact, which we apprehend rather than comprehend.

As readers and viewers of plays, we tend to reach for theme as a shorthand way to explain our understanding, as a quick way to come to terms with a play's idea and its implications. But there is also the force of a play's action on our feelings, on what the play *does* to and for readers and viewers. These are important aspects of a play's meaning. For the meaning of a play is ultimately more than any statement of theme we employ to describe it. Additionally, we should avoid thinking of theme as something hidden in a play that we somehow have to ferret out. We should resist the temptation to unlock the play's mystery with a special key (perhaps a symbolic key).

With these caveats in mind, we can consider thought and theme in *The Rising of the Moon*. First, it is a political play, taking as its context the political turmoil of a beleaguered Irish populace. To fully appreciate Lady Gregory's play we need to understand the depth of Irish bitterness toward their British overlords. Britain finally granted home rule to Ireland in 1914, but this was delayed due to the start of World War I. After the Irish War of Independence, the Irish Free State was established in 1922 but this applied only to the predominantly Catholic southern part of the country, while the predominantly Protestant Northern Ireland remained British. A bloody conflict continued over many years as the Irish underground, later the IRA (Irish Republican Army), actively worked to subvert British rule in the north.

These historical details of the political situation are not explicitly rendered in the play, largely because they would have been familiar to Lady Gregory's audience when the play was first produced. But they are alluded to with references to Granuaile, an Irish revolutionary hero. Lady Gregory's ballad singer is less a common criminal than a rebel fighting for a cause many Irish people believed in, including the Sergeant. Moreover, we are meant to side with this man who fights for the cause of Granuaile, and to see the justice of that cause and the hope of its ultimate triumph over the social and political status quo. According to the wanted man (and the play overall), a social revolution is in the making. The play alludes to a spirit of optimistic idealism and a corresponding sense that injustice and inequity will not always prevail.

This political idea is closely associated with the crisis of conscience the sergeant undergoes. His decision to trust his instinctive sympathy for the man and his cause, and his impulse to act in accordance with his reawakened youthful idealism rather than to capture the criminal, are powerfully dramatized. Even though the play ends with a question, an answer to it is clearly implied. When the sergeant asks, "am I as great a fool as I think I am?" his question directs us to the play's theme not merely as an abstract idea but as a living moment of meaningful decision-making. Our answers to the sergeant's question may vary, though one that seems endorsed by the many interrelated details of the play is: "No, you're not a fool at all. In fact, you are a good man, one who is trying to do what you believe is right."

The Rising of the Moon suggests that the sergeant is not a fool in ignoring his responsibility to uphold the law by arresting the ballad-singer. In one sense, of course, the sergeant is a fool, since he wastes an opportunity to gain a promotion and to collect a sizable reward. In another sense, though, he is no fool at all, since he knows exactly what he is doing and why. He values the man and his cause more than he values his own prospective good fortune; he values his own diminished but still living idealism more than the glory he would gain by arresting the man. Morally, the sergeant feels vindicated. Practically, he may feel some regret. It depends on what criteria we use to evaluate his decision.

Thus, as we think back to the sergeant's crisis of conscience, to the wanted man and his Irish ballads, to his friends and their effort to rescue him, to the play's dramatized conflicts of dialogue and action, to its symbolic implications, we begin to see its rich, complex meaning. Thanks to Lady Gregory's dramatic skill and art, the play's significance and implied themes continue to reverberate for us long after our encounter with the play is over.

25 Elements of the Essay—Zora Neale Hurston

"How It Feels to Be Colored Me"

As with the elements of poetry, fiction, and drama, we can also analyze essays via literary elements. As with the other genres, we'll work with a single text, an essay by Zora Neale Hurston, "How It Feels to Be Colored Me." First, the essay, then discussion of the elements of voice and tone, style, structure, and thought.

> I am colored but I offer nothing in the way of extenuating circumstances except the fact that I am the only Negro in the United States whose grandfather on the mother's side was *not* an Indian chief.
>
> I remember the very day that I became colored. Up to my thirteenth year I lived in the little Negro town of Eatonville, Florida. It is exclusively a colored town. The only white people I knew passed through the town going to or coming from Orlando. The native whites rode dusty horses, the Northern tourists chugged down the sandy village road in automobiles. The town knew the Southerners and never stopped cane chewing when they passed. But the Northerners were something else again. They were peered at cautiously from behind curtains by the timid. The more venturesome would come out on the porch to watch them go past and got just as much pleasure out of the tourists as the tourists got out of the village.
>
> The front porch might seem a daring place for the rest of the town, but it was a gallery seat for me. My favorite place was atop the gate-post. Proscenium box for a born first-nighter. Not only did I enjoy the show, but I didn't mind the actors knowing that I liked it. I usually spoke to them in passing. I'd wave at them and when they returned my salute, I would say something like this: "Howdy-do-well-I-thank-you-where-you-goin'?" Usually automobile or the horse paused at this, and after a queer exchange of compliments, I would probably "go a piece of the way" with them, as we say in farthest Florida. If one of my family happened to come to the front in time to see me, of course negotiations would be rudely broken off. But even so, it is clear that I was the first "welcome-to-our-state" Floridian, and I hope the Miami Chamber of Commerce will please take notice.

During this period, white people differed from colored to me only in that they rode through town and never lived there. They liked to hear me "speak pieces" and sing and wanted to see me dance the parse-me-la, and gave me generously of their small silver for doing these things, which seemed strange to me for I wanted to do them so much that I needed bribing to stop. Only they didn't know it. The colored people gave no dimes. They deplored any joyful tendencies in me, but I was their Zora nevertheless. I belonged to them, to the nearby hotels, to the country—everybody's Zora.

But changes came in the family when I was thirteen, and I was sent to school in Jacksonville. I left Eatonville, the town of the oleanders, as Zora. When I disembarked from the river-boat at Jacksonville, she was no more. It seemed that I had suffered a sea change. I was not Zora of Orange County any more, I was now a little colored girl. I found it out in certain ways. In my heart as well as in the mirror, I became a fast brown—warranted not to rub nor run.

II

But I am not tragically colored. There is no great sorrow dammed up in my soul, nor lurking behind my eyes. I do not mind at all. I do not belong to the sobbing school of Negrohood who hold that nature somehow has given them a low-down dirty deal and whose feelings are all hurt about it. Even in the helter-skelter skirmish that is my life, I have seen that the world is to the strong regardless of a little pigmentation more or less. No, I do not weep at the world—I am too busy sharpening my oyster knife.

Someone is always at my elbow reminding me that I am the grand-daughter of slaves. It fails to register depression with me. Slavery is sixty years in the past. The operation was successful and the patient is doing well, thank you. The terrible struggle that made me an American out of a potential slave said "On the line!" The Reconstruction said "Get set!"; and the generation before said "Go!" I am off to a flying start and I must not halt in the stretch to look behind and weep. Slavery is the price I paid for civilization, and the choice was not with me. It is a bully adventure and worth all that I have paid through my ancestors for it. No one on earth ever had a greater chance for glory. The world to be won and nothing to be lost. It is thrilling to think—to know that for any act of mine, I shall get twice as much praise or twice as much blame. It is quite exciting to hold the center of the national stage, with the spectators not knowing whether to laugh or to weep.

The position of my white neighbor is much more difficult. No brown specter pulls up a chair beside me when I sit down to eat. No dark ghost thrusts its leg against mine in bed. The game of keeping what one has is never so exciting as the game of getting.

I do not always feel colored. Even now I often achieve the unconscious Zora of Eatonville before the Hegira. I feel most colored when I am thrown against a sharp white background.

For instance at Barnard. "Beside the waters of the Hudson" I feel my race. Among the thousand white persons, I am a dark rock surged upon, and overswept, but through it all, I remain myself. When covered by the waters, I am; and the ebb but reveals me again.

III

Sometimes it is the other way around. A white person is set down in our midst, but the contrast is just as sharp for me. For instance, when I sit in the drafty basement that is The New World Cabaret with a white person, my color comes. We enter chatting about any little nothing that we have in common and are seated by the jazz waiters. In the abrupt way that jazz orchestras have, this one plunges into a number. It loses no time in circumlocutions, but gets right down to business. It constricts the thorax and splits the heart with its tempo and narcotic harmonies. This orchestra grows rambunctious, rears on its hind legs and attacks the tonal veil with primitive fury, rending it, clawing it until it breaks through to the jungle beyond. I follow those heathen—follow them exultingly. I dance wildly inside myself; I yell within, I whoop; I shake my assegai above my head, I hurl it true to the mark *yeeeeooww!* I am in the jungle and living in the jungle way. My face is painted red and yellow and my body is painted blue. My pulse is throbbing like a war drum. I want to slaughter something—give pain, give death to what, I do not know. But the piece ends. The men of the orchestra wipe their lips and rest their fingers. I creep back slowly to the veneer we call civilization with the last tone and find the white friend sitting motionless in his seat, smoking calmly.

"Good music they have here," he remarks, drumming the table with his fingers.

Music. The great blobs of purpose and red emotion have not touched him. He has only heard what I felt. He is far away and I see him but dimly across the ocean and the continent that have fallen between us. He is so pale with his whiteness then and I am *so* colored.

IV

At certain times I have no race, I am *me*. When I set my hat at a certain angle and saunter down Seventh Avenue, Harlem City, feeling as snooty as the lions in front of the Forty-Second Street Library, for instance. So far as my feelings are concerned, Peggy Hopkins Joyce on the Boule Mich with her gorgeous raiment, stately carriage, knees knocking together in a most aristocratic manner, has nothing on me. The cosmic Zora emerges. I belong to no race nor time. I am the eternal feminine with its string of beads.

I have no separate feeling about being an American citizen and colored. I am merely a fragment of the Great Soul that surges within the boundaries. My country, right or wrong.

Sometimes, I feel discriminated against, but it does not make me angry. It merely astonishes me. How *can* any deny themselves the pleasure of my company? It's beyond me.

But in the main, I feel like a brown bag of miscellany propped against a wall. Against a wall in company with other bags, white, red and yellow. Pour out the contents, and there is discovered a jumble of small things priceless and worthless. A first-water diamond, an empty spool, bits of broken glass, lengths of string, a key to a door long since crumbled away, a rusty knife-blade, old shoes saved for a road that never was and never will be, a nail bent under weight of things too heavy for any nail, a dried flower or two still a little fragrant. In your hand is the brown bag. On the ground before you is the jumble it held—so much like the jumble in the bags, could they be emptied, that all might be dumped in a single heap and the bags refilled without altering the content of any greatly. A bit of colored glass more or less would not matter. Perhaps that is how the Great Stuffer of Bags filled them in the first place—who knows?

Voice and Tone

Every essay comes to us through a writer's voice. What kind of voice do we hear in Hurston's essay? For one thing, Hurston's voice is immediately engaging; it's direct and unpretentious. She uses everyday language to describe her life story. She makes herself appealing to her readers. She seems like she is simply talking to us, directly, unpretentiously, revealing herself sincerely.

How does she do this? She tells us that she experienced pain in her initial discovery that she was Black. Even so, she reveals that she possesses an irrepressible gaiety, refusing to be depressed about the fact that she is the granddaughter of slaves. She shows herself as patient, tolerant, and understanding.

Her tone, the attitude she takes toward her subject—herself as a Black girl and woman (referred to by the word "colored")—is one of joy, even celebration. She accepts herself as she is; she appreciates who and what she is and has become. She loves herself, and her tone expresses the joyful celebration of her loved self in spades.

Structure

Seeing how an essay is organized, or structured—how it is put together, how it develops, is critical for understanding. In the first part Hurston indicates the significant change that occurred in her self-perception when she moved from Eatonville to Jacksonville. She learned there what it meant to be "a little colored girl." In the second part, Hurston makes clear that although she felt the sting of discrimination, she doesn't wallow in self-pity, but instead looks hopefully to her opportunities as a human being, a woman, and an artist, seeing the world as her oyster. Part three reveals the differences Hurston feels between herself and her white friend. It also includes the revelation that she feels most Black when she is accompanied by white people. In her essay's final section, she describes the paradoxical sense of being a small part of a complex and multifaceted cosmic whole, all the while retaining a distinctive sense of selfhood. In exploring the implied question in her title (How does it feel to be a Black woman?) Hurston provides an answer: that for her it feels just fine.

Style

Hurston's style is informal, personal, engaging. She uses short sentences and mostly simple, everyday language. One of the signal features of her style is her use of comparisons, by which she describes herself:

> A patient after an operation
> An actress on center stage
> A player in a game of "getting'
> A "dark rock surged upon, and ... covered by the waters"
> A stone statue of a lion
> A fragment of the Great Soul
> A brown bag of miscellany.

Collectively, these metaphors provide a sense of Hurston's variability and of her confidence. She is multifarious and richly alive—a survivor, an active and passionate participant in the game of life. We might consider as well to what extent her comparisons exhibit commonalities of idea. What common features, we might ask, do her comparisons about herself suggest? How are those comparisons related to the feeling she describes elsewhere in her essay?

Hurston sees herself from a number of perspectives, including as an adult looking back on her childhood and adolescence; as an observer describing scenes of white and Black people together—Eatonville; the jazz club. She reveals herself as interested in place and in history, of her experience of living in Eatonville and Jacksonville, and also by referencing the past, especially slavery and Reconstruction.

We might invite consideration of the contrasts Hurston establishes with these questions: What is the relationship between the two scenes Hurston describes? How does she feel serving as an unofficial welcoming committee for Eatonville? How does she feel while listening to music in the cabaret? What is her relationship to the white people she is with? And also: What significant differences exist for her between Eatonville and Jacksonville? How do you account for her different feelings about each place?

Hurston writes about her blackness without bitterness. She seems to prefer being "colored"—her color—seeing benefits in her blackness with possibilities unavailable to white people. She seems proud of her race. She values herself, is confident in her abilities, and secure in her sense of self. She sees herself as a performer, on center stage, with an opportunity to make a strong impression as a woman, as a Black person, and as an artist. She sees herself as a survivor, not as a problem. And she considers white people as bearing the weight of the race problem in America.

Theme–Thought–Idea

I prefer the term "thought" to "theme" generally, but especially with respect to essays. Another term and related concept I like to use is "idea." Both "idea" and "thought" suggest the act of thinking, the thinking of the writer and that of the reader. Hurston's essay is about race and race relations between Black people and white during her time. But it's also about her response to her blackness and her relationship to all those she encountered in the separate realms of Black and white America during her life. In addition, it's about her resilience and sense of self.

In thinking about what Hurston is saying, we need to account for the social, cultural, moral, and other values the work embodies. We can consider Hurston's celebration of her race—and her celebration of her unique, individual self, which combines consideration of racial identity with those of personal identity—Hurston's own identity.

Given these observations and connections, inferences and values considerations, we might write a bit about our understanding of Hurston's essay—our interpretation of it. Here are a few final thoughts about the significance of "How It Feels to Be Colored Me," in which Zora Neale Hurston reveals a Black woman's confidence in her color, her femininity, and her talent. She sees the issue of color as intrinsically skin-deep and primarily a problem for white people, and one that need not result in tragic consequences for Black people.

Hurston suggests that she does not regret being Black. Instead, she is delighted with her race, since she says, "No one on earth ever had a greater chance for glory." She sees being "colored" as an opportunity, not a drawback, and she announces her satisfaction by distinguishing herself from those who see themselves as "tragically colored." Moreover, "no brown specter" and "no dark ghost" haunt her, as they do for those with a heritage of guilt for legal and moral crimes committed against Black people.

But it is not just the idea Hurston expresses that is important. It is her attitude toward her idea and the tone in which she expresses it that matter, as well. Hurston appears to relish her chance to shine; she is thrilled to think about the opportunities she has in "the game of getting." She is also not one to weep over the past. Instead, she is "off to a flying start" toward success and the enjoyment of her life. As she puts it, she is "busy sharpening [her] oyster knife."

Interlude V
Literary Conventions

To read literature with understanding we also need to recognize its conventions, or customary and typical features. And we need to see how writers in different times and places adapt and modify the conventions they inherit. One example is the conventions of the short story—a brief narrative fiction that typically focuses on a few characters and a single incident. Other story conventions include descriptive detail and dialogue, along with a narrator who presents the story's action in first person or third person.

Another example is the conventions that govern the lyric poetic form of the sonnet. To appreciate what an individual poet does in writing a sonnet, you need to understand the conventions of the sonnet form. What is of interest, as well, is how a poet might vary those conventions, or formal elements, and what effects the poet achieves with those variations.

Although we learn to recognize literary conventions over time through wide reading, by thinking about our experience with conventions in everyday life, we can understand just how important conventions are and what characterizes them.

First, conventions *give form to reality*—the way a short story fictionalizes action in prescribed ways or a sonnet structures language. Conventions provide ways to *structure experience*. They help us know what to do and what to expect. Conventions *impose order* on what, without them, would be a rather rampant and confusing disorder.

Second, conventions are *learned*. We acquire an understanding of conventions from experience. Our understanding of wedding conventions, for example, derives largely from our having attended weddings, from having heard about them and read about them and watched them in movies and on television.

We learn literary conventions from our experience of reading literature. Through familiarity with literary forms and genres, we learn to distinguish different types of poems and plays and novels; to recognize and appreciate, for example, the formal characteristics of parable and novella, of sonnet and villanelles of drama and epic—and of genres yet to be invented.

Third, *conventions change*. The chorus, a feature of Greek tragedy, for example, is rarely found in drama from later periods. And when the chorus appears in Shakespeare's *Henry V* and Eugene O'Neill's *Mourning Becomes Electra*, it serves each author's dramatic purposes.

And so, it is important to learn to recognize and understand literary conventions across genres. With time and practice in the experience of reading literature, we gain confidence in our increasing ability to do so. And with that confidence (accompanied by increasing competence) comes one of the many pleasures literature affords us.

Part VI
Reading Literature through Critical Lenses—Twelve Takes

Prelude VI
The Value of Literary Perspectives

Literature is the supreme manifestation of language, and it makes maximum and ultimate use of language, as literary works mold, shape, and construct worlds out of words. In the process, literature provokes our thinking and stimulates our feeling; it makes us smarter and, some claim, more understanding and tolerant of others.

Literature also possesses cultural and social value; it can increase our ability to empathize with others. Literature accomplishes this feat by inviting us to participate imaginatively in the lives of others. In a form of empathic reading, we project ourselves into other worlds, other lives, other ways of thinking and feeling—and thereby extend the range of our own experience.

Whatever we might make of these various claims for the uses and the value of literature, ultimately literature gives us pleasure. Taking a hint from Northrop Frye in *The Educated Imagination*, we might take literature as a singular and amazing human invention—like painting or music or dance or film—and simply enjoy its distinctive pleasures, especially the ways it displays and reveals the capacities of the human imagination, and the ways it invites our participation in those imaginative revelations.

Another kind of pleasures literary works offer is the opportunity to engage in "thought experiments," which are more often associated with science and history. Literature presents many opportunities to engage with complex moral issues, with situations fraught with ambiguity, with problems that do not admit of easy solutions. Examples are legion, but we can cite the plays of Arthur Miller, especially *Death of a Salesman*, *The Crucible*, and *All My Sons* as a few modern American examples. The first of these plays invites consideration about what it means to be successful in terms of the "American Dream." *The Crucible* provokes us to think about the ways groupthink and crowd behavior lead people into dangerous and mistaken beliefs, with the Salem witch trials as the stimulus to thinking. *All My Sons* invites us to consider how and why ethical and moral norms can be violated in the pursuit of riches.

Literature helps us make sense of the world and helps us make sense of ourselves. It does this through putting us in conversation with writers and with each other about their creations, regardless of genre. Literature brings the past to life for us; it memorializes the present; it imagines the future. And

DOI: 10.4324/9781003620280-43

as novelist Claire Messud suggests, "Literature reminds us that we're not alone on this planet...not alone in this time...not alone in this experience... not alone in *history*" (243). Messud counterpoints this consoling thought about literature's value for us with another, that the literature we read and the writing that we do to understand ourselves, explain ourselves in, through, and with literature are ineluctably only fragments (242), little bits and pieces we have managed to salvage; in T. S. Eliot's words from *The Waste Land*, "fragments I have shored against my ruins" (*CP* 69).

For some readers (and writers) literature provides an opportunity to become politically engaged. This is yet another distinctive pleasure of literature. Literature embodies for these readers political, social, cultural, and other ideas and ideals. And so, it's not surprising that we might consider ways in which literature can enhance political understanding or even inspire political action.

Two contemporary writers for whom politics, specifically with reference to the rights of women, was critical, are Adrienne Rich and bell hooks. In whatever genre Rich wrote—poems and essays, articles and reviews, speeches, and literary criticism—she was earnestly committed to the liberation of men as well as women from prejudices that blind perception and stifle the thinking mind. And while she has been long associated with a radical form of feminism, Rich was not constrained by it. Both her poetry and her prose writings dramatize a self-discovering freedom in language and literary artistry. At her best, Adrienne Rich was less a polemicist than an artist who challenged preconceptions about women, especially in their relationships with men and their mutual obligations toward one another. She aimed for a reconstruction of the mind—her own and those of women, generally.

One place to see Rich's own reconstruction of mind is in her autobiographical writing. In "When We Dead Awaken: Writing as Re-Vision," Rich describes how she needed to change the images that represented, for her, ideals of both woman and poet, since her images of both had been dominated by men. She explores the concept of "re-vision" as an "act of looking back, of seeing with fresh eyes" (*On Lies*). This kind of re-envisioning is essential both for writers and for readers, amateur and professional. And, as Rich notes, it's essential for women living in a patriarchal society. For them it's an act of survival. Throughout her career as reader and poet, teacher and public intellectual, Rich used her own experience, especially her political experience, to illustrate how such re-vision can become part of one's intellectual, emotional life, at times saving women's lives.

Like Adrienne Rich, bell hooks was an active participant in political causes, always engaging her reading and teaching about literature with a political purpose. She saw literacy—developing critical reading, writing, and thinking skills—as essential for all learning, and especially for the future of feminism. Literacy for hooks was always more than just being able to read and write; it involved, for her, "critical consciousness," which combines critical thought with political action, with self-actualization a goal. For hooks, education occurs not just in the classroom, not only in texts, and not only in the streets, but wherever people find themselves.

In *Teaching Community: A Pedagogy of Hope*, bell hooks explains how to make the classroom a life-sustaining and mind-expanding place, where teacher and students work together in partnership to engage authentically and passionately with works of literature. Education both through literature and more broadly across disciplines was, for hooks, a practice of freedom designed to restore our sense of connections and a sense of community. Throughout her life and work, bell hooks found hope, seeing individuals positively transforming their lives and the world around them.

Literature, thus, provides many kinds of value. Literature enriches our lives, including pleasure as well as knowledge; and it provides the pleasures of knowledge. Literature is valuable in and of and for itself, for its intrinsic benefits; it is also valuable for the variety of extrinsic rewards and opportunities it offers to engage with others in a multitude of ways.

Critical Perspectives as Heuristics

One way to extend and deepen our enjoyment and appreciation of literature is through varied critical approaches we can take in reading it. The varied perspectives that literary theories offer can be considered as heuristics, methods of problem solving that can lead to thinking discoveries. Each critical approach highlights particular aspects of a literary work, providing a lens through which to view it. In each case, the change of critical lens brings out qualities that might otherwise elude attention. Each critical lens temporarily foregrounds some aspects and features of literary works while relegating others to the background.

Different literary theories also provide different "ways in" to a text, resulting in different understandings of what a work is "about" and what it says and suggests—hermeneutical concerns. Textual details analyzed through varied critical lenses direct readers toward different textual emphases and toward varied ways to understand and appreciate literary works.

The imaginative élan and intellectual provocation of multiple critical literary perspectives can drive our thinking about literary works in unexpected directions. Literary theory, in short, can help us think about our thinking about literature. That may well be its most important and most valuable contribution to appreciating and understanding of literature.

In what follows, I provide brief descriptions of major critical approaches with a minimum of jargon. You can use the questions included with each critical lens to think about literature from that critical approach or perspective. I believe that you will find the effort to do so rewarding, leading you toward a fuller, more wide-ranging set of insights into literary works, and, I believe, increased pleasure in reading them.

26 Formalist

Formalist critics emphasize the form of a literary work to determine its meaning; they focus on literary elements such as plot, character, and setting; diction, imagery and figurative language; dialogue and subtext; tone, symbolism, and point of view. Formalist critics approach literary works as largely independent systems with interdependent parts. They typically downplay approaches that consider an author's biography, a work's social and historical contexts, or its economic, political, or gender aspects. The primary concern of formalist critics is with the work itself rather than with external contexts.

What matters most to a formalist critic is how a writer conveys and embodies meaning through a work's resources of language and form. Implicit in a formalist critical approach is that readers indeed can determine the meanings of literary works and that those meanings are accessible—in short, that literature can be understood and its meanings clarified. Implied in this approach as well is that literary works (the best of them at least) are "universal," their wholeness and harmony transcending their local particularities and their specific historical, biographical, cultural, linguistic, and other contexts.

The primary method of formalism is "close reading of the text." Lyric poetry is well suited to close reading because its language tends, generally, to be more compressed and metaphorical than the language of prose. Nonetheless, formal analysis of novels and plays can also focus on close reading of key passages. Formalist critics, in addition, analyze the large-scale structures of longer works, looking for patterns and relationships among scenes and acts, characters and actions. Much of the discussion in the first four parts of this book exhibits a formalist critical perspective, though other critical approaches are included in those chapters as well.

Let's consider D. H. Lawrence's brief poem "Piano" from a formalist perspective:

> Softly, in the dusk, a woman is singing to me;
> Taking me back down the vista of years, till I see
> A child sitting under the piano, in the boom of the tingling strings
> And pressing the small, poised feet of a mother who smiles as she sings.

In spite of myself, the insidious mastery of song
Betrays me back, till the heart of me weeps to belong
To the old Sunday evenings at home, with winter outside
And hymns in the cosy parlour, the tinkling piano our guide.

So now it is vain for the singer to burst into clamour
With the great black piano appassionato. The glamour
Of childish days is upon me, my manhood is cast
Down in the flood of remembrance, I weep like a child for the past.

Formalist critics would note the poem's three-stanza structure, each stanza comprised of four lines. They would note, further, that the last line of each stanza is longer than the others. They would attend, as well, to the poem's rhyme pattern of two couplets per stanza. They would also note the repetition of the references to the poem's speaker as "me."

They would highlight the repetition of words involving song, "singing," "sings," and "singer." And they would identify other patterns of sound at play in the poem, including, for example, alliteration with the repeating "s" sounds: "softly," "singing," "sitting," "small," "smiles," "she," "spite," "song," "Sunday," "singer," and "appassionato." And these repeated "s" sounds at the beginning of words are reinforced by other words, where the "s" appears in the midst of words, among them "dusk," "vista," "pressing," "poised," "insidious," "myself," "mastery," "cosy," "appassionato," "cast," "past," as well as at the ends of words: "Betrays," "weeps," "evenings," "childish," and "remembrance."

Formalist critics would also remark on the poem's syntax, how its sentences are long, two of them, the first and second, occupying entire stanzas. These critics would also note how the lines of the poem flow into one another; they are enjambed, their meaning running over the ends of lines into the lines that follow. The two exceptions are the first line, which is end-stopped with a semi-colon, and the second line of the final stanza, which contains a period near the end of that line.

This syntactic pattern creates a continuous flow of thought and feeling in the poem. Its rhymed couplets highlight key words that describe both the poem's action and the narrator's feelings.

Formalist critics study literary works by analyzing their language and form in order to see the literary artifact in itself. They emphasize the value of literature as revealing an essentially unchanging human nature in which the unique individual transcends external forces. They seek to explain how the form and content of literary works are organically integrated. They also mediate between the reader and the text by explaining what the text says, suggests, means.

Formalist Critical Questions

1   How is the work organized or structured? How does it begin and end? What is its plot, and how is that plot related to the work's structure?

2 What is the relationship of each of the work's parts to the work as a whole? How do its parts relate to one another?
3 Who is narrating or telling the story of the work? How is this narrator, or speaker, or character revealed to the reader? How do we come to know and understand, interpret and evaluate this figure?
4 Who are the major and minor characters, what do they embody and represent, and how do they relate to each other?
5 What is the work's setting, its time and place? How is the setting related to what we know of the characters and their relationships? To what extent is the setting symbolic?
6 What kinds of language inhabit the work? What figures of speech does it employ and emphasize? What meanings do those figures of speech convey and how do they do it?

27 Reader-Response

Reader-response critics raise the question of where literary meaning resides—in the text, the reader, or the space between them. Reader-response critics differ in the degree of subjectivity they emphasize. David Bleich sees a literary work as a mirror in which readers contemplate themselves. Norman Holland focuses on the psychological dynamics of reading, and suggests that readers create their identities through reading literature. Wolfgang Iser emphasizes negotiating the text rather than the reader's feelings. Text-centered theorists like Iser highlight the temporal aspect of reading, emphasizing how readers construe texts word-by-word, line-by-line, sentence-by-sentence, making and altering their sense of what is happening in a text and what it means as they progress through it.

One of the earliest and most influential reader-response critics, Louise Rosenblatt, argues against emphasizing the reader's feelings. Like Iser, Rosenblatt keeps a focus on the text, though she finds literary meanings in the dynamic inter-relationship between readers and texts. For Rosenblatt and other reader-response critics, the meaning of a literary work does not exist until the text is performed by the reader. A text's meaning potential is only actualized as a literary work when read. The literary work, for these critics, is not an independent entity; it lives only in a reader's imagination.

Two additional points obtain for reader-response critics. One is that a reader's interpretation and understanding of a work will most likely change over time. Reading Shakespeare's *Julius Caesar* in secondary school is a distinctly different experience, and one that bears a different kind and level of understanding, than reading the play in college or in later adulthood. A second point is that, historically, readers from different times interpret literary works differently. According to this idea of reception theory, works speak to readers in different ways depending on readers' beliefs, needs, and life circumstances.

Some reader-response critics acknowledge limits to subjectivity when interpreting works of literature. For these critics, interpretation has both latitude and limits, which require a delicate balancing act between a reader's subjective experience of a work and a respect for the meanings of the words on the page. Inge Crosman Wimmers, for example, suggests that a text's

DOI: 10.4324/9781003620280-45

verbal and cultural constraints prohibit chaotic readings, while noting that any text has more than one single correct reading (xvii).

Some reader-response critics read literary works more subjectively and impressionistically than others, emphasize how they feel about a literary work, and how their feelings change in the act of reading it. Others emphasize the *process* of reading literary works, attending to the moment-by-moment *experience* of reading. They focus on the psychological processes of how readers construe texts and make meaning. They read works of literature as transactions between texts and readers. They consider how readers' responses to literary works change over time—both how individual readers' experiences may change over a period of years, and how the reception of literary works changes over decades and centuries.

Let's return briefly to Lawrence's "Piano," which we considered in the section on formalist criticism. From a reader-response perspective, we might relate to Lawrence's poem by considering a similar experience we may have had of nostalgia, remembering the past with a powerful emotional response. We need not have had this experience with music, though we might have. Nor need we have had it remembering it as a young child, with the mother a singular singing smiling presence. But our recollection should involve a memory of something we once loved that now no longer exists for us—whatever the reason for its discontinuance. And although there is much more we might say about "Piano," and its richness of language and feeling, this quick suggestion about how it taps our emotional response is among its powers and its pleasures.

Reader-Response Critical Questions

1. What is your initial emotional response to the work? How did you feel upon first reading it—while reading it, and after?
2. At what places in the text did you make inferences, fill in gaps, make predictions and guesses, and adjust your sense of what was happening or what it meant?
3. How do you respond to the characters, the speaker, the narrator? How do you feel about them, and why?
4. What places in the text caused you to do your most serious thinking?
5. How did you begin to put the pieces of the text together to make sense of it?
6. How have your second and later readings of particular works changed? How did they differ from earlier readings? How might you account for those differences?

28 Biographical

Some critics, formalists among them, insist that biographical information distracts from, even distorts, the process of understanding literary works. Biographical critics dispute this view, arguing that readers benefit from their approach in three ways. They argue that facts about authors' lived experience help explain aspects of their works. They also claim that knowing the struggles authors confronted in creating those works enhances a reader's appreciation of them. In addition, biographical critics maintain that through studying how writers modify their actual experience in creating their works, readers can better understand both the writers and the works they produce.

Knowing, for example, that Shakespeare and Molière acted in their plays increases readers' appreciation of their accomplishments. It also encourages us to consider the performance aspects of their plays and not merely their status as works of literature to be read and studied. Knowing that Ernest Hemingway revised the ending of his novel *A Farewell to Arms* thirty-nine times, and that he considered more than a dozen alternative titles, can direct our attention to aspects of the work we might otherwise overlook. And knowing that Hemingway loved bullfighting, big-game hunting, and fishing alerts us to the aspects of "manliness" and "machismo" celebrated in his fiction, which can also be related to his portrayal of women. Regardless of how we evaluate any of these matters, biographical critics claim that they enrich our understanding of writers' works.

A biographical critic can focus on a writer's works not only to enhance or enrich a reader's understanding of writers and their thematic preoccupations, but also to aid understanding of literary craft and art. In *Literary Biography*, Leon Edel suggests that what the literary biographer seeks to discover about the subject are his or her characteristic ways of thinking, feeling, and perceiving, as revealed in the writer's work (1–3). In addition, what we learn about writers from a judicious study of their works can be linked with an understanding of their world, thus serving as a bridge to appreciating the social and cultural contexts in which the writer lived and wrote (7). Edel, for example, wrote a multi-volume, highly detailed biography of Henry James, in which he situates James's fiction in the context of his life. He provides information about the seeds of James's fiction in the author's notebooks, which

DOI: 10.4324/9781003620280-46

record observations James made about situations from everyday life. While such information does not necessarily influence our perception of the quality of a work inspired by events from James's life, it certainly enriches our understanding of ways fiction and fact, story and actual experience are related.

Biographical critics examine literary works to consider aspects of writers' lives—their beliefs and actions, ideas, and attitudes. They read literary works in light of the facts of an author's life. They link a writer's life and work to social and historical contexts. They also seek a coherent and meaningful story in the writer's life. And they sometimes employ psychological analysis as part of a bio-critical perspective.

Biographical Critical Questions

1 What influences—people, ideas, events, and movements—evident in the writer's life, does the work reflect?
2 To what extent are the events described in the work a direct transfer of what happened in the writer's actual life?
3 What modifications of the actual events has the writer made in the literary work? For what possible purposes? And with what effects?
4 Why might the writer have altered his or her experience in the literary work?
5 What does the life teach us about the writer's work and what does the work teach us about the writer's life?
6 What has the author revealed in the work about his or her characteristic modes of thought, emotion, or perception? What place does this work have in the artist's literary development and career?

29 Historical

Historical critics approach literature in yet other ways: they provide background information for how works were perceived in their time; they show how literary works reflect ideas and attitudes of their historical period—either the period of their composition or the time and place of their setting. Some historical critics argue that a work of literature can only be understood as a product of its time and its environment. For these critics, understanding the social background and intellectual currents of that time and world illuminate literary works for later generations of readers. Many biographical critics also ascribe to this view, as for example Leon Edel in his life of Henry James, Richard Ellmann in his biography of James Joyce, Joseph Frank in his biography of Fyodor Dostoevsky, and Claire Tomalin in her biographies of Thomas Hardy, Jane Austen, and Mary Wollstonecraft. These biographers set their authors' lives and works in the context of the social, cultural, and intellectual forces of their times, and they do so with illuminating detail and explanatory power. But historical critics emphasize the context of history even more vigorously than do biographical critics.

To take another example: knowing something about the London of English Romantic poet William Blake's time helps readers better appreciate the power of Blake's protest against horrific social conditions, and the institutions of church and state that Blake held responsible for permitting those conditions to exist. In his poem "The Chimney Sweeper," from his *Songs of Experience*, Blake describes a chimney sweeper, typically a young child small enough to fit inside a chimney and whose parents put to work that drastically curtailed both childhood and life.

Here is Blake's poem with its indictment of parents, king, priest, and God—all of whom he holds responsible for the chimney sweeper's plight:

> A little black thing among the snow:
> Crying "weep, weep," in notes of woe!
> "Where are thy father & mother? Say?"
> "They are both gone up to the church to pray.
>
> Because I was happy upon the heath,
> And smil'd among the winter's snow:

They clothed me in the clothes of death,
And taught me to sing the notes of woe.

And because I am happy, & dance & sing,
They think they have done me no injury:
And are gone to praise God & his Priest & King
Who make up a heaven of our misery."

Blake makes clear whom he holds accountable for the child chimney sweeper's injury, misery, and general woe—parents, churchmen, and political leaders.

New Historicism

Like earlier historical approaches, new historicism considers historical contexts of literary works essential for understanding them. Unlike earlier historical critics, however, new historicists analyze historical documents with the same intense scrutiny they give to literary works. New historicist critics compare and contrast the language of contemporaneous documents and of literary works to reveal hidden assumptions, biases, prejudices, and other cultural attitudes, and to uncover their cultural assumptions.

New historicist critics examine the power relations of rulers and subjects. Other kinds of texts, not only literary works, are considered ideological products culturally constructed by and from the prevailing power structures. These include government documents, explorers' diaries, court records, child-rearing manuals, even institutions such as prisons and hospitals, which are analyzed as "texts."

While appropriating some of the methods of formalist critics, new historicists differ from them in important ways. Unlike the formalists, new historicists explain how a work reveals cultural biases and prejudices. And unlike more traditional historical critics, new historicists do not seek to provide "background" or "context" for the study of literary works. Instead, they analyze non-literary documents alongside literary works to reveal the power relations of human interactions in families and larger social organizations and structures. Historical elements and concerns get equal emphasis with the literary work.

In a study of Shakespeare's play *The Tempest* in *Learning to Curse*, for example, Stephen Greenblatt presents contemporary documents that reflect the imperialist ambitions of England during the Renaissance. Greenblatt shifts the emphasis from Shakespeare's protagonist, Prospero, as magician and stage director of a human drama, to manipulator and executor of an imperialist agenda. Analogously, Chinua Achebe's reading of Joseph Conrad's novella *Heart of Darkness* emphasizes its racist and imperialist aspects—social, cultural, political concerns rather than the imagistic, metaphorical, tonal, and structural ones that would occupy a formalist critic.

New historicist critics attempt to de-familiarize literary works, scrubbing them of encrusted prior scholarship. They emphasize the power of the state and of patriarchal structures, the process of colonialization, and the ways power is assumed, executed, and maintained. By the end of the twenty-first century, new historicism, however, was no longer new. It passed the torch to other literary perspectives and other critical approaches.

Historical and New Historicist Critical Questions

1. When was the work written? When was it published? How was it received by critics and the public? Why?
2. What does the work's reception reveal about the standards of taste during the time it was published and reviewed?
3. What social attitudes and cultural practices related to the action of the work were prevalent during the time it was written and published?
4. What kinds of power relations does the work describe, reflect, or embody?
5. How do the power relations reflected in the work manifest themselves in cultural practices and social institutions prevalent during when the work was written?
6. What other types of historical documents, cultural artifacts, or social institutions might be analyzed in conjunction with particular literary works? How might a close reading of such a nonliterary text illuminate affiliated works of literature?

30 Psychological

Psychological criticism approaches literary works as revelations of their authors' minds and personalities. Psychological critics see literary works as intimately linked with the mental and emotional characteristics of their authors, along with reflections of the writers' consciousness and mental worlds. Some psychological critics explore a writer's creative processes, reading literary works for clues to a writer's creative imagination. Psychological critics study not only the authors of literary works, but also the characters they create, Shakespeare's Hamlet, for example, or Franz Kafka's Gregor Samsa.

Psychoanalytic criticism derives from Sigmund Freud's revolutionary notion of the "unconscious," along with the mechanisms of "displacement," "fixation," and "manifest" and "latent" content, among others. According to Freud, the unconscious harbors forbidden wishes and desires, often sexual, that conflict with a person's or a society's moral standards. The individual represses or censors these unconscious desires, displacing and distorting them in dreams, disguising their real meaning.

Psychoanalytic critics rely heavily on symbolism to explain the meaning of repressed desires, interpreting ordinary objects such as clocks and towers, and natural elements such as fire and water, in terms of a literary character's sexuality. These critics also employ other psychoanalytic concepts such as "fixation" and "obsessive compulsion" linked with feelings, fantasies, and behaviors harbored and enacted by literary characters.

Among the most important and pervasively influential of Freud's categories are those of the "id," "ego," and "superego." The id, for Freud, was the repository of desires, primarily sexual, aggressive, and possessive. The superego represents parental and societal standards of ethical and moral behavior, with the ego as the middle-ground negotiator between the demands of the id and the strictures of the superego.

These varied psychoanalytic terms and concepts have been used by various critics, Freud included, to explain the hidden meanings of literary works. Freud analyzed Sophocles' tragedy *Oedipus Rex* to explain how Oedipus harbored an unconscious desire to kill his father and marry his mother, events the play accounts for. Other critics have used Freud's insights to analyze the

DOI: 10.4324/9781003620280-48

hidden motivations of literary characters. Numerous critics, for example, have psychoanalyzed Hamlet, including Ernest Jones, who used Freud's theory of the "Oedipus complex" to explain Hamlet's delay in killing King Claudius, who murdered Hamlet's father to secure his throne and his queen, Gertrude, Hamlet's mother. According to Jones, Hamlet is unable to punish (kill) Claudius because Claudius did what Hamlet wanted to do himself—kill his father and marry his mother.

Lacanian Psychoanalytical Criticism

More recent psychoanalytical criticism derives from the work of French psychoanalyst Jacques Lacan. Lacan's major emphasis is on the unconscious, not as a complex and chaotic realm, but rather as a coherent and accessible domain, structured like a language. Lacan allies the Freudian dream concepts of condensation and displacement with metaphor and metonymy, respectively. He sees the unconscious as a network of differences. For Lacan and his followers, words and meanings have a life of their own; they undermine and contradict, they override and complicate the clarities and simplifications often ascribed to external reality.

Lacan emphasizes the fractured detachment of words from their referents in the external world. He dismisses literary realism as untenable, rejecting the conventional understanding of literary characters and the process of characterization by which writers create them. Lacan deconstructs the idea of the human subject (and literary character) as a coherent consciousness, emphasizing what has been called the "mirror-stage" of human development, a time when a child recognizes itself as a distinct and separate conscious entity. The pre-conscious state Lacan calls the "imaginary stage," in which no distinction is made between the self and the other, and the later "symbolic stage," in which order and logic define difference. Realist literary works reflect Lacan's symbolic stage; anti-realist literary works embody his imaginary stage.

Whereas Freudian critics emphasize differences between the conscious and the unconscious mind of the author and of characters in literary works, and attend closely to characters' unconscious motives, Lacanian critics attend to unconscious motives and feelings in the text itself, seeking to identify phases and symptoms, such as the mirror-stage and the sovereign role of the unconscious. Whereas, Freudian critics seek to show how literary works embody classic psychoanalytic symptoms and conditions, such as Freud's stages of sexual and emotional development, Lacanian critics treat literary works in terms of "lack," "desire," or other Lacanian concepts. They also view literary works as exhibiting Lacan's views of language and the unconscious. Both types of psychoanalytical critics emphasize the "psychic" context of literary works rather than their formal properties, or their social, cultural, and historical contexts.

Psychological/Psychoanalytical Critical Questions

1. How does your understanding of the characters and character relationships in a literary work help you better understand the mental world and imaginative life of the author?
2. How does a particular literary work—its images, metaphors, and other linguistic resources—reveal the psychological motivations of its characters or the psychological mindset of its author?
3. To what extent can you employ the concepts of Freudian or Lacanian psychoanalysis to understand the motivations of literary characters or the psychology of authors?
4. What kinds of works and what types of literary characters seem best suited to a critical approach that employs a psychological or psychoanalytical perspective?
5. How might a psychological or psychoanalytic approach be productively combined with another critical approach—biographical, historicist, formalist?

31 Sociological

Sociological critics argue that literary works need to be read in terms of the social contexts in which they are inextricably embedded. These critics emphasize how power relations are played out by varying social forces and institutions, allying them, in this regard, with new historicist critics. Sociological critics concern themselves with how social, political, and cultural values are embodied and reflected in works of literature. Some sociological critics treat literary works as documentary products of social conditions. Two significant trends in sociological criticism are Marxist criticism and feminist criticism.

Marxism

Indebted to the political theory of Karl Marx and Friedrich Engels, Marxist critics examine literary works for their reflection of how dominant elites exploit subordinate groups, how people become alienated from one another, and how bourgeois values control and suppress the working classes. Marxist critics see the value of literature in promoting social and economic revolution. Such changes include overthrowing the dominant capitalist ideology and those with money, status, and privilege. Fundamentally, Marxist ideology looks toward a vision of a world in which social hierarchy and social classes have been abolished.

Marxist critics typically approach literary works as products of their era, as influenced, even determined, by economic and political forces prevalent when they were written. Marxist analyses of novels often focus on the relations among classes. In British and European novels of the nineteenth century, for example, class plays a significant role. Novels such as Charles Dickens's *Little Dorrit*, George Eliot's *Middlemarch*, and William Makepeace Thackeray's *Vanity Fair*, among many examples, portray a panoramic vision of society, with characters competing to move up in social position and status. The Marxist perspective has been used most often on fiction and least often on poetry, with drama occupying a middle position for Marxist analysis.

Marxist critics distinguish between the manifest and latent content of literary works, relating the latent or hidden subject matter to basic Marxist ideas, such as class struggle or the horrors of industrial capitalism.

DOI: 10.4324/9781003620280-49

Relating literary works to the social class of their authors, Marxist critics also explain literary works and entire literary genres, such as the novel, in terms of the historical period that produced them. And they connect works of literature to the social assumptions of the time in which they are read or consumed. In short, Marxist critics seek to demonstrate how literary forms and genres are determined by social and political forces.

Marxist Critical Questions

1   What social forces and institutions are represented in the work? How are these forces portrayed? What is the author's attitude toward them?
2   What political elements appear in the work? How important are they in determining or influencing the lives of the characters?
3   What economic issues appear in the course of the work? How important are economic facts in influencing the motivation and behavior of the characters?
4   To what extent are the lives of the characters influenced by social, political, and economic forces? To what extent are the characters aware of these forces?

Feminism

Feminist critics examine the social, economic, and cultural aspects of literary works with respect to the role, position, status, and situation of women. They often see literature both as an arena of contestation for power and control, and as an agent of social transformation. Feminist critics work to redress the imbalance of literary study through the study of women writers whose works have been neglected, marginalized, or denigrated. They also study how feminine consciousness has been portrayed in literary works by both male and female writers.

Feminist critics of the novels cited a moment ago in our discussion of Marxist criticism would shift the emphasis from social and economic matters to those of gender and power relations. A feminist perspective on Dickens's *Little Dorrit*, for example, would focus on the title character and her relations with the men in her life rather than on the functions of bureaucracy and large social forces that interest Marxist critics. Similarly, a feminist reading of Eliot's *Middlemarch* would stress the ways Dorothea Brooke's marriage to Casaubon constrains her freedom and damages her hopes for happiness. A feminist reading of Thackeray's *Vanity Fair* would view its social-climbing protagonist Becky Sharp through the causes and consequences of her rise and fall within the context of gender and power relationships.

A feminist approach to Emily Dickinson's poem "I'm 'wife'" would be alert to why the speaker compares herself to a czar and what that means in terms of her ability to exert her will and control her destiny. Feminist readers would likely also consider why the state of wifehood brings "comfort" and girlhood "pain." They would consider how such differences were reflected in marriages during Dickinson's lifetime. They might wonder also whether the insistent tone of the poem's abrupt ending "I'm 'Wife'! Stop there!" might mask an undercurrent of fear or powerlessness.

Feminist critics have enlarged the canon by discovering overlooked women writers, highlighting their importance and the value of their literary achievements and contributions. They analyze how women are represented in literature, challenging representations of women as subordinate to men. They analyze power relations and the dominance of patriarchy in literary works, while deemphasizing biological sex differences, stressing instead the social construction of gender. Feminist critics also use psychoanalysis to explore aspects of female (and male) identity through considering the role of language in representing gender. And they provide new analyses and interpretations of canonical works with more complex representations of female identity and experience.

Feminist Critical Questions

1   To what extent does the representation of women in the work reflect the time and place in which it was written?
2   How are women portrayed in the work? How are relations between men and women and between and among women presented in the work?
3   To what extent is the work presented from within a male or female sensibility or perspective? How is this manifested in the work?
4   To what extent and how do the facts of the author's life and social, economic, and political contexts relate to the presentation of women (and men) in the work?
5   How do other works by the author correspond to the work in the depiction of the power relationships between men and women?
6   How is women's sexuality presented and explored in the work?

A Note on Queer Theory

Lesbian feminism, a species of feminist criticism generally, is less inclined to emphasize the commonalities women share, and instead focus on their differences, as, for example, differences among the experience of white and black women, or cultural differences among women of Asian-American and African-American heritage. Critics who work from a lesbian and gay critical perspective make sexual orientation a basic category of textual analysis. Their writing resists homophobic attitudes and complicates simplistic stereotypical representations, descriptions, and understandings of homosexual identities and experiences. Their work often focuses on what it means to be a lesbian woman or a gay man in a homophobic and non-homocentric world.

For queer theorists, identity is not a given, but is instead constructed. Gender, they argue, is less what one is than what one does, a condition one enacts by repeated iterations of resistance to repression and subversion of socially standardized gender categories. Moreover, identity is fluid. For example, gay identity might be announced openly to friends and family, more selectively indicated at work among colleagues and employers, and perhaps concealed from institutions, such as banks and insurance companies. Queer theorists also question the stability of heterosexual/homosexual identities. Queer theorists analyze how gender is portrayed and conveyed in literary works, and especially how forms of lesbian, gay, bisexual, transgender, and queer sexuality are represented or repressed.

Queer Theory Critical Questions

1. How is gender portrayed and conveyed in the work?
2. To what extent does gender portrayal in the work extend beyond traditional heterosexual identities?
3. To what extent are forms of lesbian, gay, bisexual, transgender, and queer sexuality either represented or repressed in the work?
4. To what extent is gender shown to be fluid? In what ways and with what consequences?
5. How are gender relationships portrayed in the work? To what extent and in what ways do the portrayal of gender and gender relationships link up with issues of mastery and power?

32 Mythological

In general terms, a "myth" is a story that explains how something came to be. Every culture creates such stories to explain what it considers important, valuable, and true. The Greek myth of Persephone, for example, which describes how she is kidnapped by Pluto, god of the underworld, and returned to her mother Demeter each year, explains why the seasons change. And the biblical story of Eve's temptation by the serpent in the book of Genesis, which concludes with God's curse of the serpent, explains why snakes crawl on their bellies, and why human beings experience physical suffering, including the pains of childbirth.

Mythological criticism, however, is concerned less with such originating stories than with stories that provide universally recurring patterns. The patterns myth critics typically analyze are those that represent common human experiences, such as being born and dying, crossing the threshold into adulthood, going on a journey, engaging in sexual activity, and the like. Birth, for example, is of interest as a symbolic beginning and death as a symbolic ending. A journey symbolizes a venture into the world to engage in exploration and experience. Sleep and dreams represent modes of entrance into another realm beyond that of waking life. Physical contests and encounters serve as forms of testing challenge, initiation into advanced states of responsibility, as, for example, becoming a warrior or chief, priest or prophet, mother or monarch.

Some myth critics, those influenced by the psychologist C. G. Jung, for example, emphasize *archetypes*, universal symbols believed to be part of every individual's unconscious mind, a kind of collective unconscious all people inherit. Examples of some of these archetypes include the womanizer or Don Juan, the *femme fatale* or dangerous female, the trickster or con artist, the damsel in distress, the betrayer, the rebel, the hero.

Myth critics focus heavily on a story's plot, especially on its patterns of recurrence. Stories of the arduous quest fraught with perils are common—Harry Potter novels, Tolkien's *The Lord of the Rings*, Jason and the Argonauts, and many ancient stories, for example, as are stories of revenge, death and destruction, resurrection and transformation. Many such stories can be found in the world's religious literatures. The Christian Bible, for example,

DOI: 10.4324/9781003620280-50

contains creation stories, stories of sibling rivalry (Cain and Abel, for example, and Joseph and his brothers), destruction and forgiveness (Noah and the Ark), death and resurrection (Jesus). There are also stories of "apocalypse" or last things, such as the biblical book Revelation, which describes the catastrophes predicted to befall humankind when the world comes to an end.

Myth critics approach the study of literary works and a culture's myths in many ways, including identifying mythic figures and events in literary works, along with recognizing mythic themes and patterns. In his *Anatomy of Criticism*, Northrop Frye, for example, explains the traditional literary genres, including novel, drama, and epic, with reference to the recurrence of mythic patterns such as death and rebirth, departure and return, ignorance and insight. Frye associates the genres of romance, comedy, tragedy, and satire with the cycle of the seasons, stages in the day, and aspects of consciousness. Romance is linked with the fertility of spring, with sunrise, awakening, and the birth of the hero (186 ff.). Comedy is associated with summer, midday, full consciousness, and the triumph of the hero (163 ff.). Tragedy parallels autumn, sunset, dreams, and the hero's alienation (206 ff.). Satire reflects winter, night, sleep, and the hero's death (223 ff.).

The mythic categories can be considered with respect to epic poems, such as Homer's *Iliad* and *Odyssey*, the Hindu epics *The Ramayana* and *The Mahabharata*, as well as to dramatic works such as the Oedipus plays of Sophocles and the plays by Aeschylus about the house of Atreus, including the myths about Agamemnon and his faithless wife Clytemnestra and their vengeful children Orestes and Electra.

Mythological critics also make connections between literary works and the social science of anthropology. They also interpret works of literature in terms of large-scale concepts related to religious belief, such as the afterlife, and philosophical ideals, including that of a utopian paradise or a dystopian repressive society.

Mythological Critical Questions

1 What incidents in the work seem as if they could be symbolic or archetypal?
2 Are there any journeys, battles, contests, or reversals of fortune? Why are they important?
3 What kinds of character types appear in the work?
4 What creatures, elements of nature, or man-made objects that play a role in the work might be considered symbolic?
5 What religious or quasi-religious traditions might the work's story, characters, elements, or objects be compared to or affiliated with?

33 Structuralist

The word "structure" as used by non-structuralist critics differs from its use by structuralist literary critics. In the traditional sense, "structure" refers to the organization of a literary work—to its plot, its stanzas or other parts, its use of repetition and contrast, its patterns of imagery and sound, rhythm and rhyme, for example. For structuralist critics, however, "structure" has another meaning, one that derives from linguistics and anthropology. Structuralists speak of how language is an arbitrary system of "signs," part of a semiotic system of codes. It is these signs and codes that constitute the heart of the structuralist approach to literary analysis.

We can illustrate with the example of the word "dog." Why do the letters D-O-G when put together signify the creature who barks at the mail carrier and wags its tail while running off with our sneakers? Only because of a particular set of linguistic conventions. That the letters D-O-G represent our canine companion is an arbitrary agreement that could have been otherwise. And it is otherwise in different languages. In French, for example the English "dog" is "*chien*" (pronounced Shuh-YEN); in Italian "dog" is "*cane*" (pronounced CAH-nay), a word pronounced differently in English, and referring to a walking stick or a particular-shaped peppermint candy.

An additional structuralist linguistic element is difference. In all languages words are differentiated from one another by sound and by spelling. Thus, in English C-A-N-E can be a walking stick, but C-O-N-E and C-A-P-E, each with a single differentiating letter from "cane," signify entirely unrelated things. Structuralist critics analyze difference via "binary opposition," in which they examine a text's contrasting elements. Structuralist critics find all kinds of oppositions in literature, from small-scale elements, such as letters and syllables; through symbols, such as light and dark; to motions or directions (up and down), times (before and after), places (inside and outside), distances (far and near); to elements of plot and character, as well as gender differentiation. Such significant structural oppositions require interpretation.

Structuralist analysis can be applied to a range of subjects—everything from football games and wrestling matches to political practices and economic activity. Anything can be examined from a structuralist/semiotic perspective: fashion shows, newspaper cartoons, aerobic exercises, restaurant

DOI: 10.4324/9781003620280-51

menus, food pairings such as wine and cheese, Greta Garbo's face, Roman haircuts, and more, as Roland Barthes has demonstrated in his book *Mythologies*. And though structuralism has been deployed heavily in the analysis of narrative texts, it has also been used to analyze poems.

Structuralist Critical Questions

1. What are the elements of the work, and how do those elements reveal difference?
2. How do the characters, narrators, speakers, or other voices in the work reveal difference? And what do those types of difference signify?
3. How do the elements of the work's plot or structure suggest meaningful patterns? What changes, adjustments, transformations, shifts of tone, attitude, behavior, or feeling do you find and what is their significance?
4. What system of relationships governs the work as a whole?
5. What system of relations could link this work with others of its kind or type?
6. How do these various structuralist elements "signify" in the broadest sense of the word, to influence, affect, and determine the interpretation of literary works?

A Note on Semiotics

Semiotics is the study of signs and sign systems; more importantly, it is the study of codes, the systems we use to understand the meaning of events and entities, from poems and songs to advertisements, institutions, and cultural happenings. Culturally coded sign systems enable us to understand the implications and significance of everything from films and television game shows to football and soccer games, to parades, religious rituals, Halloween and New Year's parties.

Fairy tales and folktales have long been a popular subject for structuralist critics with a semiotic inclination. Consider, for example, Cinderella, her beauty in opposition to her stepsisters' ugliness, her poverty to their wealth, her servitude to their social superiority. Difference functions throughout the tale, including Cinderella's reversal of fortune, as a prince displaces the nasty stepmother. The Cinderella story has had many updates, as exemplified by Rossini's opera *La Cenerentola*, for example, and the films *Pretty Woman* and *Maid in Manhattan*, which update its many binary oppositions.

In the study of literature, semiotics conceives of literary works as texts, seeing them as open and incomplete. Literary meaning is made by individual readers applying codes of grammar, semantics, and culture available to them. Structuralist critics analyze prose narratives and relate them to conventions of genre, networks of inter-textual relations, and models of narrative structure.

Structuralist semioticians connect literary structures with the structures of language; they use the system of signs to analyze patterns and structures of many cultural domains, including cultural myths and monuments, as well as works of literature.

34 Deconstructionist

Deconstruction emerged as a further development of structuralism. Like their structuralist counterparts, deconstructive critics look for oppositions in literary works and in other kinds of texts, such as films, ads, and social institutions, including schools, hospitals, and prisons. According to its founding father, Jacques Derrida, "deconstruction is neither a theory nor a philosophy…neither a school nor a method. It is not even a discourse, nor an act, nor a practice" (Iser 120).

Like structuralism, deconstruction emphasizes differences, or the structure of constituent opposition in a text or any signifying system (for example, male/female, black/white, animate/inanimate). For deconstructionist critics, any meaning is constructed as the result of an opposition always ideologically grounded. Deconstructing oppositions reveals how they are not inevitable, but instead are constructed out of discourses that rely on those oppositions, such as mind/body, literal/metaphorical, nature/culture, and speech/writing.

Deconstruction differs from structuralism, however, in at once describing a pair of equally valid conflicting oppositions while also identifying a prevailing ideology that needs to be challenged, undermined, subverted. Deconstructive critics unravel the text by identifying places where it is ambivalent, contradictory, or ambiguous—in some way at odds with itself.

For deconstructive critics texts deconstruct themselves; the critic simply points out how this happens. These critics argue, further, that the contradictions found in literary and other texts are inherent in the nature of language, which functions essentially as a system of oppositions and differences that undermine its own stability, making the discovery of meaning, essentially, impossible.

Deconstructionist critics operate on the principle that language is self-contradictory and self-destroying. Since language is unstable, texts are unstable. Literary works, thus, mean more and other than their authors intended or are aware of. Terms such as "unmasking," "unraveling," "suppression," and "contradiction" are common in the lexicon of deconstruction. These terms are used to demonstrate how literary works never mean what they appear to mean, but instead betray and subvert themselves in contradictory and self-destructive ways.

DOI: 10.4324/9781003620280-52

A crucial notion for deconstructionist criticism is "difference," or "*différance*" as the seminal deconstructionist critic Jacques Derrida spells it. By *différance*, Derrida means both the usual meaning of difference (dissimilarity) and the additional idea of deferral, both derived from the two meanings of the French verb *différer*, which means "to differ" and "to defer" or "postpone." The kind of difference meant by Derrida is a deferral of meaning that is never completed because a text or utterance means whatever it means as a function of differences among its elements. Meaning thus is indefinitely postponed, endlessly deferred, and thus ever elusive and incomplete.

An essential aspect of *différance*, for Derrida, is how every claim, concept, idea, distinction, includes an alternative conception or distinction implied or hinted at but not explicitly made. One way of seeing the aim of deconstruction is as a way to recover lost possibilities beyond those claimed and articulated and argued for. In this sense, to tame it a bit, deconstructive criticism constantly reminds us that our way of thinking, analyzing, and understanding a text or a work is not the only way—that it is merely one way among many others. And that we can never get to the end of them.

Deconstructive Critical Questions

1 What oppositions exist in the work? Which of the two opposing terms of each pair is the privileged or more powerful term? How is this illustrated in the work?
2 What textual elements suggest a contradiction or alternative to the privileged or more powerful term or category?
3 What is the prevailing ideology or set of cultural assumptions in the work? Where are these prevailing assumptions most in evidence?
4 What passages of the work most reveal gaps, inconsistencies, or contradictions?
5 How stable is the text? How decidable is its meaning? What textual aspects or elements are complicit in destabilizing it?

A Note on Post-Structuralism

Post-structuralism, another way of describing deconstruction, represents a radical break with previous ways of reading and understanding literary works. Deriving from philosophy rather than from linguistics, post-structuralism posits a world of radical discontinuity and inherent opaqueness and unknowability. Post-structuralist critics refer to a decentered universe, one with no fixed reference points and no agreed upon standards by which to measure and assess anything.

Post-structuralist critics engage in deconstructing literary texts through showing their inherent contradictions, inadequacies, and incompleteness. The post-structuralist outlook has been characterized as one of "linguistic anxiety" because language is inherently unstable and unable to construct solid and certified meanings. The instability of language and the erasure of meaning lead to a deep skepticism about what literature reveals about the external world and about what it is saying about itself.

Where structuralist critics seek parallels and balances, post-structuralist critics seek shifts, breaks, and contradictions. Where structuralists seek reflections and repetitions, their post-structuralist counterparts seek conflicts. Where structuralist critics look for patterns, contrasts, and symmetry, with the goal of revealing textual unity and coherence, post-structuralist critics ferret out absences and omissions, linguistic oddities and impasses, to reveal textual disunity and instability.

35 Postcolonial

Postcolonial criticism has a strong, overt political orientation. It shares with feminist and Marxist critical perspectives a concern for power relations and imbalances, and for how political power manifests itself in works of literature. Postcolonial critics repudiate traditional literary beliefs and values about the timeless universality of literary works, emphasizing instead how they embody conflict and dissonance. Essentially, postcolonial theory attempts to understand and explain the problems created by European colonial exploitation and its consequences.

With cultural materialists, postcolonial critics share a concern with particular groups of people reclaiming their distinctive identities and their histories. Postcolonial critics devalue the colonialist ideology in all its manifestations and consequences, including ways it has marginalized and devalued native peoples and their cultural beliefs and practices.

Euro-centrism takes for granted that the values of colonizing powers are the right ones, that European values are superior to those European powers colonized. Postcolonial critics repudiate the notion that the "other"—those who differ from the white European norm—are considered in the mass rather than as individual distinct persons. Black and Asian people are homogeneously seen as strange and different, almost as a mass of undifferentiated stuff.

In her essay "On Seeing England for the First Time," Jamaica Kincaid describes how she was taught to value everything English and to celebrate the achievements of the British to the denigration of her Antiguan island culture. Kincaid explains how she and her island friends eat a big English breakfast because that's what they do in England. She describes her father wearing a wide-brimmed felt hat in the hot Antiguan climate because it bears the mark of an English manufacturer. "The world was theirs not mine; everything told me so" (336), she writes.

In *Beginning Theory*, Peter Barry describes a three-stage process in which postcolonial literatures transition from literary subservience to literary freedom (198). In the first stage, a colonized country adopts the forms of the colonizer's literature, which provides the norm of value to be emulated. In a second stage, the colonized adapt the literature of the colonizing power. This

DOI: 10.4324/9781003620280-53

adapting phase transitions to a third stage in which the colonized country declares its cultural and literary independence. Barry refers to this third stage as the "adept" stage, since colonial writers have proceeded beyond imitation and adaptation to becoming adept at creating their own distinctive literatures.

Postcolonial critics lament the situation that Kincaid describes and expose how the colonial values imposed on the colonized destroy and devalue what it uses. In Jane Austen's novel *Mansfield Park*, for example, the beautiful English estate of that name can exist only because its lord of the manor, Sir Thomas Bertram, owns and operates an estate in Antigua, in which the work of slaves on his sugar plantation makes possible his wealth and social prominence. Postcolonial critics move such observations and considerations to the center of the critical enterprise instead of keeping them in the background, neither ignoring them altogether nor minimizing their importance.

Language is another arena in which postcolonial critics challenge the assumptions and values of the colonizing powers. They ask: Whose language is the language of power and prominence? Whose English is admired and celebrated, and whose English is reviled and denigrated? How do literary works describe and reveal, portray and conceal conflicting linguistic ideologies?

A number of Irish writers take up these questions in various ways. Poems by William Butler Yeats and Seamus Heaney, and plays by Lady Gregory represent arenas in which the King's English, the dominant English style and idiom, lords it over other English idioms and dialects. In the southwestern United States where Spanish is a significant linguistic presence, we might ask: What is the relationship between English and Spanish? How do speakers and writers fluent in both languages demonstrate, reveal, and conceal their conflicting cultural and linguistic loyalties?

Postcolonial critics reveal how more traditional critical perspectives make unjustified assumptions about the centrality of Eurocentric beliefs, customs, ideas, and attitudes. They study the representation of other cultures in works of literature. They expose how classic literary works remain silent about colonial and imperialist ambitions and consequences. They also highlight questions about cultural difference and analyze their appearance in literary works. And they invest the concept of the "other" with value and importance, as a source of purpose and power.

Postcolonial Critical Questions

1 How are the colonizers and the colonized depicted in the work?
2 Which are the norms that define the central and dominant values of the work? Whose norms are they?
3 To what extent are competing languages or dialects at play in the work?
4 To what extent is cultural otherness, difference, and diversity celebrated or denigrated in the work?

5 What kinds of social, economic, and cultural privileges (or the lack thereof) are revealed in character relationships in the work?
6 To what extent might various kinds of ugliness, unpleasantness, nastiness, brutality, and other forms of oppression have been masked, obscured, or otherwise hidden in the work?

36 Ecocritical

Ecocritics study the relationship between literature and nature. Ecocriticism has its origins in the writings of three important nineteenth-century American writers: Ralph Waldo Emerson, Margaret Fuller, and Henry David Thoreau. Among the goals of these and other transcendentalist writers and thinkers was to separate themselves from the influence of European writers, and declare their intellectual, literary, and cultural independence.

Emerson's first important book from an ecocritical perspective was *Nature* (1836), in which he explores how nature impacts human life and thought. For Emerson, nature is beneficent; it brings good things to human beings, among them joy and freedom and exhilaration. Nature, for Emerson, is also a moral teacher whose truths are eternal and unchanging (26–31).

Margaret Fuller's *Summer on the Lakes* (1843) offers her reflections in journal form about the power and grandeur of nature. She sees in nature "a perpetual creation" and "an incessant, indefatigable motion" (4). Fuller's book represents what was to become a popular form of nature writing—the journal of time spent alone amid the sublime beauty and majestic nature of the physical world. Works such as John Muir's *The Mountains of California* and *My First Summer in the Sierras* provide notable examples.

Thoreau's classic *Walden*, which recounts the two years and two months he spent in a cabin he built on the shore of Walden Pond in Massachusetts, is among the best-known works representing the return to nature. In one chapter, Thoreau invites his readers to "spend one day as deliberately as Nature" (399), encouraging them to experience the natural organic rhythm of a day rather than the artificial measure of mechanical time imposed by clocks.

In England, nature writing has had a long tradition, primarily as pastoral poetry. Pastoral poems have been written from as early as the Middle Ages, becoming especially popular during the Renaissance. Pastoral motifs can be found in many of Shakespeare's plays, especially in the comedies. During the nineteenth century British literature (along with American and continental European literatures) reflected an increased emphasis on nature. Poetry and prose by writers such as Jane Austen, William Blake, Samuel Taylor

DOI: 10.4324/9781003620280-54

Coleridge, Thomas Hardy, Gerard Manley Hopkins, John Keats, Percy Bysshe Shelley, and William Wordsworth—in England alone—make nature both powerfully visible and a dominant symbol and idea.

Peter Barry identifies four areas in which nature attracts ecocritical attention:

- The Wilderness (deserts, oceans, uninhabited continents)
- The Scenic Sublime (forests, lakes, mountains, cliffs, waterfalls)
- The Countryside (hills, fields, and woods)
- The Domestic Picturesque (parks, gardens, lanes)

Barry suggests that we can consider a movement from "wilderness" to "the domestic picturesque" in relation to culture—with wilderness reflecting an absence of culture, the scenic sublime and countryside an increasing impact of culture, and the domestic picturesque with its parks and gardens an acculturated form of nature—nature tamed and domesticated (255–256).

Considering canonical works from an ecocritical perspective foregrounds nature and the environment. Nathaniel Hawthorne's "Roger Malvin's Burial" and "Young Goodman Brown" ecocritically shift readers' attention from the moral and psychological concerns of Puritanism to the forest as "character" and symbol. This significant aspect of nature in Hawthorne's stories contrasts an ecocritical perspective civilization and the village and what their symbolic link with moral and psychological concerns.

In *The Song of the Earth*, in an ecocritical reading of John Keats's ode "To Autumn," Jonathan Bate suggests that the world of the poem resembles "a well-regulated ecosystem" (106). Bate claims that Keats possesses an "intuitive understanding of the underlying law of community ecology" (106), and that this is displayed through the ways Keats creates contiguity between and among elements, making the poem itself a system of "networks, links, bonds and correspondences" (105), all of which serve to "renounce the quest for aesthetic transcendence" and instead "embrace[s] the immanence of nature's time, the cycle of the seasons" (109).

Ecological critics investigate the representation of nature and the natural world in literary works. In their analysis of literature, they employ ecocentric concepts such as growth and decay, symbiosis and sustainability. They also broaden the categories of literature to include "nature" writing, travel writing, essays, and other forms of non-imaginative literature. And they value in works of literature and call out their presence or absence such aspects as ethical responsibility, consideration of others, including animals and other living things.

Ecocriticism Critical Questions

1   How is nature depicted in the work? What aspects of the natural world are highlighted?

2 What is the relationship in the work between the human and the natural worlds?
3 To what extent are aspects of the natural world in conflict with one another or with the human world?
4 What "green" values does the work embody or celebrate, disparage or mask?

37 Influence and Values

Another way to think about literature from the perspective of theory is that of literary influence and values. Literary influence can cause a writer considerable "anxiety," according to Harold Bloom, whose *The Anxiety of Influence* describes how later writers wrestle with precursors, trying to overcome their influence through metaphorically "killing them off." Bloom argues that a writer breaks free of powerful precursors by rewriting their works anew, deliberately "misreading" them and, in the process, "correcting" the earlier literary masters.

Each successor derives something of importance and value from the poetic precursor. In order to make that derivation productive, however, the successor needs, if not to "kill" the literary predecessor, to at least circumvent the direct powerful influence, which would otherwise be debilitating. Underlying Bloom's theorizing are Freud and Nietzsche, and prior to them lie the biblical Adam and Satan.

Bloom's concept of misreading requires the later poet to find a way to re-conceptualize the influential master poet's work. For Bloom, poetic misreading is an act of survival for the later poet. Although John Keats needs William Wordsworth as model and influence, he also needs to move beyond him, if not to surpass him; Keats needs to find another direction for his poetic impulse; he needs to find a way to make Wordsworth's poetry matter, but without allowing his precursor's influence to stifle his own poetic originality.

Bloom's later book *The Anatomy of Influence* traces the concept of influence further and explores it differently. Bloom considers how writers influence themselves—how a writer's early work influences the later work. This kind of "self-influence," Bloom argues, is as powerful and important as the influence of earlier writers on later ones. It causes similar kinds of "anxious expectations" (14) and equally complex struggles to works of literature that develop a writer's literary mastery in spite of the influence of his earlier work.

Let two examples suffice. The first, Thomas Hardy, was a talented and well-regarded novelist, even a popular one. However, once his novels began to deal with controversial topics, including sex, the critical response to his work became entangled in Victorian morality. Embittered by the response to novels such as *Tess of the D'Urbervilles* and *Jude the Obscure*, Hardy abandoned novel writing and devoted himself to poetry, which he wrote, exclusively, for the last thirty years of his life. And so, Hardy became a kind of victim, if not directly, of literary influence, of changing mores and shifting attitudes towards what was acceptable in the public's reception of novel writing.

A second example is William Butler Yeats, whose influence has been confined within a small domain. It's less a matter of Yeats's influence on later poets, Wallace Stevens among them, perhaps, than of Yeats's "influence" on himself—with his earlier poems influencing his later ones.

The Value of Literature

Literature is one of language's supreme manifestations. Literary works make maximum, ultimate use of language as they mold, shape, and construct worlds out of words. In the process, literature provokes our thinking. Literature raises serious questions, as Marjorie Garber notes in *The Use and Abuse of Literature*: "What is the use of literature? Does it make us happier, more ethical, more articulate?" (8). Behind these questions lies an assumption: that literature might have, perhaps even must have, a practical purpose, a use to which it can be put. Garber continues in this vein, asking an additional series of purpose-driven questions. She asks, for example, whether literature might "make us more human" and "better rounded individuals" (8).

The fundamental question Garber asks is whether literature is somehow "good" for us. Whatever answer we might make to that question is another related aspect of literature: the extent to which it gives us pleasure—the extent to which we simply enjoy reading literary works. This aspect of literature we might simply call its "feel-good" aspect.

We thus have two distinct and distinctive ways of thinking about literature—as something that is somehow "good for us," and as something that in some way makes us "feel good" (10). These two values suggest, additionally, how literature can be personally valuable for us, either as self-enhancing approval, suggests Andrew Elfenbein in *The Gist of Reading*, or as self-criticism, highlighting our limitations and deficiencies (174).

Literature also possesses cultural and social value; it can increase our ability to empathize with others. Literature invites us to participate imaginatively in the lives of others. In a form of empathic reading, we project ourselves into other worlds, other lives, other ways of thinking and feeling—and thereby extend the range of our own experience.

In *A Little History of Literature*, John Sutherland claims that literature provides us with a representation of "the human mind at the height of its ability to express and interpret the world" (6). Its value is that "it enlarges our minds and sensibilities" (6) so that we can deal more competently with life's complexities. Literature, in Sutherland's words, "helps make sense of the infinitely perplexing situations" (4) in which we find ourselves as human beings.

We read literature because it enriches our lives; literature helps us navigate the challenges life presents.

Literature helps us make sense of the world and helps us make sense of ourselves. It does this through putting us in conversation with writers and with each other about their books in various genres.

Literature brings the past to life for us; it memorializes the present; it imagines the future. Literature breaks down barriers of time and place, as Walt Whitman famously and beautifully suggests in "Crossing Brooklyn Ferry":

> It avails not, time nor place—distance avails not,
> I am with you, you men and women of a generation, or ever so many generations hence,
> Just as you feel when you look on the river and sky, so I felt,
> Just as any of you is one of a living crowd, I was one of a crowd....
>
> What is it then between us?
> What is the count of the scores or hundreds of years between us?
> Whatever it is, it avails not—distance avails not, and place avails not....

For the time and effort we invest in reading and analyzing it, literature provides many kinds of value. Literature enriches our lives, providing pleasure as well as knowledge. It is valuable in and of and for itself; it is valuable for its intrinsic rewards, as well as for the variety of extrinsic benefits it affords us.

Influence and Values Critical Questions

1. Which literary works—or other kinds of philosophical, psychological, sociological, or anthropological works—had an impact on the literary work?
2. What kind of influence or impact did that earlier work—or those earlier works—have?
3. What values—social, political, cultural, religious, and more—does the work embody or reflect?
4. What values does the work reject?
5. How do the values embedded or embodied in and/or endorsed by the work connect with the values of readers?

Appendix
Writing about Literature

Why write about works of literature? One answer is that writing about literary works deepens our understanding and appreciation of them. Writing stimulates our thinking about literature. Writing about literature triggers questions about what we read.

We can approach the challenge of writing about literature with the following framework: response, interpretation, evaluation. Three types of questions are essential; each is linked with a specific purpose for writing.

- Questions that invite reaction and response; writing to understand.
- Questions that encourage interpretation; writing to explain.
- Questions that require evaluation or judgment; writing to evaluate.

In writing to understand, we write to make sense of literary works for ourselves.

This writing is exploratory, and may involve annotating, listing, freewriting, and making notes.

In writing to explain, we focus on interpreting, making inferences based on our observations about works. This writing is more formal and is directed toward others. It is more explanatory than exploratory.

In writing to evaluate, we consider why works of literature matter. We consider both their value and their values. We make judgments about their aesthetic quality and their effectiveness; we also consider the social, moral, cultural, and other values they reflect, or embody, or endorse.

Responding

When you read a poem or story, a play or essay, your thoughts and emotions may be stirred. You are likely to respond. When you are moved by a work, when it makes a strong and meaningful impression, you begin to live with it and let it live in you. It may affect how you think about the world, even how you think about and live your life. Your response is personal; it's based upon your own experience and your subjective reactions to what you read.

To respond fully to any work of literature, you have to give it time to work on you, speak to you, time to engage your thinking and feeling. Your response will vary as you read different literary works. And it will vary as you read a single work at different times, including different stages of your life.

In the following poem, "When I Heard the Learn'd Astronomer," Walt Whitman describes the reaction of a person (the poem's speaker) listening to an astronomy lecture. As you read, consider why the speaker responds as he does, and how you might respond in his situation.

> When I heard the learn'd astronomer,
> When the proofs, the figures, were ranged in columns before me,
> When I was shown the charts and diagrams, to add, divide, and measure them,
> When I sitting heard the astronomer where he lectured with much applause in the lecture room,
> How soon unaccountable I became tired and sick,
> Till rising and gliding out I wander'd off by myself,
> In the mystical moist night-air, and from time to time,
> Look'd up in perfect silence at the stars.

Exercise 1

How do you respond to Whitman's poem? Take into account both the lecture room experience and the nature experience described. How does your experience compare with the poem's speaker?

Interpreting

When we interpret a literary work, we ask what the work means, what it suggests rather than how it affects us. Interpretation aims at understanding, at intellectual comprehension rather than emotional apprehension. Where response is primarily subjective, interpretation aims for something more objective.

In reading a poem, for example, we notice details about its language and structure—its rhyme or lack of it, its stanza structure or form, its word choice and sentence patterns. In reading a novel, we attend to its plot and structure, its characters and their relationships, its setting, recurring patterns of image and event, its use of dialogue and description.

In reading a play, we notice its setting and staging, its props and stage directions, its dialogues and monologues, its subtext, organization into acts and scenes and smaller structural units—its dramatic action. In reading an essay, we focus on idea and evidence, on how writers reveal and support their thinking, how the mind makes itself known and felt on the page.

Interpretation requires intellectual risks, involving speculation about the significance of a work and its details. Literary interpretation is based on inferences we make, as we connect and relate a work's details and begin wondering what they might suggest. The interpretation we make of any work is subject to revision—to change based upon further noticing, deeper thinking, additional experience.

Interpretation involves making sense of a work. To interpret we do the following:

- We make observations about its details.
- We establish connections among our observations.
- We develop inferences based on those connections.
- We formulate a conclusion based on our inferences.

You can follow a similar procedure to interpret Whitman's poem. Use the following questions as a guide through the process of making observations, establishing connections, developing inferences, and formulating an interpretive conclusion.

Exercise 2

Making observations:

- What do the following words have in common: *proofs, figures, columns, charts, diagrams, add, divide, measure*? Where do these words occur? Why might that be significant?
- How many sentences are in the poem? How many stanzas? If you were to divide the poem, where would you break it, and why?
- What human figures appear in the poem? What natural elements? How often does the word "I" occur?

Establishing connections:

- What relationship exists between the first four lines and the last four? Describe that relationship.
- What is the relationship between the words identified in question 1 and the following words: "mystical moist night-air" and "perfect silence"?
- How are these sets of details related: noise and quiet; sitting and standing and walking out; inside and outside; being with others and being alone.

Developing inferences:

- What do you infer from the speaker's getting up and walking out of the lecture room?
- What do you infer from the applause the lecturer receives?
- What do you infer about the speaker's experience as described in the last line?

Formulating a conclusion:

- Do you think that Whitman's poem is about education? About different kinds of learning? If so, how might they be described or characterized? What else might the poem be "about"?
- To what extent, for example, can we see the poem as being about "nature," or about the relationship between nature and people?

Exercise 3

Based on your answers to the previous exercise questions, write a couple of paragraphs formulating your interpretation of Whitman's "Astronomer." What do you think the poet is saying to his readers? On what basis—on which of the poem's details of language and structure—do you base your interpretation?

Evaluating

Normally, when we speak of evaluation, we mean making a judgment about quality, about an achievement, about the expressive qualities of a work. Another way to think about evaluation, however, is as an appraisal of a work's social, moral, cultural, and aesthetic ideals. In doing this second kind of evaluating, we bring to bear our own values, norms, and beliefs, on the work.

Evaluation is complex. It involves not only our individual convictions and knowledge, but also our assumptions and biases and lack of knowledge. Moreover, as our lives and outlooks change, our beliefs and values may alter as well. A film we once admired may come to seem trivial or even offensive. A painting or piece of music we once disliked we may later find interesting and even engaging. So too with works of literature.

And just as our individual tastes may change over time, so too do cultural tastes in art, music, and literature change. Since works of literary art are created in particular moments of time, and place, which carry with them varied social and cultural attitudes, beliefs, and dispositions, those works can reflect and embody those values. And to complicate matters further, works of literary art are sometimes, perhaps often, at odds with the social and cultural values of their time. Particular works, as well as entire styles of literature, can go in and out of fashion, waxing and waning in popularity and cultural relevance over time.

Exercise 4

Think of a literary work that conveys interesting and significant social, cultural, political, religious, or other values. What values does the work reflect, convey, or embody? How do those values relate to your own values? To what extent have the values reflected, conveyed, or embodied in the work had an impact—on you, on others, on other works of literature?

The Writing Process—an Overview

Whenever we write we need to identify a topic and develop an idea about it. We also need to create an organizational structure that suits the evidence you present to develop and support your ideas. In doing these things, writers typically follow a three-stage process that consists of prewriting, drafting, and revising. Two additional smaller steps—editing and proofreading—follow the larger stages of the writing process.

Prewriting

Prewriting involves initial efforts. It includes making lists, jotting annotations, posing questions, freewriting, and other preliminary reading/writing/thinking strategies. We can use the following sonnet by William Shakespeare to illustrate some prewriting strategies.

> That time of year thou may'st in me behold
> When yellow leaves, or none, or few, do hang
> Upon those boughs which shake against the cold,
> Bare ruin'd choirs, where late the sweet birds sang.
> In me thou see'st the twilight of such day
> As after sunset fadeth in the west,
> Which by and by black night doth take away,
> Death's second self, that seals up all in rest.
> In me thou see'st the glowing of such fire
> That on the ashes of his youth doth lie,
> As the death-bed whereon it must expire,
> Consum'd with that which it was nourish'd by.
> This thou perceiv'st, which makes thy love more strong,
> To love that well which thou must leave ere long.

Listing

In preparing to write an analysis of this sonnet, you might list details you observe. Your list might look something like this:

that time	sunset
me	black night
yellow leaves	glowing fire
no leaves	ashes
few leaves	youth
bare boughs	death-bed
ruined choirs	love

238   *Appendix*

Such a list can help you isolate particular details and images. You might notice, for example, images of time, of death, of cold and warmth. You might then group your details like this:

yellow leaves / few leaves / no leaves / bare boughs
twilight / sunset / night
cold / ashes / death-bed / consumed
sunset / glowing /
consumed / nourished

As you think further about your understanding of the poem, and as you begin to develop an idea about it, you can use details from your list as evidence to support your interpretation.

Asking Questions

Questions provoke thought; their very openness of form invites response. Ask yourself about the details you listed and the connections you've been noticing. Ask questions about your annotations. Here are a few questions you could ask about Shakespeare's sonnet 73:

- What season is the poet/speaker describing?
- What time of day is emphasized?
- Why are the "choirs" "bare," and "ruined"?
- What is death's "second self"?
- What is being "consumed"?
- What is fading?
- What patterns of repetition do you notice?

Focused Freewriting

Like other prewriting techniques, including annotation, focused freewriting is preliminary writing you do for yourself as a form of discovery, rather than more formal writing you do for others. Focused freewriting can help you generate ideas without worrying about how you will organize or support them just yet.

Focused freewriting is unstructured, yet zeroes in on a topic. When you freewrite around a topic, such as the images in a poem, you jot down the first thoughts you have. You try to write quickly, in part to free you unconscious mind. And you write for yourself to see where your thinking might lead you. Use freewriting together with other prewriting techniques. Here is a sample of freewriting about Shakespeare's sonnet:

> That time of year—what time? Autumn when leaves fall in the fall. Speaker equals seasons? Poem about seasons of life? Shift from day to night, youth to age.

Does night or twilight = Fall? Day = Life? Night = Darkness, Death?

Fire is life; ashes death. Puzzling line about fire consumed by what it is "nourished" by?

Poem is 14 lines; 4-line segments + rhyming ending—a couplet = a sonnet.

Meaning of conclusion? We love things we will lose? We love them more BECAUSE they don't last?

Lots of images—day and night, fire burning and dying out—birds, leaves, trees.

Figure out how images work in each section of poem?

Here, the writer jots thoughts as they come, ideas suggested for later development. The freewriting contains leads to explore—questions to consider. Use freewriting to see where your thinking takes you. In a second pass develop the more promising, interesting bits from your first freewriting.

Exercise 5

Do some focused freewriting by working from details you noticed about the work, from annotations, or from questions you raised. See what you can develop further with freewriting.

Summarizing, Paraphrasing, and Analyzing

A *summary* is a succinct account of a work; it compresses and condenses. A *paraphrase* converts the words of a work into your own words. A paraphrase of Shakespeare's sonnet 73 would have the same number of lines; it would proceed in a line-by-line "translation." A summary would be shorter and tighter.

A summary differs from an analysis, which presents evidence for ideas and not just a compressed statement of them. Summarizing requires identifying the central idea of a work and supplying evidence to support that idea.

Writing a summary helps you analyze because it requires a consideration of a work's details and structure. Summary and analysis are typically woven together in academic writing.

Here is a summary and analysis of the imagery in Shakespeare's sonnet 73:

> The sonnet's central images appeal to three senses: sight, hearing, and touch. The first four lines include images that evoke each of these senses. We see the yellow leaves and bare branches; we feel the cold wind that shakes the boughs; we hear the singing birds in summer.
>
> Collectively, these images become metaphors, ways of speaking about one thing in terms of something else. Autumn, for example, is "That time of year" when leaves turn yellow and fall to the ground, leaving trees' branches bare. Shakespeare compares the barren branches to an empty

choir loft because the chorus of singing birds has departed with the coming of cold weather. And because Shakespeare's speaker says that "you" can behold autumn in him, we realize that he is talking about aging in terms of seasons.

In lines 5–8, the poem's second quatrain, the metaphor of autumnal aging gives way to another: that of twilight presaging the end of day. These lines describe the setting of the sun and the coming on of night. The emphasis here is on "black" night taking away the light of the sun; the sun's setting is seen as a dying of its light. The comparison of night with death is directly stated in line 8, where night is described as "Death's second self." But while night's rest is temporary, death's rest is final; its sealing up ends life.

These metaphors of autumn and evening highlight the gradual coming of death. Autumn precedes winter and twilight precedes night just as illness precedes death. The poem's speaker knows that. He is in the autumn of his life, the twilight of his time on earth. This metaphor is continued in a third image in lines 9–12: the dying of the fire, which in its fading of light and loss of heat, symbolizes the dying out of the speaker's life. In addition, the speaker's youth is compared with "ashes," which serve as the "death-bed" on which he will "expire."

Literally, these lines say that the fire will expire as it burns up the fuel that feeds it. In doing so, the fire glows with light and heat. The glowing fire than becomes a metaphor for the speaker's life, which is still "glowing," but which, like the fire, is beginning to die out as it consumes itself. Like the dying fire, the speaker's youth has turned to ashes. Also, like the dying fire, the speaker's life is "Consum'd with that which it was nourish'd by"—the speaker's very life itself. The fire consumes itself by burning up the logs that fuel it. The speaker's life, like the fire, in its very glowing, burns towards its own extinction.

Drafting

First drafts tend to be rough drafts, even with prewriting preparation. Your idea initially may be fuzzy and unclear. Use the drafting process to focus and clarify your idea.

Your first draft charts a course—a direction for your thinking. Write your first draft quickly. Identify details that will become your evidence and explore thinking that can lead to a main idea.

Decide on your purpose. Are you writing to analyze a work? To provide historical background? To explain something about the writer's vision and style?

Your explanation begins an interpretation, which is an attempt to persuade your reader(s) to see things as you do. You gain persuasiveness from the kinds and amount of supporting evidence you provide.

How will you organize your draft? What will you do in the beginning, middle, and end? Your beginning introduces your central idea. Your middle presents supporting evidence as you develop and deepen your idea. Your ending offers a perspective on the work and provides a sense of completion for your essay.

Common strategies for organizing an analysis and interpretation are these: (1) order of importance, or climactic order, from least to most important; (2) order of time sequence, or chronological order, from earliest to latest.

Revising

Once you have a first full draft, you are ready to revise. Ideally, you should allow time between drafts. Your revision process should include conceptual revision, organizational revision, and stylistic revision.

Conceptual revision involves reconsidering your main idea, clarifying and deepening it. Your original idea may be vague or overly general; it may be overly simple. Further thinking can improve and deepen your idea.

Organizational revision, or structural revision, involves reconsidering the arrangement of the parts of your draft. Is your organization clear? Does it make sense? Is anything out of order, missing or in need of development? How does your introduction set up what comes in the middle of your essay? How is your middle organized? What are its major parts? How does each part follow from what comes before; how does it prepare for and connect with what comes after?

Does your conclusion follow logically from what precedes it? What is the relationship of your conclusion to the middle of your essay? How does your conclusion connect with your introduction?

Stylistic revision requires attention to your words, phrases, and sentences. To what extent are your sentences clear and concise? Are some sentences wordy? Is your tone consistent? Is your level of language consistent and appropriate for your topic and audience?

Writers make moves as they develop a piece, especially as they work through its body or middle. Do you need an example or two? Do you need to define a term? Introduce an analogy? Provide a contrast? Reference another text? Ask a question? Introduce an objection or a qualification? Cite an authority?

Beginnings and endings often require rewriting. They present challenges for both inexperienced writers and professionals. The other major challenge for organizational revision comes with designing and developing the middle. How many parts should the middle of the piece have? What should those parts include? In what order should they be presented? How should it develop? How might it cohere, so that it flows seamlessly, one segment into the next?

Stylistic revision requires attention to words, phrases, and sentences. Do concrete and specific words balance and illustrate abstract and general words and concepts? Are phrases and clauses balanced and parallel? To what extent are the sentences clear and concise? Are some sentences wordy; how might they be trimmed?

Is the level of language appropriate for the topic and the audience? Is the writing engaging? Does the writing convey a person, a human being thinking and speaking behind the language? How does the voice of the writing sound? Is there a voice at all?

Editing and Proofreading

Editing focuses your attention on small details—of spelling and punctuation, of grammatical consistency and proper usage. A handbook or style guide can help with editing.

Look for these things as you edit:

- Grammatical errors: inconsistencies in verb tenses and subject–verb agreement.
- Inconsistencies with pronouns and their referents.
- Sentence fragments and comma splices.
- Errors in spelling and punctuation.

Proofreading is the final step. It's a chance to ensure that you didn't miss anything while editing. If you notice an omitted word, you can add it. You can correct any misspellings as well.

Here are a few proofreading suggestions:

- Read your draft aloud to hear places where sentences get tangled, where something doesn't sound right.
- Read your paragraphs beginning with the last sentence and going back to the first.
- Look for omitted words in sentences and missing letters in words.

Print a copy. Also, save a copy electronically, so you have your work in digital form as well.

Writing about Fiction and Drama

I follow here with a few additional thoughts on writing about fiction and drama (though some of what I say applies to poems as well). Among the more common ways of writing about these genres is analysis. In writing an analytical essay about a short story, novel, or play, your goal is to explain something about the work's significance. You might do this by identifying a key theme of the work—its questioning of authority, for example, or its dramatization of the dangers of public disorder. You might do it by focusing on an aspect of the work's style—on its irony, for example, or on the role setting plays in conveying a sense of the work's world. You might analyze its characters to explain how their relationships reveal an author's view of power, of love, of what matters in life—and death—and more.

Another approach is to compare two works—two stories or novels or plays, for example—focusing on one aspect or element, their imagery or symbolism, for example, their plots, or character relationships.

Additionally, you might write to show how one critical perspective—feminism, for example, or ecocriticism, sheds light on important dimensions of the work's significance. Or you might examine a key aspect or element of a story, novel, or play from multiple perspectives to show how different critical approaches bring into relief a work's power relations, or its psychological, or stylistic features, for example.

The following questions focus on one or another literary element of a fictional or dramatic work. They provide a starting point for your thinking. You might jot brief, informal responses to jump-start your thinking about the work you are analyzing. Once you've used some prewriting techniques—annotation, questioning, freewriting—you can begin to produce a more formal analysis of the work.

Questions about Fiction and Drama

Plot and Structure

- How are the incidents of the work arranged? Chronologically? With flashbacks from later to earlier action? With foreshadowing events to come later? With what effects?
- What patterns do you discern in the plot and structure of the work? To what extent do repetition, balance, and/or contrast play a role? How, and with what effect(s)?
- What external or internal conflicts occur in the work? Does the work drive toward a climactic action or culminating revelation? With what effect(s)?

Character and Characterization

- To what extent do the work's characters change? To what extent do they represent particular human types and kinds of behavior? How believable are the characters? What is the nature of their relationships with one other?
- How does the author portray the characters? How are they revealed to us? How do we come to know and understand them?
- What functions do the work's minor or lesser characters serve? What would be lost without their presence?

Setting

- Where and when does the action of the work take place?
- To what extent are elements of the work's time and/or place symbolic?
- What if the time or place of the story were altered? How might that affect its characters and action? How might it affect our response to it?

Symbolism

- Are any objects or events in the work symbolic? How might you decide?
- Do any of the work's symbols convey multiple, ambivalent, or ambiguous meanings?
- What do any symbols contribute to the overall significance or meaning of the work?

Language and Style

- What is distinctive about the author's style—its use of language, especially diction, imagery, and figurative language, including metaphor and tone?
- To what extent might the work be ironic? How would you decide?

Theme

- To what extent can a clear theme (or set of themes) be identified?
- Is that theme, or those themes, presented directly or indirectly?
- Can you identify key passages where the theme appears?
- Is there more than one theme? If so, how are those themes related?

Point of View (Fiction Only)

- Who narrates the short story or novel?
- Is the work presented from a single point of view, or does the point of view change or shift? Is the narrator completely knowledgeable about the work's characters? Partly knowledgeable?
- Does the narrator participate in the work's plot and action, or is the narrator essentially an outside observer?
- What is the effect of the writer's narrative choice?
- Can we trust the narrator—that is, do we have a "reliable," "unreliable," or partly reliable narrator? What are the implications of that choice by the writer for our experience of the work?

Dialogue

- How can the voices of the characters be described? How does the dialogue advance the work's plot and/or its theme(s)?
- How does the work's dialogue display character and reveal motivation?
- What particular exchanges of dialogue, or renderings of a character's thoughts, are especially important for revealing character?
- Why and how do those moments aid our understanding of the work?

References

Achebe, Chinua. "An Image of Africa: Racism in Conrad's 'Heart of Darkness.'" *Hopes and Impediments*. Penguin, 1990.
Aristotle and Michael Heath. *Poetics*. Penguin, 1997.
Auden, W. H. "Musée des Beaux Arts." *Collected Poems*. Random House Vintage, 1991.
Austen, Jane. *Mansfield Park*. Penguin, 1996.
Austen, Jane. *Pride and Prejudice*. Penguin Classics, 1996.
Bacon, Francis. "Of Youth and Age." *The Essays*. Penguin Classics, 1986.
Barry, Peter. *Beginning Theory*, 4th edition. Manchester University Press, 2017.
Barthes, Roland. *Mythologies*. Hill & Wang, 1957.
Bate, Jonathan. *The Song of the Earth*. Harvard University Press, 2000.
Bentley, Eric. *The Life of the Drama*. Applause Books, 1991.
Blake, William. "The Chimney Sweeper." *The Complete Poetry and Prose*. Edited by David V. Erdman. Random House, 1965.
Bleich, David. *Subjective Criticism*. Johns Hopkins University Press, 1978.
Bloom, Harold. *The Anxiety of Influence*. Oxford University Press, 1973.
Bloom, Harold. *The Anatomy of Influence*. Yale University Press, 2011.
Booker, Christopher. *The Seven Basic Plots: Why We Tell Stories*. Bloomsbury, 2019.
Briggs, Kate and Renee Gladman. Conversations: "Renee Gladman and Kate Briggs Talk Translation and Form." *Yale Review*, Winter 2021, Volume 109, No. 4.
Carr, Nicholas. *The Shallows*. Norton, 2010.
Chopin, Kate. "The Story of an Hour." *The Awakening and Selected Stories*. Bantam, 1985.
Cohen, Richard. *How to Write Like Tolstoy*. Random House, 2016.
Coleridge, Samuel Taylor. *The Major Works, Including Biographia Literaria*. Oxford University Press, 1817/1985.
Collins, Billy. "In The Deep Heart's Core." *Light the Dark*. Edited by Joe Fassler. Penguin, 2017.
Conarroe, Joel, editor. *Six American Poets*. Vintage, 1991.
Conrad, Joseph. "Heart of Darkness." *The Portable Conrad*. Penguin, 2007.
Crane, Stephen. *Stephen Crane: Prose and Poetry*. Edited by J. C. Levinson. Library of America, 1984.
Davis, Lydia. *Essays One*. Farrar, Straus and Giroux, 2019.
Derrida, Jacques. *Of Grammatology*. Johns Hopkins University Press, 2016.

Diaz, Hernán. "The Heart of Fiction: Storytelling, Experience, and Truth." *Yale Review*, Summer 2021, Volume 109, No. 2, 53–66.
Doty, Mark. *The Art of Description*. Graywolf Press, 2010.
Edel, Leon. *Literary Biography*. University of Toronto Press, 1957.
Elfenbein, Andrew. *The Gist of Reading*. Stanford University Press, 2018.
Eliot. T. S. "The Waste Land." *Collected Poems 1909–1962*. Harcourt, Brace and World, 1963.
Emerson, Ralph Waldo. "Nature." *Emerson: Essays and Lectures*. Library of America, 1983.
Epstein, Joseph. *A Literary Education*. Axios Press, 2014.
Flower, Dean. "Notes Toward a Supreme Fiction." *The Hudson Review*, Spring 2025, 89–99.
Freud, Sigmund. *Selected Writings*. Edited by Robert Coles. Norton, 1996.
Frost, Robert. "Stopping by Woods on a Snowy Evening." *Collected Poems, Prose, and Plays*. Library of America, 1995.
Frye, Northrop. *Anatomy of Criticism*. Princeton University Press, 1957.
Frye, Northrop. *The Educated Imagination*. Indiana University Press, 1964.
Fuller, Margaret. *Summer on the Lakes*. Penguin, 2017.
Garber, Marjorie. *The Use and Abuse of Literature*. Pantheon, 2012.
Gioia, Dana. "The Imaginary Operagoer." *Hudson Review*, Winter 2024.
Greenblatt, Stephen. *Learning to Curse*. Routledge, 1990.
Hardy, Thomas. *The Complete Poems of Thomas Hardy*. Macmillan, 1982.
Hass, Robert. *A Little Book of Forms*. Ecco, 2017.
Hawthorne, Nathaniel. "Roger Malvin's Burial" and "Young Goodman Brown." *Complete Short Stories of Hawthorne*. Doubleday, 1959.
Hemingway, Ernest. "The Revolutionist." *In Our Time*. Boni-Liveright, 1924.
Hemingway, Ernest. *A Farewell to Arms*. Charles Scribner's Sons, 1929.
Hemingway, Ernest. "A Clean, Well-Lighted Place," "The Short Happy Life of Francis Macomber." *The Short Stories*. Scribner, 1995.
Hirsch, Edward. *How to Read a Poem and Fall in Love with Poetry*. Mariner Books, 1999.
Hirsch, Edward. *The Heart of American Poetry*. New American Library, 2022.
Hoagland, Tony. *The Art of Voice*. Norton, 2020.
Hoagland, Tony. *real sofistikashun*. Graywolf Press, 2006.
Hogan, Michael. *Walking Each Other Home*. Sinn Fein Editions, 2024.
Holland, Norman. *The Dynamics of Literary Response*. Norton, 1975.
Homer. *Iliad*. Translated by Robert Fagles. Penguin, 1998.
Homer. *Odyssey*. Translated by Robert Fagles. Penguin, 1999.
hooks, bell. *Teaching Community: A Pedagogy of Hope*. Routledge, 2003.
Hopkins, Gerard Manley. "Spring and Fall: *to a young child*." *Poems and Prose*. Penguin, 1953.
Hurston, Zora Neale. "How It Feels to Be Colored Me." *The World Tomorrow*. 1928.
Iser, Wolfgang. *How to Do Theory*. Blackwell, 2006.
James, Henry. "Daisy Miller." *The Portable Henry James*. Viking, 1977.
James, Henry. *The Portrait of a Lady*. Penguin, 2003.
Jamison, Leslie. "A Street Full of Splendid Strangers." *The Atlantic*, December 15, 2019.
Jones, Ernest. *Hamlet and Oedipus*. Norton, 1949.
Jung, Carl Gustav. *Archetypes of the Collective Unconscious*. Princeton University Press, 1959.

Kafka, Franz. "The Metamorphosis." *The Metamorphosis and Other Stories.* Penguin, 2008.
Keats, John. "To Autumn" and "On First Looking into Chapman's Homer." *Complete Poems.* Edited by Jack Stillinger. Harvard University Press, 1982.
Kincaid, Jamaica. "On Seeing England for the First Time." *Putting Myself Together.* Farrar, Straus and Giroux, 2025.
Klein, Ezra. "What a Poetic Mind Can Teach Us About How to Live." Interview with Jane Hirshfield. *The New York Times*, March 3, 2023. nytimes.com.
Lacan, Jacques. *Four Fundamental Concepts of Psychoanalysis.* Norton, 1981.
Lawrence, D. H. *The Complete Poems of D. H. Lawrence.* Penguin, 1994.
Lesser, Wendy. *Why I Read.* Farrar, Straus and Giroux, 2014.
Lewis, C. S. *The Reading Life.* HarperCollins, 2019.
Marvell, Andrew. "To His Coy Mistress." *Poems.* Knopf, 2004.
Mendelson, Edward. "She Talk Her Mind." Review of Zadie Smith, *The Wife of Willesden. The New York Review*, March 7, 2024, 24.
Messud, Claire. "Words on Paper Will Outlast Us." *Light the Dark.* Penguin, 2017.
Mikics, David. *Slow Reading in a Hurried Age.* Harvard University Press, 2013.
Miller, Madeline. *Song of Achilles.* Ecco, 2012.
Miller, Madeline. *Circe.* Little, Brown, 2018.
Milton, John. *Paradise Lost.* Penguin, 2003.
Modiano, Patrick. "Patrick Modiano Says Good Books Make Good People." *New York Times Book Review*, January 15, 2023. newyorktimes.com.
Newkirk, Thomas. *The Art of Slow Reading.* Heinemann, 2012.
Newkirk, Thomas. *Minds Made for Stories.* Heinemann, 2014.
Nims, John Frederick and David Mason. "Western Wind." *Western Wind*, 4th edition. McGraw-Hill, 2005.
Orwell, George. "A Hanging." *George Orwell: Essays.* Everyman's Library, 2002.
Parks, Tim. "Reading Against the Novel." *The New York Review*, July 18, 2024, 43.
Paterson, Don. *The Poem.* Faber and Faber, 2019.
Persse, Isabella Augusta, Lady Gregory. "The Rising of the Moon." *Lady Gregory: Selected Writings.* Penguin, 1955.
Pinker, Steven. *How the Mind Works.* Norton, 2009.
Poe, Edgar Allan. "The Cask of Amontillado." *The Portable Edgar Allan Poe.* Penguin, 2006.
Porter, Katherine Anne. "Rope." *Collected Stories and Other Writings.* Library of America, 2008.
Pound, Ezra. *Selected Poems of Ezra Pound.* New Directions, 1957.
Pound, Ezra. *ABC of Reading.* New Directions, reprint, 2010.
Reynolds, Michael. *The Young Hemingway.* Blackwell, 1986.
Rich, Adrienne. *On Lies, Secrets, and Silence: Selected Essays 1966–1978.* Norton, 1979.
Rich, Adrienne. *Collected Poems: 1950–2012.* Norton, 2016.
Rosenblatt, Louise. *Literature as Exploration.* Open Library, 1933.
Ryan, Kay. *Synthesizing Gravity.* Grove/Atlantic, 2020.
Saunders, George. *A Swim in the Pond in the Rain.* Random House, 2021.
Schulz, Kathryn. "Wait for It: Suspense in Literature and Life." *The New Yorker*, May 27, 2024. newyorker.com.
Shakespeare, William. *The Riverside Shakespeare.* Houghton Mifflin, 1974.
Shaw, George Bernard. *Arms and the Man. Plays Pleasant.* Penguin, 1946.

Shelley, Percy Bysshe. "A Defence of Poetry." *The Prose Works of Percy Bysshe Shelley*. Oxford University Press, 1993.
Smith, Barbara Herrnstein. *Poetic Closure*. University of Chicago Press, 1968.
Smith, Zadie. *Feel Free*. Penguin, 2018.
Steiner, George. "The Uncommon Reader." *No Passion Spent*. Yale University Press, 1996.
Strindberg, August. *The Stronger*. Translated by F. I. Ziegler. *Poet Lore*, Spring 1906, Number 1, 46–50.
Sutherland, John. *A Little History of Literature*. Yale University Press, 2013.
Thomas, Dylan. "The force that through the green fuse drives the flower." *The Collected Poems of Dylan Thomas*. New Directions, 2010.
Thoreau, Henry David. *Walden*. Library of America, 2009.
Twain, Mark. *Adventures of Huckleberry Finn*. Penguin, 2014.
Virgil. *Aeneid*. Translated by Robert Fitzgerald. Random House, 1983.
Wasserstein, Wendy. "Tender Offer." *Antaeus: Plays in One Act*. 66: 1991.
Whitman, Walt. "Crossing Brooklyn Ferry," "One's Self I Sing," "Proud Music of the Storm," "Song of Myself," "When I Heard the Learn'd Astronomer," "When Lilacs Last in the Dooryard Bloom'd." *Poems and Prose*. Library of America, 1982.
Williams, William Carlos. "Landscape with the Fall of Icarus." *Selected Poems*. New Directions, 1963.
Wimmers, Inge Crosman. *Poetics of Reading*. Princeton University Press, 1988.
Wolf, Marianne. *Reader, Come Home*. Harper, 2018.
Wollstonecraft, Mary. *A Vindication of the Rights of Woman*. Dover, 1996.
Woolf, Virginia. "How Should One Read a Book?" *The Common Reader*, Second Series. Harcourt, Inc., 1932.
Woolf, Virginia. *The Common Reader*, First Series, annotated edition. Mariner Books, 2002.
Yeats, William Butler. "An Irish Airman Foresees His Death", "In Memory of Major Robert Gregory". *The Collected Poems of W. B. Yeats*. Revised Second Edition. Edited by Richard Finneran. Scribner, 1996.
Zapruder, Matthew. *Why Poetry*. HarperCollins, 2017.

Index

1984 76

Abdiel (character) 154
absurdist drama 107–108
Achebe, Chinua 208
Achilles (character) 32–35
Adam (biblical character) 153, 156–158, 230
Adventures of Huckleberry Finn 41, 65
Aeneas (character) 35–38
Aeneid 35–38
Aeschylus 218
aesthetic values 130–131
Agamemnon (character) 32–34, 218
Ahab, Captain (character) 63
Alboni, Marietta 27
alliteration 145, 149, 150, 153
All My Sons 197
"American Dream" 197
Anatomy of Criticism 218
Anna Karenina 76
annotations 115–119
Anticlea (character) 34
Antigone 83
Antigua 132–134, 224–225
Anxiety of Influence, The 230
"Araby" 159–166
Archer, Isabel (character) 43, 63
archetypes 217
Aristotle 105, 106
Arms and the Man 99–104
art: and fiction 66–69; as imitation of life 42; and poetry 24–28; Renaissance 66; *see also* art history
art history 66–67
Art of Voice, The 10
assonance 145, 149, 150, 153
Athena (character) 34
Atlantic, The 124

Attenborough, David 141
Auden, W. H. 3, 24–26
Augustus Caesar 36, 115, 117
Austen, Jane 227; biography 207; irony 76–78; *Mansfield Park* 225; *Pride and Prejudice* 46, 63–64, 76–78

Bacon, Francis 115–119
Barone, Joshua 27
Barry, Peter 224–225, 228
Barthes, Roland 220
Bate, Jonathan 228
Beckett, Samuel 108
Beginning Theory 224
Bentley, Eric 83, 178
Best American Essays 2020, The 124
Bettini, Alessandro 27
Bible 217–218; *see also* Genesis; Revelation
biographical criticism 205–206
Biographies 1–2
biopics 141
Blake, William 154, 207–208, 227
Bleak House 76
Bleich, David 203
Bloom, Harold 230
Booker, Christopher 42
Brueghel, Pieter 24–26
Briggs, Kate 42
Brooke, Dorothea (character) 63
Brooklyn Museum 126
Brothers Karamazov, The 76
Burns, Ken 141

caesura 20, 150
Calypso (character) 34
capitalism 213
Carthage 36–38
"Cask of Amontillado, The" 55–62

Catcher in the Rye, The 41
Catholicism 60, 163, 186
Caulfield, Holden (character) 63
Celan, Paul 9
Cenerentola, La 220
Cézanne, Paul 67–69
characters 145, 164, 243; in drama 179–181, 243
"Chimney Sweeper, The" 207
Chopin, Kate 70–75
Christianity 152
Ciceronian style 153
Cinderella stories 106, 220
Circe (book) 35
Circe (character) 34
"Clean Well-Lighted Place, A" 67
"cliffhangers" 46–47
Clytemnestra (character) 34, 218
codes 220
Cohen, Richard 44
Coleridge, Samuel Taylor 84, 227–228
Collins, Billy 9
Collins, Wilkie 46
colonization 133, 208, 224–225; *see also* postcolonial criticism
comedy 105–107, 218; romantic 106–107; satiric 107, 218
comparisons 12, 54, 191
Conarroe, Joel 7
conceptual revision 241
conflict 178–180, 183–184
Conrad, Joseph 208
Copperfield, David (character) 63
Cosmus 115, 117
couplet 12, 13
Crane, Stephen 22–23
creation stories 218
critical consciousness 198
critical perspectives: biographical 205–206; deconstructionist 221–223; ecocritical 227–229; formalist 200–202; as heuristics 199; historical 207–209; influence and value 230–232; mythological 217–218; postcolonial 224–226; psychological 210–212; reader-response 203–204; sociological 213–216; structuralist 219–220
"Crossing Brooklyn Ferry" 232
Crucible, The 197
cultural biases 208
cultural values 130, 133–134, 197, 231, 236
Cupid (character) 37
Cyclops (characters) 34, 38

Daedalus (character) 24
Daisy Miller 79
dance 84
Davis, Lydia 45
Dead Christ, The 67
Death of a Salesman 107, 197
decision-making 42–43
deconstruction 221
deconstructionist criticism 221–223
"Defence of Poetry, A" 8
Derrida, Jacques 221–222
Desdemona (character) 61, 94–96, 106
dialogue: in drama 94–96, 108, 180–181, 244; in fiction 44–45, 63–64, 244
Diaz, Hernán 42
Dickens, Charles 47, 76, 213, 214
Dickinson, Emily 9, 214–215
diction 145, 148
Dido (character) 36–38
différance 222
digital reading 1–3
Disasters of War, The 67
documentary films 141
Doll's House, A 107
Donne, John 9
Dostoevsky, Fyodor 76, 207
Doty, Mark 8–9
drama 83–108; absurdist 107–108; as an active art 84; as a communal experience 83; as a composite art 84; conflict 178–180, 183–184; dialogue 94–96, 108, 180–181, 244; idea 185; as an immediate art 84; as an interactive art 84; interrupted reading 99–104; irony 76, 183–185; language 94–96; literary elements 167–186; mental performance 85–91; as a mimetic art 83; pleasures of 83–85; plot 177–178; realism in 107–108; setting 181–183, 243; sound effects 97–98, 183; subtext 92–93; symbolism 183–185; theme 185–186; thought 185–186; types of 105–108
dramatic irony 76, 184–185
Dubliners 163

e-books 2
ecocriticism 227–229
Edel, Leon 205, 207
editing 242
Educated Imagination, The 197
electronic technologies 2
Elfenbein, Andrew 231
Eliot, George 47, 63, 213, 214

Eliot, T. S. 198
Ellmann, Richard 207
Emerson, Ralph Waldo 227
Engels, Friedrich 213
enjambment 20, 150
enslavement 43
epic poetry 32–38, 218; literary elements 152–153
Epstein, Joseph 113
essays 111–142; analytical 112; annotation 115–119; argumentative 112; attunement 113; establishing connections 129, 132–133; evaluation 130–134; exploratory 112; expository 112; idea 111–113, 192; inferences 130, 131, 133; interrupted reading 135–140; literary elements 187–192; narrative 112; observations 129, 131, 132; pleasures of 111–112; purpose of 111; reading as conversations 113–114; reading framework 129–134; slow reading 113, 124–128; spectrum 112; structure 190–191; style 120–123, 191–192; theme 192–193; thought 113, 192–193; tone 120–123, 190; types of 112; video 141–142; voice 190
Euro-centrism 224, 225
Euryclea (character) 34
evaluation 130–134, 236
Eve (biblical character) 153, 156–158
Eyre, Jane (character) 63

fairy tales 220
Farewell to Arms, A 67–69
feminism 198, 214–215
Feynman, Richard 130
fiction 41–80; and art 66–69; benefits of 41–43; dialogue 44–45, 63–64, 244; form 47; and history 65–66; interrupted reading 70–75; literary elements 159–166; pleasures of 41–47; plot 41–42, 46, 145, 163–164, 243; questions 48–54; and reality 43, 193; rhythm 45–46; setting of a story 164–165, 243; surprises 55–62; suspense 46–47; theme 48, 76, 78, 166; tone 64, 76–78; and truth 42; voice 63–64
film 83
Finn, Huckleberry (character) 43, 63, 76
Fitzgerald, F. Scott 63, 65
Flaherty, Robert 141
Flaubert, Gustave 65
Flower, Dean 80

focused freewriting 238–239
Foix, Gaston de 115, 117
folktales 220
form: fiction 47; poetry 10–14, 150
formalist criticism 200–202
Frank, Joseph 207
Freud, Sigmund 210–211
Frost, Robert 29–31
Frye, Northrop 197, 218
Fuller, Margaret 227

Garber, Marjorie 231
Garden of Eden 152–153, 156–158
Gatsby (character) 63
gender 214–216
Genesis 152, 217; *see also* Bible
Gioia, Dana 9
Giotto 66
Gist of Reading, The 231
good guesses 130
Goya, Francisco de 67, 69
Granuaile 186
Great Depression 141
Great Gatsby, The 63, 65
Greek tragedy 106, 193
Greenblatt, Stephen 208
Gregory, Lady 167–186, 225
Gregory, Robert 15, 18
Gregory, Sir William 167

Hamlet (character) 211
Hamlet (play) 211
"Hanging, A" 135–140
Hardy, Thomas 46, 228; biography 207; literary influence 230–231
Hass, Robert 11
Hawthorne, Nathaniel 228
Heaney, Seamus 225
Heart of Darkness 208
Heaven 154–156
Hejinian, Lyn 11
Hell 154–155
Hemingway, Ernest: "A Clean Well-Lighted Place" 67; *A Farewell to Arms* 67–69, 205; *In Our Time* 65, 66, 67; "The Revolutionist" 65–67; "The Short Happy Life of Francis Macomber" 44, 46; *The Sun Also Rises* 67
Henry V 193
hermeneutics xii–xiii
Hermogenes 116, 117
Hirsch, Edward 10
Hirshfield, Jane 9–10

historical criticism 207–209
history 65–66
Hoagland, Tony 7, 10, 22
Hobbit, The 76
Hogan, Michael 3–4
Holland, Norman 203
homage 36
Homer 12, 32–38, 218
hooks, bell 198–199
Hopkins, Gerard Manley 147–151, 228
Hortensius 116, 117
Howe, Irving 79
"How It Feels to Be Colored Me" 112, 187–192
"How Should One Read a Book" 8
Hughes, Langston 112
Hurston, Zora Neale 112, 187–192
hyperbole 20
hyperlinks 1–2
hyper-reading 2

Iago (character) 61, 94–96, 105
iambic pentameter 12, 153
iambic tetrameter 20
Ibsen, Henrik 83, 107
Icarus (character) 24–26
idea 146; drama 185; essay 112–113, 192–193
Iliad 32–35, 218
imagery 145, 149
imperialism 208
"I'm wife" 214–215
inferences 130, 131, 133
In Our Time 65
internet 1
interpretation 131, 183, 234–236; provisional 133–134
interrupted reading: drama 99–104; essays 135–140; fiction 70–75; poetry 29–31
Inuit people 141
Ionesco, Eugène 108
"Irish Airman Foresees His Death, An" 15–18
irony 23, 60–61, 74, 76; in drama 183–185; of incident 184; of language 60–61, 184; of situation 76, 184; verbal 76
Iser, Wolfgang 203
Ithaca 34

James, Henry 63; biography of 205–207; *Daisy Miller* 79; on novella 78; *The Portrait of a Lady* 43

Jamison, Leslie 124–128, 130
Jane Eyre 41
Jason and the Argonauts story 217
Jesus Christ 152
Johnson, Denis 44–45
Jones, Ernest 211
Joyce, James 159–166, 207
Jude the Obscure 231
Julius Caesar 115, 117
Julius Caesar (play) 203
Jung, C. G. 217

Kafka, Franz 79
Keats, John 12, 228
Kincaid, Jamaica 129–134, 224
Klein, Ezra 9

Lacan, Jacques 211
La Cenerentola *see* Cenerentola, La
Landscape with the Fall of Icarus (painting) 24–26
"Landscape with the Fall of Icarus" (poem) 24–26
language: in drama 94–96, 181; ironic 60–61, 184; and poetry 10; postcolonial criticism 225; religious 165; as a system of "signs" 219; as self-contradictory 221
Latinate style 153
Lawrence, D. H. 200–201, 204
Learning to Curse 208
Leaves of Grass 26
lesbian feminism 215
Lesser, Wendy 84
Levertov, Denise 11
Lewis, C. S. 10
Life of the Drama, The 83
Lincoln, Abraham 27
linguistic conventions 219
listing 237–238
literacy 198
Literary Biography 205
literary conventions 193–194
Literary Education, A 113
literary elements: drama 167–186; epic poetry 152–158; essay 187–192; fiction 159–166; lyric poetry 147–151; value of 145–146
literary genres 218
literary influence 230–231
literary perspectives 197–199; *see also* critical perspectives
literary tact 131
Little Dorrit 213, 214

Little History of Literature, A 83, 231
Livy (Titus Livius Patinus) 116, 117
Lolita 78
Lord of the Rings, The 217
"Lottery, The" 55

Macbeth 97–98, 107
Macomber, Francis (character) 44
Madame Bovary 65
Mahabharata, The 218
Maid in Manhattan 220
Mansfield Park 225
Mantegna, Andrea 66–67, 69
Marriage of Heaven and Hell, The 154
Martyrdom of St. Sebastian, The 67
Marvell, Andrew 19–21
Marx, Karl 213
Marxism 213–214
Masaccio 66
Master Builder, The 83
Maupassant, Guy de 55
Melville, Herman 63
mental theater 85–91
Messud, Claire 198
Metamorphoses 24
Metamorphosis, The 79–80
metaphor 211, 240
meter 145, 149–150, 153
metonymy 211
Middlemarch 63, 213, 214
Mikics, David 113
Miller, Arthur 107, 197
Miller, Madeline 35
Milton, John 152–158
Minds Made for Stories 41
"mirror-stage" 211
Moby-Dick 63
Modiano, Patrick 43
Molière 205
"Monkey's Paw, The" 55
monologue 180–181
moral issues 197, 210
moral norms 197
moral values 43, 130
Mountains of California, The 227
Mourning Becomes Electra 193
Muir, John 227
Muldoon, Paul 9
Muse, the 32, 153
"Musée des Beaux Arts" 25–26
music 26–28, 84
My First Summer in the Sierras 227
mythological criticism 217–218

Mythologies 220
myths 217–218

Nabokov, Vladimir 78
Nanook of the North 141
National Theatre Society 167
Nature (book) 227
nature (concept) 227–229
new historicism 208–209
Newkirk, Thomas 9, 41, 113
"Notes On Form" 47
novellas *see* short novels
novels: benefits of reading 42–43; as modes of knowing 80; and novellas 78–80; of the past 42; *see also* fiction; short novels

observations 129, 131, 132
O'Connor, Flannery 76
octave 12
Odysseus (character) 33–35, 37–38
Odyssey 33–35, 218
Oedipus (character) 105–106, 210–211
"Oedipus complex" 211
Oedipus Rex 106, 107, 210
Oedipus the King *see* Oedipus Rex
"Of Youth and Age" 115–119
O. Henry (William Sydney Porter) 55
O'Neill, Eugene 193
"One's Self I Sing" 11
"On First Looking into Chapman's Homer" 12
"On Seeing England for the First Time" 129–134, 224
online reading 1–3
opera 27–28
organizational revision 241
Orwell, George: *1984* 76; "A Hanging" 135–140; "Shooting an Elephant" 112
Osmond, Gilbert (character) 43
Othello (character) 61, 94–96, 105–106
Othello (play) 61, 94–96, 105–107
Ovid 24

painting 24–26
Paradise Lost 152–158
paraphrasing 239–240
Parks, Tim 42
pastoral poems 227
Paterson, Don 10, 11
Persephone (character) 217
Persse, Isabella Augusta *see* Gregory, Lady
photography 126–128

254   Index

"Piano" 200–201, 204
Piero della Francesca 66
pietas 38
Pinker, Steven 42
plots 145; in drama 177–178; in fiction 41–42, 46, 145, 163–164, 243
Poe, Edgar Allan 55–62
poetic closure 13–14
Poetic Closure (book) 13
Poetics 105
poetry 3–4, 7–38; argument in 19–21; and the arts 24–28; conventions 193; diction 145, 148; form 10–14, 150; imagery 145, 149; impact of 7–8; interrupted reading 29–31; and language 10; literary elements 147–153; memorization of 9; meter 145, 149–150, 153; and music 26–28; and painting 24–26; pleasures of 7–14; rhyme 145, 149–150; rhythm 7, 10, 11, 14, 26, 145, 149–150; situation 147; sound 7, 9, 14, 15, 17, 149, 201; speaker 15–18, 22, 23, 147; structure 15–18, 201; syntax 17, 148–149, 201; theme 150–151; tone 22–23; value of 8–10; *see* also epic poetry
political plays 181, 185
politics 198; *see also* political plays
Porter, Katherine Anne 48–54
Portrait of a Lady, The 43, 63
postcolonial criticism 224–226
post-structuralism 222–223
Pound, Ezra 9, 181
power relations 208–209, 214
prejudices 208
Pretty Woman 220
prewriting 237
Pride and Prejudice 46, 63–64, 76–78
print reading 1–3
proofreading 242
"Proud Music of the Storm" 27
psychoanalytical criticism 210–212
psychological criticism 210–212

quatrains 12, 13, 240
queer theory 215–216
questions 9–10, 48–54

race 43
racism 208
Ramayana, The 218
reader-response criticism 203–204
reading aloud 13, 31, 86, 125, 180
reading technologies 1–2

realism 107–108
real sofistikashun 7, 10, 22
reception theory 203
Renaissance 66, 107, 208, 227
Revelation 218; *see also* Bible
revision 241–242
"re-vision" 198
"Revolutionist, The" 65–67
Reynolds, Michael 68
rhyme 145, 149–150
rhythm: in fiction 45–46; in poetry 7, 10, 11, 14, 26, 145, 149–150
Rich, Adrienne 9, 198
Rising of the Moon, The 167–186
"Roger Malvin's Burial" 228
romantic comedies 106–107
Rome 36–37
"Rope" 48–54
Rosenblatt, Louise 203
Rossini, Gioachino 220
Ryan, Kay 9

Sagan, Carl 141
"Salvation" 112
Satan (character) 153–158, 230
satiric comedies 107, 218
Saunders, George 43
Schulz, Kathryn 46
science documentaries 141
scientific knowledge 130
Scipio Africanus 116, 117
scrolls 1
sculpture 84
semiotics 220
Septimius Severus 115, 117
sestet 12
setting: in drama 181–183, 243; in fiction 164–165, 243
Seven Basic Plots, The 42
Shakespeare, William 205; *Hamlet* 211; *Henry V* 193; *Julius Caesar* 203; *Macbeth* 97–98, 107; *Othello* 61, 94–96, 105–107; pastoral motifs 227; sonnets 12–14, 237–240; *The Tempest* 208; "When in Disgrace with Fortune and Men's Eyes" 13
Shaw, George Bernard 99–104, 107
Shelley, Percy Bysshe 8, 228
"Shooting an Elephant" 112
"Short Happy Life of Francis Macomber, The" 44, 46
short novels (novellas) 78–80
short stories 44, 78, 193
Sirens 34

slow reading (concept) 113, 124–128
The Art of Slow Reading (book) 9
Slow Reading in a Hurried Age 113
Smith, Barbara Herrnstein 13–14
Smith, Zadie 41, 43–44
social class 213–214
social interactions 42–43
social values 130, 197, 231, 236
sociological criticism 213–216
"Some Notes on Organic Form" 11
Song of Achilles 35
"Song of Myself" 26–27
Song of the Earth, The 228
Songs of Experience 207
sonnets 11–12, 237–240; Petrarchan 12, 13; Shakespearean 12–14; structural parts 12–14
Sophocles 83, 105–106, 210, 218
sound: in drama 97–98, 183; in poetry 7, 9, 14, 15, 17, 149, 201
"Spring and Fall: to a young child" 147–151
staging 182–183
stanza 10–11, 14
"Steady Hands at Seattle General" 44–45
Stevens, Wallace 9, 231
"Stopping by Woods on a Snowy Evening" 29–31
"Story of an Hour, The" 70–75
"Street Full of Splendid Strangers, A" 124–128
Strindberg, August 86–91
Stronger, The 85–91
structuralist criticism 219–220
style 165; Ciceronian 153; essay 120–123, 191–192; Latinate 153
stylistic revision 241
subtext 92–93
summarising 239–240
Summer on the Lakes 227
Sun Also Rises, The 67
suspense 46–47
Sutherland, John 83, 231
symbolism 165, 183–185, 210, 243
Synge, John Millington 167
syntax 17, 148–149, 201

Teaching Community: A Pedagogy of Hope 199
Tempest, The 208
Tender Offer 92–93
Tess of the D'Urbervilles 231
Thackeray, William Makepeace 213, 214

theater 83, 84; of the absurd 107, 108; mental 85–91; *see also* drama
theme 145–146, 244; in drama 185–186; in epic poetry 32, 37–38; in essays 192–193; in fiction 48, 76, 78, 166; in lyric poetry 150–151
Thomas, Dylan 3
Thoreau, Henry David 227
"thought experiments" 197
"To Autumn" 228
"To His Coy Mistress" 19–21
Tolkien, J. R. R. 76, 217
Tolstoy, Leo 76
Tomalin, Claire 207
tone 76; in essays 120–123, 190; in fiction 64, 76–78; in poetry 22–23; *see also* irony
Torah 1
tragedy 105–106, 218; Greek 106, 193; Shakespearean 106
tragicomedy 107
Tranströmer, Tomas 9
Trojan Horse 35, 37
Trojan War 32–33, 36, 37
truth 42
Tully (Marcus Tullius Cicero) 116, 117
TV documentaries 141
Twain, Mark 43, 65, 76

unconscious, the 210–211
Use and Abuse of Literature, The 231

values 70; aesthetic 130–131; and appraisal of literary work 130–134; cultural 130, 133–134, 197, 231, 236; of literary elements 145–146; of literature 197–199, 230–232; moral 43, 130; of poetry 8–10; social 130, 197, 231, 236
Vanity Fair 213, 214
video essays 141–142
Vindication of the Rights of Woman, A 120–123
Virgil 35–38
voice 63–64, 190

Walden 227
Walking Each Other Home 3
Walpole, Horace 105
"War Is Kind" 22–23
Wasserstein, Wendy 92–93
Waste Land, The 198
"Western Wind" 8

"When I Heard the Learn'd Astronomer" 234–235
"When in Disgrace with Fortune and Men's Eyes" 13
"When Lilacs Last in the Dooryard Bloom'd" 27
"When We Dead Awaken: Writing as Re-Vision" 198
Whitman, Walt 11, 26–28, 232; "When I Heard the Learn'd Astronomer" 234–235
Why I Read 84
Why Poetry 8
Williams, William Carlos 24–26
Wilson, Robert (character) 44
Wimmers, Inge Crosman 203–204
Winogrand, Garry 126–128
Wollstonecraft, Mary 120–123, 207
women's rights 120–123, 198
Woolf, Virginia 7–8
Wordsworth, William 228
Works Progress Administration 141
writing 233–244; drafting process 240–241; editing 242; evaluating 236; about fiction and drama 242–244; interpreting 234–236; overview of the process 237–242; proofreading 242; responding 233–234; revising 241–242; *see also* focused freewriting; prewriting

Yeats, William Butler 15–18, 167, 225, 231
"Young Goodman Brown" 228
YouTube 142

Zapruder, Matthew 8, 11

For Product Safety Concerns and Information please contact our EU representative GPSR@taylorandfrancis.com
Taylor & Francis Verlag GmbH, Kaufingerstraße 24, 80331 München, Germany

www.ingramcontent.com/pod-product-compliance
Ingram Content Group UK Ltd.
Pitfield, Milton Keynes, MK11 3LW, UK
UKHW020053040426
469672UK00019B/440